The Baltic States

The National Self-Determination of Estonia, Latvia and Lithuania

Edited by

Graham Smith

*Fellow of Sidney Sussex College, Cambridge
and Lecturer in Geography, University of Cambridge*

First edition 1994
Reprinted (with alterations) 1996

Published by
MACMILLAN PRESS LTD
Houndmills, Basingstoke, Hampshire RG21 6XS
and London
Companies and representatives
throughout the world

ISBN 0–333–57101–0 hardcover
ISBN 0–333–66580–5 paperback

A catalogue record for this book is available
from the British Library.

10   9   8   7   6   5   4   3   2   1
05   04   03   02   01   00   99   98   97   96

Printed and bound in Great Britain by
Antony Rowe Ltd, Chippenham, Wiltshire

Published in the United States of America 1996 by
ST. MARTIN'S PRESS, INC.,
Scholarly and Reference Division
175 Fifth Avenue, New York, N.Y. 10010

ISBN 0–312–12060–5 (cloth)
ISBN 0–312–16192–1 (paperback)

THE BALTIC STATES

Also by Graham Smith

PLANNED DEVELOPMENT IN THE SOCIALIST WORLD
THE NATIONALITIES QUESTION IN THE SOVIET UNION
FEDERALISM: THE MULTIETHNIC CHALLENGE
HUMAN GEOGRAPHY: SOCIETY, SPACE AND SOCIAL SCIENCE
  (WITH D. GREGORY AND R. MARTIN)
THE NATIONALITIES QUESTION IN THE POST-SOVIET STATES

Contents

List of Figures

List of Tables

List of Contributors

Aadne Aasland, Institute of Russian and East European Studies, University of Glasgow.

Michael Bradshaw, School of Geography and Centre for Russian and East European Studies, University of Birmingham.

Phil Hanson, Centre for Russian and East European Studies, University of Birmingham.

Nicholas Hope, Faculty of Modern History, University of Glasgow.

David Kirby, School of Slavonic and East European Studies, University of London.

Richard Mole, Department of Geography, University of Cambridge.

Andrus Park, sometime Faculty of Philosophy, Politics and Law, Estonian Academy of Sciences, Tallinn.

Denis Shaw, School of Geography and Centre for Russian and East European Studies, University of Birmingham.

Aleksandras Shtromas, Department of History and Political Science, Hillsdale College, Michigan.

Graham Smith, Department of Geography, University of Cambridge and the Post-Soviet States Research Programme, Sidney Sussex College, Cambridge.

James D. White, Faculty of Modern History and Institute of Russian and East European Studies, University of Glasgow.

Preface

Few events in the latter half of the twentieth century can be so momentous as the geopolitical disintegration of the Soviet Union. Not only did it bring to an end state socialism in the first country to embrace a socialist route to modernity but it also brought into being fifteen nation-states, including the rebirth of the three Baltic States of Estonia, Latvia and Lithuania. Despite their small size, with a combined population of only 8.8 million, these three republics emerged to play a key part in contributing to the end of the USSR. While initially displaying a willingness to engage in Mikhail Gorbachev's plans for economic and political reform, the Baltic peoples quickly became the pacesetters in the struggle to achieve greater national self-determination. Following the August 1991 coup in Moscow they again rejoined the international community of sovereign states.

The underlying rationale of this book is that it is only possible to understand fully the prominent contribution of the Baltic peoples to this geopolitical transformation by locating the Baltic States within the wider context of their twentieth-century struggle for national self-determination. Part I of this book therefore examines the Baltic nations from their national awakening in the nineteenth century through to securing their independent statehood during the interwar years and finally their incorporation into the Soviet Union. In Part II we explore their transition towards the re-establishment of independent statehood and the problems linked to their political rebirth as sovereign states in the 1990s. Although the Baltic States have shared a remarkably similar fate throughout the twentieth century, we have also attempted to signal the marked differences which exist between them, in their national cultures, economies and social structures, providing what we hope is a more balanced comparative examination of these societies.

The major acknowledgement which an editor of a volume such as this needs to make is to the contributors. All of them responded with enthusiasm to the project, and I am particularly grateful for their willingness to follow editorial guidelines, which, we hope, provide the coherence in approach and balanced coverage that was intended. I am also grateful to Ian Agnew for his usual high standard of cartographic artistry and to Clare Andrews, editor at Macmillan, for her steady guidance.

Graham Smith
Sidney Sussex College, Cambridge
June 1993

xi

Preface to the 1996 Reprint

I have taken the opportunity to make some minor corrections to the 1994
hardback edition and to update Chapter Eight. This edition is dedicated
to the memory of Andrus Park, one of the contributors, whose untimely
death leaves Baltic studies that much poorer.

Graham Smith
August 1995

Figure 1　The Post-1991 Baltic States

Introduction: The Baltic Nations and National Self-Determination

Graham Smith

In 1991, after a lapse of just over half a century, the Baltic peoples of Estonia, Latvia and Lithuania rejoined the world community of nation-states. The Baltic States were of course hardly unique among the former Soviet Union's republics in taking advantage of the failure of the short-lived period of perestroika or reform communism (1985–90) to establish themselves as sovereign states. What however does distinguish them is that this was not the first time their peoples had struggled successfully for a historically sustained period of independent statehood. In being able to look back upon such an era of recent statehood (1918–40), all three Baltic nations possessed powerful national symbols to mobilise their peoples' support for independent sovereignty. This recourse to a unique political history undoubtedly contributed both to the character of their national reawakenings and to the role that their republics were to play in leading the way in challenging the territorial legitimacy of the Soviet empire.

In the early months of reform communism there was little indication to suggest that the question of Baltic national self-determination was likely to prove such an apocalyptic problem for Mikhail Gorbachev's administration. Indeed for the new reform-minded leadership in Moscow, it seemed that of all the nationality-based republics, Estonia, Latvia and Lithuania were likely to prove the most amenable to its unfolding agenda for economic, social and political reform. Here after all were nations whose national cultures were endowed with many of the features judged by Moscow as important to its reform programme including, most importantly, a recent pre-Soviet experience of both pluralist democracy and market-type economies. However by taking advantage of the new climate of glasnost offered by Moscow, regionally-based social movements emerged which while initially supportive of the centre's reform programme, quickly developed into organisations calling for their peoples' national self-determination and for the re-establishment of sovereign nation-states.

That support for the idea of national self-determination should emerge so easily and quickly in all three Baltic republics can only be fully appreciated by recourse to history. Indeed the underlying rationale of this book is that it is impossible to fully understand the recent transition towards independent

1

statehood without locating the question of Baltic national self-determination within a broader historical perspective. Although of twentieth-century vintage, the idea of constituting modern nation-states began with their respective national awakenings in the latter half of the nineteenth century. While Lithuanians can rightfully boast of a medieval kingdom which stretched from the Baltic to the Black Sea, for all three peoples a modern sense of national consciousness developed only during the nineteenth century when the region constituted part of the Russian empire. In Chapter 1 the emergence and nature of this national consciousness amongst these overwhelmingly peasant peoples is explored in which the social formation of indigenous educated élites and the appearance of literary vernaculars were to play a fundamental part. This national awakening also coincided with the region's transition from feudalism to capitalism linked to agrarian reforms which got under way earlier in Estonia and Latvia than in Lithuania and other parts of the Empire, and to the region's rapid industrial development. Accompanying these important processes of economic restructuring was the emergence of an indigenous class of urban professionals who were to play a key part in championing the cause of their peoples' national self-determination. Yet as this chapter also makes clear, the economic restructuring of this region during the late nineteenth century meant that socialism also played a crucial part in shaping events as shown by the role that the region's cities played in the 1905 and 1917 revolutions. With the collapse of both the Russian empire and Germany, however, the Baltic peoples were able to take advantage of the geopolitical situation to achieve their own independent sovereign states.

While independent statehood may have been short-lived, it was nonetheless marked by a period of intense state-building in which the economies, political institutions and national cultures of all three were reshaped in ways which invite comparison with their cultural neighbours, the interwar Scandinavian states. As Chapter 2 shows, this was far more evident for the predominantly Lutheran and economically more developed Estonia and Latvia than Roman Catholic and less industrial Lithuania. What in effect emerged were small but economically successful agrarian countries whose emphasis on self-education, cultural pluralism and co-operative agriculture resembled many of the hallmarks of Scandinavian liberalism. Yet liberal democracy did not last. In Lithuania it quickly gave way to authoritarian rule, with Estonia and Latvia following seven years later in 1934.

The establishment of the Baltic States did not however secure an enduring stability in a region where Great Power rivalries and interests remained largely indifferent to the Baltic peoples' struggles to maintain their political sovereignty. For the new Soviet state, in particular, the *pribaltika* represented a vulnerable buffer zone in which Russia's rival in the area, Germany, also had long-established interests. Chapter 3 examines the nature of the Great Power rivalry, focusing on the events which culminated in the signing of the 1939 Secret Protocol between Stalin and Hitler and which paved the way for the incorporation of all three Baltic States into the Soviet Union.

With the reinstatement of Soviet rule following three turbulent years of German occupation (1941–4), the redesignated Baltic republics were rapidly restructured both economically and socially to fit the template of Stalinism. From the late 1940s, all three republics were subject both to the rapid industrialisation of their urban economies and to the forced collectivisation of their countryside. Soviet-style economic transformation also went hand in hand with the mass deportation of thousands of Balts. Soviet power also signalled an abrupt end to any forms of cultural or political behaviour which could be interpreted as a challenge to the new political order. Yet as Chapter 4 shows, although sporadic armed resistance by the Balts had come to an end by the early 1950s, and despite the totalitarian methods employed by the Soviet State, Baltic dissent continued to manifest itself in a number of ways, both formally and informally. Occasionally dissent found an outlet amongst a local Communist party political leadership concerned about Moscow's insensitivity towards local cultural and economic interests, most notably in Estonia in 1950 and in Latvia in 1958–9. However such dissenting apparatchiks had little room for political manoeuvre, and were simply replaced by loyal Moscow functionaries. Yet dissent, which invariably took on a strong national flavour, also found other productive outlets in underground movements such as the human rights movement and in religious organisations, the latter especially evident in Catholic Lithuania. It was these movements which were to provide an important building-block to organising the national reawakening of late 1980s and in politicising the identific linkages between issues of freedom, democracy and social justice with resolving their respective national questions.

The remarkable stability that was characteristic of social and political life in the Baltic republics throughout the two decades preceding the Gorbachev administration cannot however be explained only by the recourse to state terror. Other forms of control also existed, not least the way in which Moscow was able to effectively incorporate the Baltic political leadership into what had become by the eve of perestroika a regime of political stasis. Yet as Chapter 5 suggests, just as an emerging native intelligentsia had played such a crucial part in forwarding the cause of national self-determination in the previous century, so it was this stratum, particularly those drawn from the humanistic professions, who were also at the forefront of the second national awakening. In taking advantage of the new political and social spaces opened up by Moscow's twin policies of glasnost and democratisation, the Baltic intelligentsia along with and their newly installed radical governments were able to organise and mobilise their peoples successfully behind their respective independence movements.

The re-establishment of independent statehood raises a whole variety of questions about the nature and problems associated with polities undergoing transition, notably the role and reconstitution of political leaders during transition, the problems of economic restructuring that these states now face following fifty years of being part of a Soviet economy, and of how decolonisation has resulted not in the creation of idealised nation-states but rather in multi-ethnic polities. In Chapter 6 the role of the political leadership during this transitional period (1985–91) is examined in which it is argued that in all three republics a number of changes in leadership occurred, at each stage associated with the cumulative radicalisation of Baltic politics. With the establishment of independence, however, it also becomes clear that the Baltic states are not unusual amongst post-communist states in that it is their national intelligentsia, having led the struggle for statehood, who emerge to comprise a new post-independence political élite.

For the newly independent Baltic States, economic self-determination has also emerged as a major issue triggered off by the early importance given by the Gorbachev regime to Baltic economic autonomy within its unfolding reform programme. Chapter 7 examines how the economies of all three Baltic republics became inextricably bound up with a centrally planned system of regional specialisation of production and the consequences which such a legacy of interdependency has bequeathed to national economies wishing to realign themselves along more sovereign lines. Indeed it was precisely the highly centralised character of economic management and of the way in which the Baltic economies had been structured to fit the economic priority of Stalinist development that received such critical questioning by radically-minded Baltic economists during the period of reform communism. Having, however, secured statehood the Baltic States are now embarking upon far-reaching programmes of economic restructuring designed to reconnect their national economies with Western markets and with a privatised sector more in keeping with the interwar years than with Soviet-style central planning.

While independent statehood led to a resolution of Baltic national self-determination it has not resolved the tensions inherent in the regions multi-ethnic character. For the Baltic republics the issue of who in a multi-ethnic polity should enjoy national citizenship has dominated their political agendas. The issue has centred on the Russian community, a large proportion of whom settled in the Baltic States during Soviet rule. With independence these migrants, at one time secure in their Soviet citizenship, have found membership of the new states highly contested and uncertain. Chapter 8 examines the evolution of the citizenship debates in the transitional period towards independence and the impact that their formalisation is having on shaping the nature of inter-ethnic relations, particularly in relation to the community most affected by it, the Russians.

TRIALS OF TRANSITIONS

The unique twentieth-century experience of the Baltic States in having secured independent statehood both at the beginning and end of the twentieth century inevitably invites comparisons between these two transitions not only because this may help us to understand the nature of the more recent political secession and the problems that these states now face but also because a keynote of the recent national awakening has been a desire by many Baltic politicians to go back to the future, in effect to reconnect with the pre-Soviet 'golden age' and to use that past era of independent statehood as a basis to reconstruct their polities, economies and national cultures. Indeed it is precisely because the Baltic States have the opportunity to revitalise past models of liberal democracy and *laissez-faire* economics that some commentators have been more optimistic about their political and economic prospects compared with other post-Soviet states. Thus for Fukuyama 'there is no reason to suggest that Lithuania or Estonia will be less liberal than Sweden or Finland once given their national independence'.[1]

More sober observations however suggest that there is nothing inevitable about either the transition to *laissez-faire* economics going hand in hand with the development of liberal democracy or that these new states in having contributed to the end of one form of totalitarian rule are unlikely to return to authoritarian-nationalism. Indeed, five decades of isolation within Baltic society from pluralist debates has reinforced what Lieven calls an 'unanalysed nostalgia'[2] for the interwar period, in which the relatively short-lived era of liberal democracy is equated with the totality of Baltic statehood and the rise of authoritarian-nationalism during the 1930s as an aberration. In short, it is too early to know what eventual form and shape such transitional societies will take, let alone declare either an 'an end to history' or 'a return to the past'. What, however, is certain is that the economic, political and social problems that these transitional societies and their polities face in the 1990s are greater than in the 1920s.

In both 1918 and 1991 the Baltic States were brought into existence out of the chaos of revolutionary change at the heart of Empire. On both occasions they chose the path of nationalism over socialism and, at least initially, liberal democracy over authoritarianism. As new states, their economic and social situations compared very favourably with the states from which they seceded. Although overwhelmingly agrarian in social composition, the new republics created in November 1918 were amongst the most urbanised and industrialised of the former regions of the Russian empire, with one in four of their combined population living in cities. Literacy was also widespread; the 1897 tsarist census records over four-fifths of the populations of Estonia and Latvia as proficient at both reading and writing, a figure which most Soviet regions did not attain until the 1930s. Similarly, on the eve of the end of the Soviet Union, the Baltic States were the most urbanised of the Soviet republics, with around 70 per cent of each republic's population living in cities. Living standards were also amongst the highest in the USSR which was also reflected in their peoples' well-above-average national incomes. By 1988, Estonia, Latvia and Lithuania ranked respectively first, second and third out of the fifteen Soviet republics in their per capita national incomes.[3] And finally, in 1918 as well as in 1991, a new beginning entailed a desire to turn away from Russia and of what was an image of an essentially non-European Asiatic Russia, to creating nation-states which looked towards the political, economic and social models of Western Europe and Scandinavia as bases to reconstruct their societies and provide the regional security architecture to ensure their continuing statehood.

The commitment to *laissez-faire* economics and to restructuring their national economies to maximise integration into 'the New Europe' was as evident in 1918 as it is in the 1990s. In 1918 this proved comparatively painless for a number of reasons. The Baltic region was already well integrated into a Europe-wide system of trading. Earlier industrialisation than elsewhere in the Russian empire, especially in Estonia and Latvia, had already established the Baltic region at the forefront of the Empire's trade with the rest of Europe. As part of capitalist Europe, the region had already in place entrepreneurial social classes well qualified and equipped to facilitate the transition towards a fully functioning market economy. As already well-established agrarian economies they also had much to offer major industrial trading partners and in return became major importers of Western manufacturing goods, especially from Britain, France, Germany and the Scandinavian countries. Thus within a very short time-frame, the Baltic States had successfully completed the wholesale reorganisation of their national economies and their economic disentanglement from Russia.

Table 1.1 Population and social structure of the interwar and post-Cold War Baltic States

	Interwar			Post cold war		
	Estonia (1922)	Latvia (1925)	Lithuania[1] (1923)	Estonia (1989)	Latvia (1989)	Lithuania (1989)
Population ('000s)	1107	1845	2171	1566	2667	3673
Nationality (%)						
Eponymous	87.6	73.4	80.1	61.5	52.0	79.6
Russian	8.3	10.5	2.3	30.3	34.0	9.4
German	1.7	3.8	4.1			
Jewish	0.4	5.2	7.1	8.2	14.0	11.0
Other						
Urban	27.4	34.3	15.8	71.0	71.0	68.0
Rural	72.6	65.7	84.2	29.0	29.0	32.0

[1]Includes Klaipeda/Memel territory (data from 1925).
Sources: Data for the interwar years calculated from the censuses of each state, and for 1989 from the Soviet census.

Estonia was fairly typical: whereas in 1922, 25 per cent of trade was with Russia, by 1935 this had fallen to 3 per cent.

Such a reorientation, however, is unlikely to prove so easy in the 1990s. Five decades of Soviet rule has bequeathed to all three Baltic States highly industrialised and specialised economies inextricably bound up with and dependent upon Russia and the other post-Soviet states. The development of heavy manufacturing industry, in particular, has meant an inordinate reliance on Russian raw materials and energy in a region largely deficient in both. Moreover, in contrast to 1918, the Baltic economies have to establish afresh market niches in the West for their products, a task not made any easier by the highly regionalised structure of a Europe dominated by the European Union. So however much the Baltic States would like to distance themselves from their recent economic past, trade with Russia will of necessity continue to be high, with all the geopolitical implications that this may carry. Given their similar economic structures, plans to strike up a Baltic *troika* of free-trading nations, something which was tried during the interwar years, is as unlikely now as then to reap much economic benefit.

In both 1918 and 1991, regime stability was dependent upon the dominant social groups who form the core of the new society. As overwhelmingly peasant societies in 1918 it was the peasant farmer who was the mainstay of regime stability, a process secured by the 1920s agrarian reforms which replaced the large estates of the Baltic German nobility in Estonia and Latvia and of the Polish aristocracy in Lithuania, with societies based on small-scale peasant farming. The significance of this rural stratum was also reinforced by the high profile given by the regimes to prioritising their designation as agrarian states rather than as fully industrialised economies, an outcome welcomed by those on the Right of the political spectrum fearful that the growth of an urban-industrial proletariat, possibly sympathetic to Bolshevism, might destabilise the regime. In the 1990s, the dominant socio-demographic core of the Baltic republics has long since been replaced by that of the urban-industrial worker. A disproportionately large number of this social stratum are also Russians. For this class, particularly those employed in state-owned and over-manned heavy industries, economic reform is likely to mean a considerable social upheaval, involving retraining, employment shift, and loss of jobs. Irrespective of the scale or speed of privatisation, there is greater prospect of this being a more turbulent transition than that in the 1920s.

Finally, there is the relationship between new ruling élites and the eponymous nations. In both 1918 and 1991, nationalism led to state formation: nationalism legitimised the claim to statehood and laid the foundations for shaping it. The largely middle-class eponymous-based counter-élites who led the independence struggles replaced *anciens regimes* dominated by largely non-eponymous élites. While the power enjoyed by the Baltic Germans was weakened primarily as a result of land reforms, initially at least these states were widely praised for their liberally-minded constitutions and for introducing far-sighted policies which protected the cultural, social and economic rights of their ethnic minorities. With the establishment of authoritarian-nationalist rule, however, the political representation of their non-eponymous peoples was drastically reduced and their cultural rights came under attack. In 1991, the Baltic States also inherited an ethnic legacy of decolonisation, the presence of large Russian-speaking communities, but which, at least in the case of Estonia and Latvia, citizenship legislation has not fully resolved. Consequently, for the Baltic States in the 1990s the politics of ethnicity is being reshaped in ways which are proving far more problematic than in the initial period of interwar state-building.

NOTES

1. F. Fukuyama, *The End of History and the Last Man* (London: Hamish Hamilton, 1992) p. 37.
2. A. Lieven, *The Baltic Revolution. Estonia, Latvia, Lithuania and the Path to Independence* (New Haven and London: Yale University Press, 1993), p. 55.
3. A. Kovalev, 'Kto pochemu za chertoi bednosti', *Ekonomicheskaya gazeta*, no. 25, 1989, p. 11.

Part I
From National Awakening
to Incorporation

1 Nationalism and Socialism in Historical Perspective

James D. White

Because it is customary to think in terms of nation-states, it is easy to slip into the anachronsim of saying that in the eighteenth century Estonia, Latvia and Lithuania were incorporated into the Russian Empire. In fact, in the eighteenth century neither an 'Estonia' nor a 'Latvia' existed or ever had existed; and only Lithuania had experienced independent statehood. By then, however, Lithuania no longer had any separate identity, having become an integral part of the Polish Commonwealth. The Estonian, Latvian and Lithuanian states which achieved independence at the end of the First World War were, therefore, not so much conquests of the Russian Empire, as entities which came into being in the context of the Russian Empire.

Livland and Estland were won from the Swedes by Peter the Great, giving Russia the valuable Baltic ports of Riga and Reval. Latgale, which formed part of Vitebsk province, was acquired by Catherine II in the First Partition of Poland in 1772. The Third Partition of Poland in 1795 brought Russia the Duchy of Kurland as well as the provinces of Vilna, Kovno and Grodno.

These territorial gains brought most of the Baltic peoples within the boundaries of the Russian Empire. The Estonians inhabited Estland and the northern part of Livland; the Latvians occupied the southern part of Livland, Kurland and Latgale, while the Lithuanians lived in the provinces of Vilna, Kovno and Grodno. An important centre of Lithuanian settlement, however, was to remain outside the Russian Empire. This was the area around Königsberg, which formed part of East Prussia.

The previous history of the lands settled by all three Baltic peoples had left them with a social structure in which class coincided with nationality. In the thirteenth century the Latvians and Estonians had been conquered by the German knights, so that by the eighteenth century the upper classes – the landowning nobility, the merchants and the clergy – were German,[1] while the peasants were either Latvian or Estonian. The Lithuanians had successfully resisted the Germanic conquest, but a long period of union with Poland had created a situation in which the landowners and clergy were either Poles or Polonised Lithuanians, and the peasants were Lithuanian. In East Prussia the peasantry was Lithuanian, and the landowners and clergy German. The Latvians and Estonians, who had taken their Christianity from the Germans, were predominantly Lutheran, whereas most Lithuanians, who had taken their Christianity from the Poles were Roman Catholic.

On being annexed by Russia, the Baltic territories were not assimilated into the Russian state, but were left with considerable local autonomy. Livland, Kurland and Estland each had its own nobles' assembly or 'Landtag', and the powers of this institution within the particular province were extensive. The Landtag could also take the initiative in legislation and had the right to petition the tsar.[2]

Until the middle of the nineteenth century Latvian, Estonian and Lithuanian speakers were almost exclusively peasants, and although these languages were rich in folklore, they possessed no substantial body of academic or artistic literature.[3] This meant that learning and culture were only open to a Latvian or Estonian if he succeeded in mastering German, or to a Lithuanian if he learnt Polish. For all three peoples, education meant the adoption of a new nationality; an educated Latvian, Estonian or Lithuanian was held to be a contradiction in terms. Important developments for the emergence of Baltic nationhood were consequently the formation of educated élites among the three peoples and the appearance of literature in their languages. These developments were to take place in the course of the nineteenth century.

AGRARIAN REFORM

A major factor in the emergence of national élites in the Baltic territories were the agrarian reforms carried out in the first half of the nineteenth century. These reforms facilitated the rationalisation of agriculture, making it among the most productive in the Russian Empire. They also had the effect of giving the social structure of the Baltic countryside its distinctive features compared with that of the Russian hinterland. Whereas in the Russian villages it was common for a large number of peasants to cultivate small allotments, in the Baltic provinces, it was more typical to find a small number of peasant householders farming relatively large holdings of land.[4] In these provinces, however, the great majority of peasants owned or rented no land at all, but worked as farm labourers.[5]

Even at the time the Baltic territories were acquired by Russia, their agrarian structure differed significantly from that of Russia proper. Whereas in Russia a peasant commune or *mir* was still in existence, and this distributed both resources and obligations among the various households, this type of institution no longer existed in the Baltic region, so that there the household was the basic unit of social organisation. This was reflected in the pattern of settlement: in the Baltic provinces – with the exception of Latgale – peasants lived in scattered individual dwellings rather than in villages, as was the custom in Russia proper.[6]

During the last years of Swedish rule in Livland and Estland there had been an improvement in the economic position of the peasantry at the nobility's expense. When these provinces were acquired by Peter the Great, however, he immediately set about reversing this policy, and restoring the privileges of the German aristocracy. Peter's successors, especially Catherine II, continued to support the nobility to the detriment of the peasants, with the result that the latter experienced increasing hardship, and expressed their discontent in sporadic revolts.[7]

In 1804 Tsar Alexander I approved a scheme of agrarian reform for Livland and Estland. This sought to alleviate peasant obligations by reviving the Swedish practice of setting out in special documents (*Wackenbücher*) the exact amount of labour service that should be performed for the quantity and quality of land made available to the peasant household. It also made tenures more secure by stipulating that land assigned for peasant use could be withdrawn only in exceptional circumstances.[8]

The landowners, however, especially those of Estland, found that they could not afford the expense of the land-surveys necessitated by the new regulations, and they considered that these regulations infringed their property rights to the land. The means chosen by the Estland nobility to escape this predicament was the liberation of the peasantry. This was first discussed in 1810, but the process of legislation was interrupted by the war against Napoleon. In May 1816, however, the law received the approval of the Emperor.[9]

In 1814 the Landtag of Kurland, which had still to institute any peasant reforms, put forward a proposal based on the Livland law of 1804. An imperial rescript of 5 December 1816 gave the Kurland nobility the choice of implementing this proposal or adopting a law similar to the one enacted by the Estland Landtag. The latter alternative was chosen, and in August 1817 the law freeing the peasants in Kurland was passed. Livland then followed the example of its neighbour and promulgated a law freeing its peasants in March 1819.[10]

The reforms of 1816–19 gave the peasants their personal freedom, and allowed them to settle anywhere in the province – providing the landowner had no objection – but left all the land, including that which had formerly been reserved for peasant use (*Bauerland*), in the hands of the nobility. To earn a livelihood the peasants now had to rent their allotments from the landowner. The two parties would now make a free contract in which the peasant would receive a lease of the land in return for labour services on the landowner's estate.[11]

The emancipation legislation, therefore, did not bring about any great change for the better in the economic position of the peasantry; in fact they had now lost the protection given by the 1804 laws and the traditional *Wackenbuch* arrangements. The landowners were able to take advantage of this circumstance to rationalise their agriculture, and in the process to annex peasant allotments to their estates. These clearances (*Bauernlegen*) evoked a series of major peasant disturbances. These were especially severe in the 1840s, and troops were required for their suppression. At that time it came to be widely believed among Latvian and Estonian peasants that the Russian government was willing to grant them freedom and land, but that an obstacle to receiving these things was their Lutheran faith. Consequently, Latvian and Estonian peasants converted *en masse* to Orthodoxy.[12]

The peasant disturbances compelled the landowners to undertake new reforms. Laws were enacted for Livland in 1849 and Estland in 1856 extending leases of allotments and facilitating the sale of land to the peasants. The reforms also encouraged the payment of rents in money instead of labour service. In Kurland there was no such law. But even without special legislation developments proceeded there in the same direction as in the other two provinces. Agriculture became increasingly commercial, and labour services steadily gave way to money rents.[13]

The 1850s, therefore, saw the emergence of distinctive economic and social patterns in Livland, Estland and Kurland. These provinces had a rational landlord economy, based on advanced farming methods and making extensive use of hired labour. Those peasant householders who were able to buy their allotments or obtain a long-term lease were also able to attain some degree of prosperity. Only a minority of peasants, however, possessed land of any description, the vast army of landless peasantry being a characteristic feature of the Baltic countryside.[14]

In preparing the legislation to free the Russian peasantry the government of Alexander II was determined not to follow the example of the Baltic provinces in freeing the serfs without land. It decided that the peasants should be liberated with at least some land, and that the existing peasant commune should be retained. In this way the freed peasants would not be without the means to maintain themselves and would be attached to a stable social unit.[15]

The liberation edict of 1861, which was originally intended to apply to the Lithuanian provinces and Latgale, was based on the amount of land the peasantry had at its disposal at that time, and the allotments were assigned on that basis. In January 1863, however, the Polish rebellion erupted, the insurgents receiving significant support from the gentry in the Lithuanian provinces. To prevent the rebellion spreading among the peasantry, the government revised the terms of the emancipation settlement as they related to Lithuania and Latgale, as well as Belorussia and the Right-Bank Ukraine, in a manner advantageous to the peasants. They were given the unconditional entitlement to purchase allotments of land; they were accorded the status of peasant proprietors without having to go through the transitional stage of 'temporary obligation'; and the redemption payments for their land were reduced by 20 per cent.[16]

The land reforms carried out in the Lithuanian provinces between 1861 and 1867 appreciably improved the position of the peasantry at the expense of the nobility. As a result of the reforms, the peasants of the province of Vilna had 16 per cent more land in 1867 than they had possessed in 1861, those of Kovno province 19 per cent more, and those of Grodno province 12 per cent more. Many landless peasants in these provinces were also provided with small parcels of land.[17] Thus, as in Livland, Kurland and Estland, the formation of comparatively large consolidated farms producing for the market was a common phenomenon in the Lithuanian countryside. An important difference, however, was that in the Lithuanian provinces there were considerably fewer landless peasants. For this reason agrarian disturbances in 1905 were rarer and less severe than in the neighbouring Livland.

THE RUSSIAN CONTEXT OF THE BALTIC NATIONAL MOVEMENTS

The mass conversion of Livland peasants to the Orthodox faith in the early 1840s exposed an ambivalence in the ideology of official Russian nationalism, and established the pattern for the future orientation of the national movements in the Baltic provinces. For while the conversions deeply embarrassed the provincial Lutheran clergy and German nobility, they could scarcely be condemned by a government which professed to uphold the values of 'autocracy, Orthodoxy and national character'. A division was revealed between those in court circles who supported the privileges of the German aristocracy and those who applauded the Baltic peasants for their pro-Orthodox – and therefore pro-Russian – stance.[18]

The peasants found a powerful champion in the person of Yury Samarin, a prominent figure among the Slavophiles, and one of the architects of the peasant liberation in Russia. He visited Riga in 1848 and wrote a report on the plight of the peasants, advocating that the Baltic provinces be thoroughly integrated into the Empire. His 'Letters from Riga' were widely circulated in manuscript. The pro-German party at court soon gained the upper hand, however, and Samarin was imprisoned in the Peter and Paul Fortress in St Petersburg for two weeks.[19]

Samarin continued to advocate the Russification of the Baltic provinces in the newspaper *Den'*, which he edited with Ivan Aksakov, and the theme was taken up by the influential conservative publicist Mikhail Katkov in the newspaper *Moskovskie vedomosti*. After the Polish insurrection of 1863 the tide turned decisively in favour of those who advocated Russification of the Baltic provinces. They were then able to argue that the underlying cause of the rebellion had been the incomplete assimilation of the Polish territories into the Russian Empire, and that only Russification could guarantee political stability. That policy was carried out in the Polish and Lithuanian provinces, the local governmental and educational systems being remodelled on the Russian pattern.[20]

Samarin and Katkov had been advocates of the relatively generous land-distribution to the peasants in the Lithuanian provinces. But in favouring the Lithuanian peasants in one respect the Russification measures disadvantaged them in another. To wean them away from the baneful influence of the Poles, in 1864 the use of roman type was forbidden in Lithuanian publications; henceforth only Cyrillic type was permitted.[21]

The argument for Russification was then applied to the provinces under German domination, and in his book *Okrainy Rossii* written in 1868 Samarin drew a parallel between the situation in the Polish territories and that in the Baltic provinces. Samarin urged that the 1861 peasant reforms should be extended to the Baltic area and that the privileged position of the German nobility should be ended.[22]

In 1869 Karl Schirren, the professor of history at Dorpat University published a reply to Samarin in which he defended the Baltic Germans and condemned the principle of 'race' on which Samarin had allegedly based his position.[23] The immoderate tone of the pamphlet, however, compelled most Baltic Germans to dissociate themselves from it, and Schirren was forced to leave his university post and settle in Germany.[24]

A more systematic reply to charges by Russian conservatives that Latvian and Estonian peasants were oppressed by the German landowners appeared in 1868, when Friedrich von Jung-Stilling produced a collection of statistics on agrarian conditions in Livland.[25] This caused the polemic to turn on matters requiring precise factual information, thereby putting Katkov and his associates at some disadvantage. They were helped, however, by a group of young Latvian intellectuals who were involved in the fledgling national movement, and were prepared to make common cause with the Russian conservative and Slavophile press against the common adversary, the Baltic Germans. These 'Young Latvians' were able to supply first-hand factual material on agrarian conditions in the Baltic area and even to write for Slavophile publications themselves. In return, Katkov helped the Young Latvians establish a Latvian-language newspaper in St Petersburg.[26]

It was with the accession to the throne of Alexander III that Slavophile influences finally gained full sway over government policy. In the 1880s Russification of the Baltic provinces became one of the government's principal social policies. The reforms of the 1880s and 1890s were aimed at the full assimilation of the Baltic provinces into the Russian Empire, and involved the reorganisation of the local administration, judiciary and education system on the Russian model. The measures were an inconvenience to the Germans rather than a serious threat, and never undermined their dominant position. The policies, moreover, were relaxed in the wake of the 1905 revolution.[27]

THE GERMAN INTELLECTUAL BACKGROUND TO THE BALTIC NATIONAL MOVEMENTS

When Karl Schirren claimed in his reply to Samarin that the Germans had brought considerable intellectual benefits to the Latvians and Estonians, he did so with some justification. The German Reformation and Counter-Reformation had left their marks in the Baltic area. As the disputing parties tried to win support among the local population they published tracts in Latvian and Estonian, so that the earliest documents in these languages were of a theological character. German scholars also provided translations of the Bible into these two languages.[28]

The Pietist current within Lutheranism was also strong in the Baltic area. Its emphasis on individual Bible study encouraged the spread of literacy; and the importance it attached to personal worth gave it a markedly democratic connotation. It preferred the simple but virtuous life of the common people to the sophisticated but irreligious one of their social betters. Pietism was to be a major inspiration for German thought at the end of the eighteenth century, some of which was to influence national movements in the Baltic.[29]

As well as providing the basis for the Latvian and Estonian literary languages, the Germans also supplied the intellectual underpinnings of the Baltic national movements. The dominant figure of the period was of course, Immanuel Kant, a native of Königsberg, who published his famous

Critiques in Riga. It was in Riga too that some of Kant's ideas were elaborated first by Hamann and then by Herder in a way significant for the development of Baltic perceptions of nationality.

Hamann took up the contrast Kant had drawn between the concreteness of immediate sense perceptions and the colourlessness of abstract thought. In his epigrammatic way, Hamann set this contrast in a historical framework, speculating that 'poetry is the mother-tongue of the human race', or in other words that in the intellectual development of mankind artistic creation had preceded reasoned discourse. Herder took this idea further by suggesting that whereas the concepts employed by modern educated society were universal and cosmopolitan, the traditional artistic creation of the common people was imbued with specific characteristics of the nation to which it belonged. Not only did Herder attach a new significance, replete with Pietistic overtones, to folk culture by his theoretical writings, but he also initiated the collection of folk-songs by making a compilation which included Lithuanian, Latvian and Estonian material.[30]

The idea that folk culture embodied the ethos of a particular nation was received with enthusiasm in Germany, and given special urgency by the wars against Napoleon. For Arnim, Brentano, Görres and other writers of the Romantic movement the traditional songs and stories of the German people represented the repository of the national spirit. Thus, in the first decades of the nineteenth century the emergence of German national consciouness was closely associated with the culture of the *Volk*.[31]

As the identification of folk culture with national particularity originated in the Baltic area and drew upon Baltic material, it was natural that this should be a vital concept for the Baltic national movements. For the Latvians and Estonians, who were constantly exposed to German culture, a major preoccupation was the collection of folk material and the organisation of song festivals.[32]

The Lithuanians were to receive this version of national awareness through East Prussia, where it served as the driving force behind the appearance of a modern Lithuanian secular literature. In Königsberg a special school had been established in 1718 to teach the Lithuanian language, principally to students of theology. One of these, a Lithuanian Pietist, Kristijonas Donelaitis, was to compose a remarkable poem in his native language, *Metai* (The Seasons). It depicted the life of the Lithuanian peasants of East Prussian throughout the year. Although written between 1765 and 1775 it remained unknown until 1818, when it was published by Ludwig Rhesa, a Lithuanian admirer of Herder.[33] It was to give a significant impetus to the formation of a national awareness among the Lithuanian population of the Russian Empire, and served as an inspiration for later works in Latvian and Estonian.

THE BALTIC NATIONAL MOVEMENTS

The Latvian and Estonian national movements were to a large degree the product of the agrarian reforms of the first half of the nineteenth century. These had created a class of relatively prosperous peasant farmers who were able to send their sons to university at their own expense, without the help and good graces of Lutheran pastors or German landowners. And whereas it had been normal until the end of the 1850s for young Latvians and Estonians who received higher education to lose their former national-ity and enter the ranks of educated Germans, the new generation wished to acquire education and still retain its Latvian or Estonian identity.[34] The national movements were therefore directed towards achieving equality for the Baltic languages and cultures with those of other European peoples – with the Germans in particular. This was done within a German intellectual environment, and with materials supplied by German culture.

The Latvians

The movement known as the 'Young Latvians' began as a small group of Latvian students at Dorpat University in 1856. Its members held 'Latvian evenings' and published a small journal called *Majar viesis* (House Guest), which campaigned against the 'lack of regard in which the Latvian people and the Latvian language were held'.[35] The Baltic Germans referred to the group ironically as the 'Young Latvians', on analogy with the 'Young Ger-many' movement, a parallel which the Latvian students accepted willingly.[36]

Although the early aims of the Young Latvians were scholarly and liter-ary, they quickly acquired more far-reaching goals. They wished to eman-cipate the peasant population from the domination of the German nobility and clergy and to replace the all-pervasive German influence by a purely Latvian culture.[37] They were deeply critical of the 1817–19 reforms, deny-ing that they had really brought freedom to the Latvian peasantry. They contended that if genuinely free competition were to be introduced it would mean the end of the Baltic Germans' privileged position.[38] The Young Latvians compared the Baltic agrarian reforms unfavourably with that recently implemented in Russia, and called for the 1861 Russian peasant reform to be extended to the Baltic area.[39]

After graduating from Dorpat, some of the Young Latvians transferred their activities to St Peterburg. One of their number, Krišjanis Valdemars, made contact with Katkov and the Slavophiles, and it was in return for the Young Latvians' co-operation in their polemic against the Baltic Germans that Katkov enabled Valdemars and his circle to publish a Latvian language newspaper in St Petersburg. This was *Pēterburgas Avīzes* (St Petersburg newspaper), which first appeared in June 1862. Its contributors included many of those active in the Young Latvian movement, Valdemars, Juris Alunāns, Krišjānis Barons, Kaspars Biezbārdis, etc.[40]

Pēterburgas Avīzes was extremely influential paper, not only in the awakening of Latvian national consciousness, but also as an example for the other Baltic peoples to follow. It did not, however, survive long; in 1865 the Baltic Germans succeeded in having it closed down through their influence in court circles.[41]

After the demise of *Pēterburgas Avīzes,* Riga became the centre of the Young Latvian movement. The Riga Latvian Association was formed there in 1868 and during the following decade it organised song festivals and conferences on Latvian folklore. In 1869 the Association began to publish the newspaper *Baltijas Vēstnesis* (Baltic Herald), edited by its chairman Bernhards Dirikis; this was conceived as a successor to *Pēterburgas Avīzes.*[42]

At the end of the 1860s Dorpat regained its significance for the Young Latvians. Their spiritual leader in Dorpat was Atis Kronvalds. A lecturer at the Dorpat Teachers' Training College, Kronvalds revived the 'Latvian evenings' for students at the University, carrying on a tradition begun by Valdemars. It was while at Dorpat that Kronvalds published his essay *Nationale Bestrebungen* (1872) which defended the Latvian national movement from attacks by the Baltic Germans, and which became one of the principal manifestos of Latvian nationalism.

The Estonians

Dorpat was also an important centre for the Estonian national movement. It was there that the movement's first newspaper *Eesti Postimees* (The Estonian Postman) was published between 1864 and 1880. Its editor, Johan Jannsen, though concerned to promote Estonian national awareness and self-confidence, tried to avoid open conflict with the Baltic Germans by concentrating as far as possible on cultural matters.[43] He was involved, for example, in organising Estonian song festivals and the Estonian choral society 'Vanemuine'. Jannsen's restraint and moderation towards the Baltic Germans, however, was deplored by the more radical wing of the Estonian national movement which was centred in St Petersburg.[44]

From the 1850s there had existed in the Russian capital a group of Estonian intellectuals who referred to themselves as the 'St Petersburg Patriots'. The group included the artist Johan Köler, an admirer of the Italian 'Risorgimento', and Carl Robert Jakobson who had recently graduated from the teachers' training college in Walk run by the Latvian educationalist Janis Cimze. Although Jakobson, like Jannsen attached great importance to educating the Estonian people and securing for them a place among the European nations, he was also concerned to end the privileged position of the Baltic Germans. He believed that the effective way of doing this was to follow the example of the Young Latvians and form an alliance with the Slavophiles. Jakobson, as the chief proponent of the so-called 'eastern orientation' in the Estonian national movement found himself increasingly in conflict with Jannsen, who was unwilling to adopt this policy.[45]

In St Petersburg Jakobson and Köler had close connections with the Latvian national movement through Valdemars. The latter, for his part, helped the St Petersburg Patriots obtain permission from the Russian government to publish an Estonian language newspaper on the model of *Pēterburgas Avīzes*. He was also able to enlist the support of Katkov's *Moskovskie vedomosti* on behalf of the Estonians. The resistance of the Baltic Germans was such, however, that Jakobson's paper, *Sakala* did not appear until 1878.[46]

Sakala, which was published in Fellin, was a more radical paper than *Eesti Postimees*, though its radicalism was moderated to meet the requirements of the censor. The political orientation of *Sakala* was similar to that of its Latvian predecessor, *Pēterburgas Avīzes*, in that it demanded an extension of the Russian peasant reform of 1861 to the Baltic provinces. It also demanded the fixing of an upper limit for land prices and land rents paid by Estonian peasants to German landowners. It suggested that Estland should be united with the ethnic Estonian parts of Livland into a single province. As far as it was possible within the censorship restrictions *Sakala* criticised the special position of the Baltic Germans and advocated measures which in effect would bring it to an end, such as the extension of the Russian judicial reforms to the Baltic provinces and the subordination of schools in the Estonian provinces to the Russian Ministry of Education.[47]

Understandably, the Baltic Germans tried to have *Sakala* closed down and even succeeded in 1879 in stopping its publication for eight months. It reappeared, however, with increased popularity, and maintained its radical orientation until Jakobson's death in March 1880. The leadership of the radical wing of the Estonian national movement then passed to J. Järv and the newspaper *Virulane*.[48]

The Lithuanians

With the example of the Latvians and the Estonians before them it was natural that the Lithuanians should try to repeat the tactics which had proved so successful and try to win the support of the Russian government. This was in fact attempted, but unsuccessfully, so that the Lithuanian national movement did not repeat the pattern of the Latvian and Estonian ones. Lithuanians were identified in the minds of the Russian authorities with the rebellious Poles, and were not regarded in the same favourable light as the Latvians or Estonians. The identification of Lithuanians with Poles was reinforced by the actions of the Lithuanians themselves after the use of the Roman alphabet had been banned.

For the Lithuanians this prohibition was a particularly traumatic event, because the use of the Roman alphabet was something which distinguished the Catholic Lithuanians from the Orthodox Russians. It had consequently a deep religious significance. It was in view of this significance that the opposition to the ban on roman type was led by the Lithuanian clergy. Motiėjus Valančius, the Bishop of Samogitia, denounced the printing of Lithuanian books in Cyrillic as contrary to the Catholic faith, and with the help of the Protestant clergy in East Prussia arranged to have books and pamphlets published there and smuggled across the border.[49] The illegality of these measures undermined attempts to induce the Russian government to assist in furthering Lithuanian national aspirations.

The secular wing of the Lithuanian national movement began to appear around 1870 with the formation of Lithuanian student societies at St Petersburg and Moscow universities. These societies produced the leaders of the Lithuanian national movement in the 1880s, Jonas Basanavičius, Jonas Šliupas and Petras Vileišis. The appearance of the Lithuanian societies was warmly welcomed by the Young Latvians. Valdemars and other Young Latvians in Moscow discussed with Basanavičius and Šliupas the possibility of publishing a Lithuanian language newspaper following the example of *Pēterburgas Avīzes*. Accordingly, Basanavičius and Šliupas attempted to form the same kind of alliance with the Russian government against the Poles as the Latvians had formed against the Baltic Germans.[50]

In 1884 Šliupas presented a memorandum to the Governor General of Warsaw arguing that if the Lithuanians were allowed the use of the Roman alphabet all anti-government activity in Lithuanian would cease, book-smuggling would stop, and there would take place a 'spiritual communion with Russia'. Šliupas also pointed out that by supporting Lithuania's claim to separate cultural identity the Russian government would undermine the international prestige of the Poles; Polish writers born in Lithuanian territories (Mickiewicz, Kraszewski, Kondratowicz, etc.) would have to be considered Lithuanian.[51]

Lack of enthusiasm by the Russian authorities prevented any such bargain being struck. In any case, at the time Šliupas was negotiating with the Russians, *Aušra* (Dawn), the first newspaper of the Lithuanian national awakening, was already being printed in East Prussia and being smuggled across the border in the traditional manner for Lithuanian publications.

In the first issue of *Aušra*, which appeared in March 1883, its editor, Basanavicius, explained the objectives of the newspaper, which were: to propagate the idea of Lithuanian nationality; to foster a love for the Lithuanian country and its language; to acquaint the readers with Lithuania's history and to demand Lithuanian schools. Šliupas, who later acted as editor, stressed that the welfare of the country depended on its economic development and that it should be the duty of every true patriot to engage actively in trade and industry.[52]

By the time *Aušra* ceased publication in 1886 it was clear that any overtures to the Russian authorities to allow the legal publication of a Lithuanian newspaper were doomed to failure, and the Lithuanian national movement would not be able to enjoy the privileged position of the Young Latvians. *Aušra*'s successor, *Varpas* (The Bell), which appeared between 1899 and 1905 under the editorship of Vincas Kudirka, accordingly adopted an increasingly critical stance towards the government. The journal also continued the interest in social and economic questions displayed by Šliupas in *Aušra*. By the turn of the century *Varpas* was looked upon practically as a socialist journal, many of its contributors at that time belonging to socialist groups in Lithuania.[53]

INDUSTRIALISATION OF THE BALTIC PROVINCES

Many of the landless peasants moved to the towns in search of employment, especially with the expansion of industry at the end of the nineteenth century. As a result, the urban population of Baltic towns underwent considerable expansion. This was especially true of Riga: in 1867 it had a population of 103 000; by 1897 it was 282 000.[54]

Urbanisation, as well as the development of industry, was stimulated by the building of railways. These linked the seaports on the Baltic coast – Riga, Libau, Narva, etc. – with the internal provinces of Russia, in particular with Russia's chief grain producing areas in the central black earth region and the Lower Volga. The Baltic ports thus benefited from Russia's expanding export trade in grain.[55]

From 1868 onwards the Russian government adopted a policy of erecting high tariff barriers to protect native industry by discouraging imports. Rather than achieving this, however, the high customs duties encouraged German and other foreign firms to set up branches in the Baltic provinces. This process, which became general throughout the Russian Empire, gave a considerable stimulus to industrial expansion.

In the case of Riga and Reval the growth of industry attracted peasants from the surrounding areas, so that the growth of population made Riga more Latvian and Reval more Estonian in national composition. This was not so in the case of Vilna, however. Throughout the nineteenth and early twentieth centuries Vilna had a minoriy of Lithuanians, most of the urban population consisting of Jews, Poles and Russians.[56] In the Lithuanian provinces industry remained small-scale, and offering few opportunities for well-paid employment. Vilna, therefore, did not become the destination of Lithuanian peasants looking for jobs in industry. These went further afield, to industrial centres outside the Lithuanian provinces, such as Riga, Moscow or St Petersburg.[57]

SOCIALISM

The Lithuanians

Baltic social democratic organisations appeared initially in Vilna, where they took the form of workers' study circles, the first such group being formed about 1887. Its members included a number of intellectuals influenced by the Polish socialist party 'Proletariat', such as Leo Jogiches (Tyszka), Tsemech Kopelzon and Wacław Sielicki.[58] The composition of this first group of social democrats was multi-national, but as propaganda activities were extended among the local workers, this early unity was lost. Propaganda in Jewish workers' circles was carried on in Russian, while Polish was used in groups containing Polish and Lithuanian workers. When the Polish socialist Stanisław Trusiewicz visited Vilna in 1890 he found there two separate groups of social democrats – one Jewish and one Polish-Lithuanian.[59]

Very few of the Jewish workers in Vilna, however, could read Russian, though they were eager to learn the language for professional advancement.[60] The intellectuals who ran the study groups for Jewish workers, notably Julius Martov and Alexander Kremer decided that a wider audience could be reached if, instead of conducting propaganda in Russian among workers in study groups, one were to address larger, more informal meetings using agitational literature in Yiddish.[61]

This idea was abhorrent to the members of the Jewish workers' circles, who felt themselves to be betrayed by the intelligentsia and deprived of the opportunity to become literate in Russian.[62] The new tactic was defended, however, in a pamphlet written by Kremer entitled *On Agitation* and published in Geneva in 1896. The essay subsequently exerted a profound influence on social democracy throughout Russia. The production of agitational literature for Lithuanian workers, on the other hand, was met with some enthusiasm, but it led to serious divisions within social democracy in Lithuania.

In 1893 leadership of the Sielicki group passed to Alfons Morawski and Andrius Domaszewicz, both belonging to the local gentry and both graduates of Russian universities. They were joined in 1895 by Stanisław Trusiewicz, a member of Proletariat who had been active in Minsk. None of this group could speak Lithuanian, and initially its members confined themselves to distributing Polish socialist literature and organising Polish-speaking workers.[63] In order to reach Lithuanian workers Domaszewicz and his associates formed an alliance with the *Varpas* group to publish social democratic agitational literature in Lithuanian.[64]

In 1896 the social democratic group constituted itself into the Lithuanian Social Democratic Party (LSDP) at a congress held on 1 May.[65] At this congress Trusiewicz objected that collaboration with the *Varpas* group had diverted the social democrats from their real purpose, and was leading them in a nationalist direction. Trusiewicz therefore dissociated himself with the LSDP and established his own social democratic group – the Workers' Union in Lithuania (*Związek robotniczy na Litwie*).[66] In 1900 the Workers' Union joined the party recently formed by Leo Jogiches and Rosa Luxemburg, the Social Democracy of the Kingdom of Poland (SDKP) to form the Social Democracy of the Kingdom of Poland and Lithuania (SDKPiL).[67] Trusiewicz's secession from the LSDP, however, did not remove from it all the internationalist elements, so that debates within its ranks between nationalists and internationalists were to continue for many years to come.[68]

As the LSDP gained wider support, it also became more Lithuanian, as opposed to Polish, in character. And since relatively few Lithuanians were urban workers, the LSDP began to draw its support increasingly from rural districts. The tendency was strengthened in 1899 when Domaszewicz, Trusiewicz and most of the old leadership were arrested and were succeeded by people of Lithuanian peasant origin, such as A. Janulaitis, S. Kairys and V. Sirutavičius.[69]

The Latvians

Latvian social democracy was also closely connected with the national movement, though in the Latvian provinces social democracy was based on a numerous industrial Latvian working class. The first working-class organisations in the Latvian towns were not political, but concerned with providing workers with mutual aid, education and entertainment. The earliest of these mutual aid societies appeared during the 1860s, and by 1890 there were 250 of them in Riga alone. These societies became the forum for social democratic agitation by the radical Latvian intelligentsia at the turn of the century.[70]

In 1886 the Riga Mutual Aid Society for Latvian Artisans began to publish the newspaper *Dienas Lapa* (Daily Paper) under the editorship of F. Bergmanis. The Latvian intellectuals who contributed to it belonged to the same circle as that grouped around the Riga Latvian Association's *Baltijas Vēstnesis*.[71] In the leading article of the first number *Dienas Lapa* promised to work for the all-round progress of the Latvian people. Pēteris Stučka, a law graduate of St Petersburg University took over as editor in 1888 and in the following year *Dienas Lapa* published an article by J. Berziņš entitled 'A New Current among the Latvian People' from which came the name New Current (*Jaunā strāva*), later applied to the democratic and socialist movement which the newspaper represented.[72]

The New Current saw itself as continuing the tradition of the Young Latvians and following the original purpose of the Riga Latvian Association in working for the benefit of the Latvian people. It believed, however, that the Riga Latvian Association had become distracted from this aim by national and cultural pursuits, and had neglected the needs of the growing number of urban workers and agricultural labourers.[73] Besides Stučka, the chief representatives of the New Current were the poet Jānis Pliekšans (who wrote under the pseudonym Rainis), Fricis Rozins, Janis Jansons-Brauns, Pauls Dauge and other representatives of the more radical Latvian students at the Universities of St Petersburg, Moscow and Dorpat.

In August 1893 Rainis attended the Third Congress of the Socialist International at Zurich. He took the opportunity of visiting Bebel, who provided him with a large amount of socialist literature to take back to Riga. In the autumn of 1893, after Rainis's return from Zurich, *Dienas Lapa* began to disseminate Marxist ideas and the first social democratic circles began to appear among Latvian workers.[74]

The authorities first began to take an interest in these developments at the end of 1896. In May of 1897 mass arrests took place of people active in the New Current, and in June 1897 *Dienas Lapa* was closed down. Almost all of the most prominent figures in the New Current – Stučka, Rainis, Jansons-Brauns – were sentenced to internal exile. Some, such as Rozins and Dāvids Bundža, managed to escape abroad, to Britain and the USA, where they set about producing Latvian language journals promoting social democracy. In Boston, USA, Bundža formed the Union of Latvian Social Democrats, which produced the journal *Auseklis* (Morning Star). The West European Latvian Social Democratic Union in London, headed by F. Rozins published the journal *Latviu stradnieks* (Latvian Worker).[75]

By the summer of 1905 the Latvian Social Democratic party had about a thousand members. The Riga students were also successful in extending social democratic propaganda to the countryside,[76] thus rendering social democracy in the Latvian, as in the Lithuanian, provinces a peasant as well as a workers' movement.

The Estonians

The Estonians had no parallel with the New Current. Only in the small group of Dorpat intellectuals around the writer Eduard Vilde in the second half of the 1890s was there any resemblance to be found with the Latvian movement.[77] In 1901 Vilde, M. Martna and Konstantin Päts collaborated in producing the newspaper *Teataja* (The Herald). This paper gave special prominence to economic questions, maintaining that progress was determined primarily by the economic relations between classes.[78] The ideas expressed in *Teataja* were opposed by the more conservative group of Estonian intellectuals who published the newspaper *Postimees* (Postman). The newspaper's editors Jaan Tõnisson and Villem Reiman believed that the best means for Estonians to advance themselves was through education and by constructive cooperation with the Germans.[79]

Tõnisson was inclined to see the solution to social and economic problems in the extension of the co-operative movement. He considered that Estonians should concentrate on trying to promote reforms locally and not meddle in Russian affairs. This local orientation was not shared by Vilde, Päts and their associates, who thought it necessary to support the Russian democratic movement in the hope that its victory would redound to the benefit of the Estonians.[80]

THE 1905 REVOLUTION

The events of 9 January 1905 in St Petersburg when troops opened fire on peaceful demonstrators, drew an immediate response in the Baltic region, strikes taking place in the main towns – Vilna, Kovno, Riga an Reval. These strikes lasted until the third week in January. At the beginning of February the strikes were resumed, this time on economic grounds, for higher wages and shorter working hours.[81]

The industrial strikes very quickly spread into the countryside, especially around Riga and in the Estonian part of Livland.[82] In all of the Baltic provinces this was at least partly due to the success of social democratic agitation in the countryside, social democrats often addressing peasants who had gathered for church services.[83] The agricultural strikes were for higher wages, lower rents and a shorter working day.

The tsar's manifesto of 17 October granting new political freedoms, including that of assembly, made possible some political initiatives by the liberal groups in the Baltic provinces. In 1904 the prohibition on the use of the Roman alphabet had been lifted, allowing newspapers to be published legally in Lithuania.[84] One of the first newspapers to appear was the liberal *Vilniaus žinios*(Vilna News), edited by Petras Vileišis.The group of people associated with this paper organised elections for an assembly to be held in Vilna. The 'Vilnius Sejm' duly met on 21 November, all parties and groups being represented. In addition to the Lithuanian Social Democratic Party these included the Lithuanian Democratic Party (which consisted of non-socialist members of the *Varpas* group), the Christian Democrats and the Peasants' Union. The resolutions of the Sejm demanded Lithuanian autonomy and a national assembly in Vilna.[86]

Following the Manifesto of 17 October, the group associated with *Postimees* founded the Estonian National Progressist party. This party, which was headed by Tõnisson, adopted a programme similar to that of the Constitutional Democrats in Russia.[87] It was the Progressivist party which was instrumental in organising the Congress of People's Representatives which met in Dorpat on 27 November in the assembly hall of the university. Of the 800 delegates present, most were peasants. In its resolutions the Assembly called on the Estonian people to overthrow the tsarist regime, to boycott government institutions and courts, and to form popular committees of self-government.[88]

In many respects the resolutions of the Dorpat Congress of People's Representatives echoed those of the Congress of Peasants Delegates which had been held in Riga on 19–20 November. The Riga Peasants' Congress had resolved to break off all relations with the government, ignore its orders, refuse to pay taxes, organise people's militia, and elect local committees of popular self-government.[89] In many parts of the Baltic provinces peasant 'executive committees' were set up during the course of November. In Livland and Kurland alone at least 346 such committees were established. These for a time became the real power in the area.[90]

In the Baltic provinces the Russian example of forming soviets was not widely followed. Only in Reval was a Soviet of Workers' Deputies set up.[91] All the social democratic parties in Lithuania and Western Belorussia, especially the Jewish Bund, were against the formation of soviets. Their argument was that since 90 per cent of the local workers belonged to socialist parties it was not necessary to create soviets to organise the working class. It was a different matter in Russia, where most of the workers were unorganised. Similar considerations prevented Latvian social democrats from following the Russian example.[92]

The months of November and December were the climax of the peasant movement in the Baltic provinces, especially in the Latvian and Estonian areas. By the end of the year, 460 estates had been destroyed by arson in the Latvian, and 120 in the Estonian provinces.[93] In the Lithuanian provinces the destruction of estates was rare, but strikes by farm labourers were widespread.[94] By the end of the year, however, the army had come to the rescue of the beleaguered German barons, and a number of punitive expeditions were sent into the Baltic provinces to suppress the rebellion both in town and country. The Baltic German press encouraged Russian military intervention by asserting that the Latvians and Estonians intended to establish independent republics.[95]

The punitive expeditions, assisted extensively by the German landowners, acted with great ferocity towards the Latvian and Estonian populations. Between December 1905 and May 1909 about 700 people in the Latvian and Estonian provinces were condemned to death by military tribunal. Over 8000 were imprisoned or exiled to Siberia. In the Lithuanian provinces about 2900 people were arrested. Many Latvians, Estonians and Lithuanians emigrated abroad after the 1905 revolution, some to Great Britain but mostly to the USA.[96]

WAR, REVOLUTION AND INDEPENDENCE

The First World War and the Revolution in Russia created the fluid domestic and international situation in which the independence of the Baltic states could be achieved. During this period one can distinguish a number of phases by which the Baltic states achieved independence and some factors which led to this outcome.

The Latvians and Estonians entered the war with some enthusiasm. The Latvian Duma deputies J. Goldmanis and J. Zālitis were instrumental in overcoming the resistance of the Russian High Command and establishing Latvian Rifle Battalions. The Latvian Riflemen proved to be among the most effective and disciplined troops in the Russian army, though inefficiency of the High Command led them into useless sacrifice.[97]

By 1915 all the Lithuanian provinces and Kurland had been occupied by the advance of the German army. Riga was captured in August 1917. Many Latvians and Lithuanians fled to the interior of Russia, forming Latvian and Lithuanian colonies in several parts of the country. Industrial enterprises from the occupied area were dismantled and transported to Russia along with some 90 000 Baltic industrial workers. To cater for the needs of this vast number of refugees welfare organisations were established, which were to became important centres of political activity in Russia.[98]

In the occupied territories of the Baltic the Germans established a military administration, *Oberbefehshaberost* (usually contracted to Ober-Ost) headed by Marshall Hindenberg. All political organisations and public meetings were prohibited. The region's economy had to provide for not only the occupying army, but also to submit to requisitions of both agricultural and industrial produce to be sent to Germany. Plans were also made for the permanent annexation of Lithuania and Kurland and their incorporation into the German Empire.[99]

After the tsarist regime was overthrown in February–March 1917 representatives of the refugee organisations urged the Provisional Government to consider ethnic Latvian, Estonian, and Lithuanian territories distinct administrative units to be called 'Latvia', 'Estonia' and 'Lithuania' respectively. Only the Estonians were successful in this endeavour, the Russian Provisional Government issuing a decree that all districts with an Estonian majority were to be united into a single province. Jaan Poska, the Mayor of Reval, was appointed commissar for Estonia, and a Provincial Council (*Maapäev*), was established.[100]

Soviets of Workers' Deputies on the Petrograd model appeared in Tallinn and Riga in the first days of March, subsequently spreading rapidly to other Baltic towns.[101] Throughout the spring and summer of 1917 there was a continuous trial of strength between the soviets and the local representatives of the Provisional Government in Petrograd. In the course of the year Latvian and Estonian soviets underwent a steady radicalisation, falling increasingly under Bolshevik control. In May the Latvian Rifle Battalions went over in their entirety to the side of the Bolsheviks, an event of considerable importance for the outcome of the revolution in Russia and a cause of deep vexation to the Latvian middle classes.[102]

Following the Bolshevik revolution soviet governments were established in Estonia and the unoccupied part of Latvia. These regimes were of short duration, being brought to an end by the breakdown of Soviet–

German peace negotiations at Brest Litovsk and the advance of the German armies as far as Narva.

Shortly before the German invasion, on 24–25 February 1918, Konstantin Päts, Jüri Vilms and Konstantin Konik on behalf of *Maapäev,* which now regarded itself as the body in which national sovereignty resided, declared the existence of an independent Republic of Estonia. A provisional government headed by Päts was created, and an appeal for help was made to the Entente Powers, in the expectation that the latter, especially Britain, would be unwilling to countenance German domination of the Baltic seaboard. The Allies, however, were sympathetic, but initially unresponsive, as they wished to avoid the partition of the former Russian Empire.[103]

On 3 March the Brest-Litovsk Treaty was signed, and by a protocol agreed in Berlin on 27 August the sovereignty of the Baltic territories was transferred from Russia to Germany. The Germans meanwhile made arrangements to separate Livland and Estland from Russia and make the entire territory a German protectorate, whose ruler would be the king of Prussia.[104]

In Vilna the Germans authorised the convocation on 18 September of a congress of 214 Lithuanian delegates and the election of a 20-member 'Taryba' or council. This on 16 February proclaimed an independent Lithuanian state, which Germany recognised with the proviso that there be a 'perpetual alliance' between Lithuania and Germany. On 11 July the crown of Lithuania was offered to the Duke of Urach, Wilhelm von Würtemberg as King Mindaugas II, though the offer was subsequently withdrawn. An interim presidium was formed, which on 5 November designated Augustinas Voldemaras as prime minister of independent Lithuania.[105]

Following the military collapse of Germany in November 1918 the Latvian National Council, assembled in Riga, proclaimed the independence of Latvia. Jānis Čakste and Karlis Ulmanis were elected president of the republic and prime minister respectively.[106] The Estonian provisional government met in Reval on 11 November and once more proclaimed the independence of Estonia. Päts, released from German internment, resumed his post as premier.[107]

At the end of 1918 the Soviet government planned an offensive by the Red Army to counter the threat of invasion from the south and to carry the revolution to Germany and Poland. This involved crossing Baltic territory; and to avoid the accusation of invading independent countries, Lenin decided that Soviet governments would be established in the path of the advancing Red Army.[108]

On 29 November Soviet forces under Jukums Vācietis entered Narva and the Estland Workers' Commune was established under the leadership of Jaan Anvelt. The Päts government ordered a general mobilisation, and on 12 December a British naval squadron under Rear-Admiral Sinclair arrived in Narva. On 23 December Colonel Johan Laidoner was appointed commander-in-chief of the Estonian forces, Sinclair supplying him with weapons and two captured Soviet destroyers. In January 1919 Laidoner started a counter-offensive helped by 2000 Finnish volunteers, and the following month he was able to report that Estonia was virtually cleared of Soviet troops.[109]

During December 1918 Vācietis's forces advanced through Latvian territory, taking Riga on 3 January 1919. A soviet government was established there headed by Pēteris Stučka The Ulmanis government sought refuge in Libau, where it was protected by the Germans and a British cruiser and six destroyers.[110] With the entry of the Red Army into Vilna on 5 January 1919, a Lithuanian Soviet government headed by Vincas Kapsukas was installed, the Taryba moving to Kaunas.

The Latvian nationalist government in Libau, having no armed forces of its own, was forced to seek help from the Germans. Following the Armistice a volunteer force had been formed on Latvian territory from remnants of the VIII Army reinforced by recruits from Germany. This 'Iron Division' was commanded by General Rüdiger von der Goltz, who had ambitions to retain the Baltic area as a sphere of German influence. In return for military assistance the Ulmanis government agreed to grant German soldiers Latvian citizenship. Von der Goltz, however, regarded the Latvian government as little better than the Bolsheviks, and on 16 April, at his instigation, the Ulmanis's government was overthrown and replaced by that of the pro-German Latvian pastor Andrieve Niedra.[111]

Von der Goltz began his offensive against the Red Army in Latvia at the beginning of March and captured Riga on 23 May, bringing down Stučka's Soviet regime. Pushing northwards, von der Goltz's forces and the Baltic German *Landeswehr* were stopped near Wenden by a combined Estonian and Latvian nationalist force. In the battle of 19–22 June the Germans were defeated and had to retreat towards Riga.[112]

By the summer of 1919 the Allied powers had become convinced that the danger presented by the Bolsheviks had receded, and that now the most serious threat was presented by the continued German presence in the Baltic area. After repeated demands by General Hubert Gough, the head of the Allied Military Mission to the Baltic countries, von der Goltz laid down his command and returned to Germany. He had, however, encouraged the troops of the Iron Division to enlist in the anti-Bolshevik army of Bermondt-Avalov, and ostensibly in Russian services, remain on both Latvian and Lithuanian territory. It took the threat of Allied sanctions against

Germany for the Berlin government to order the evacuation of German troops from the Baltic. Those in Russian service, however, were now outside Germany's control.[113]

On 8 October 1919 under the pretext of trying to reach the Bolshevik front, Bermondt began an offensive in the direction of Riga. In response, the Latvian General Jānis Balodís deployed his troops to face the new threat, and, helped by the artillery of four French destroyers, defeated the Germans, who eventually retreated to East Prussia through Lithuania. Only Latgale remained under Bolshevik control, but this province was cleared by Balodis with the help of Polish forces sent by Piłsudski.[114]

Lithuanian–Polish relations were not so harmonious. The Poles regarded Vilna as their own and were determined to claim it. As a safeguard against Polish attack the Lithuanian Soviet Republic united with the neighbouring Belorussian Republic to form a single Soviet state Litbel. Meanwhile the government in Kaunas had begun to recruit German volunteers to retake the capital, but before this could be done Polish troops under Piłsudski moved up from the south and marched on Vilna. After three days of bitter fighting the Kapsukas government fell, and on 21 April Vilna was captured by the Poles.[115]

The Kaunas government immediately began an intensive diplomatic campaign for the return of Vilna. This met with no success until the summer of 1920, when in return for British help in the Polish war against the Soviet Union, the Poles reluctantly agreed to cede Vilna to the Lithuanians. The Lithuanian state, however, was not long in possession of its capital, for in October 1920 on Piłsudski's orders General Żeligowski retook the city for the Poles.[116]

In November 1919 the Soviet government opened peace negotiations with Estonia, leading to a peace treaty signed in Dorpat on 2 February 1920 between Russia and Estonia, the treaty giving Estonia *de jure* recognition. Similar agreements between the Soviet government and the other two Baltic states followed, a treaty between Russia and Latvia being concluded on 1 August 1920, and one between Soviet Russia and Lithuania on 12 July 1920.[117] The Allied powers recognised Estonia and Latvia *de jure* in January 1921 and Lithuania in December 1922.[118]

NOTES

1. In sources published prior to the First World War the German-speaking inhabitants of the Baltic provinces are invariably referred to as 'die Deutschen' (Germans) or 'die baltische Deutschen' (Baltic Germans), the adject-

ive being used in a geographical sense. From about 1920 one begins to encounter the term 'die Deutschbalten' – literally 'German Balts'. This ethnic contradiction in terms is now common in German works, especially those written by Baltic Germans.

2. Alexander von Tobien, *Die Agrargesetztgebung Livlands im 19 Jahrhundert*, vol. I, (Riga, 1899), p. 29.
3. Julius Eckardt, *Die baltischen Provinzen Rußlands*, (Leipzig, 1869), pp. 23–4.
4. P.P. Maslov, 'Razvitie zemledeliya i polozhenie krest'yan do nachala XX veka', L. Maslov et al. (eds) *Obshchestvennoe dvizhenie v Rossii v nachale XX-go veka*, vol. I, (St Petersburg, 1909), p. 26.
5. M.I. Kozin (ed.) *Ocherki ekonomicheskoy istorii Latvii 1860–1900* (Riga, 1972), p. 83.
6. L.C.D. Bray, *Essai critique sur l'histoire de la Livonie*, vol. III, (Dorpat, 1817), p. 61; V.A. Aleksandrov, N.V. Shlygina (eds), *Sel'skie poseleniya Pribaltiki (XIII-XX vv.)*, (Moscow, 1971), passim.
7. Tobien, *Die Agrargesetztgebung...*, vol. I, p. 101.
8. Ibid. pp. 206–7.
9. Axel von Gernet, *Geschichte und System des baüerlichen Agrarrechts in Estland*, (Reval, 1901), p. 145.
10. Tobien, pp. 288–372.
11. A. Rikhter, *Istoriya Krest'yanskogo sosloviya v prisoedinennykh k Rossii pribaltiyskikh guberniyakh*, (Riga, 1860), pp. 22–66.
12. Alexander von Tobien, *Die Agrargesetztgebung Livlands im 19 Jahrhundert*, vol. II (Riga, 1911), pp. 113–16.
13. Ibid., pp. 124–61; Rikhter, pp. 140–85.
14. Kozin, p. 34; *Istoriya Estonskoy SSR*, vol. II (Tallin, 1966), p. 80.
15. A. Skrebitsky, *Krest'yanskoe delo v tsarstvovanie Imperatora Aleksandra II* (Bonn, 1862), pp. 1–11.
16. P.A. Zayonchkovsky, *Otmena krepostnogo prava v Rossii* (Moscow, 1968), pp. 214–18.
17. Ibid., p. 223; Jerzy Ochmański, *Historia Litwy* (Wrocław, 1967), p. 180.
18. Alexander von Tobien, *Die Agrargesetztgebung Livlands im 19 Jahrhundert*, vol II (Riga, 1911), pp. 113–19.
19. P. Yosifova, 'Yu. F. Samarin i ego "Pis'ma iz Rigi"', *Vestnik Moskovskogo Universiteta*, Seriya Istoriya, 6/1990, pp. 3–13.
20. V.A. Tvardovskaya, *Ideologiya poreformennogo samoderzhaviya* (Moscow, 1978), p. 36.
21. Jerzy Ochmańaski, *Litewski ruch narodowo-kulturalny w XIX wieku* (Białystok, 1965), pp. 111–12.
22. Yury Samarin, *Okrainy Rossii*, Seriya pervaya, Russkoe Baltiyskoe pomorie, Vypusk I (Prague, 1868), pp. 17–18.
23. Karl Schirren, *Livländische Antwort an Herrn Juri Samarin* (Leipzig, 1879).
24. Reinhard Wittram, *Baltische Geschichte* (Munich, 1954), p. 192–3.
25. Friedrich von Jung-Stilling, *Statistisches Material zur Beleuchtung livländischer Bauer-Verhältnisse* (St Petersburg, 1868).
26. Alexander von Tobien, *Die livländische Ritterschaft in ihrem Verhältnis zum Zarismus und russischen Nationalismus*, vol. II (Riga, 1925), pp. 129; *Istoriya Latviyskoy SSR*, vol. II (Riga, 1954), p. 106.

27. See Edward C. Thaden, ed., *Russification in the Baltic Provinces and Finland, 1855–1914* (Princeton, 1981).
28. Wittram, pp. 62, 81, 98, 151.
29. See Peter C. Erb (ed.), *Pietists: Selected Writings* (London, 1983); Eckhardt, pp. 21, 197, 409.
30. J.G. Herder, *Sämtliche Werke*, vol. I, ed. B. Suphan (Berlin, 1877), p. 153; R. Haym, *Herder nach seinem Leben und seinen Werken*, vol. I (Berlin, 1880), pp. 139–40.
31. See H. Levin, *Die Heidelberger Romantik* (Munich, 1922); Ralph Tymus, *German Romantic Literature* (London, 1955).
32. Thaden, pp. 240, 269; Andrejs Plakans, 'Peasants, Intellectuals, and Nationalism in the Russian Baltic Provinces', *Journal of Modern History*, no. 3, September 1974, pp. 468–9.
33. L.J. Rhesa, *Das Jahr in vier Gesaengen* (Königsberg, 1818); Jurgis Lebedys, *Lituanistikos baruose*, vol. II (Vilnius, 1972), pp. 182–3, 196.
34. Otto Kronwald, *Nationale Bestrebungen* (Dorpat, 1872), p. 8.
35. Alexander von Tobien, *Die livländische Ritterschaft in ihrem Verhältnis zum Zarismus und russischen Nationalismus*, vol. II (Berlin, 1930), pp. 142–4.
36. G. Libermanis, *Jaunlatvieši: No latviešu ekonomiskas domas vēstures* (Riga, 1957) pp. 1–15.
37. Tobien, *Die Agrargesetztgebung...* vol. II, pp. 260–4.
38. [K. Valdemars], *Baltische namentlich livländische Bauerzustände* (Leipzig, 1862).
39. Tobien, *Die Agrargesetztgebung...*, vol. II, pp. 261–4.
40. Libermanis, p. 130.
41. Ibid., p. 231.
42. Ernests Blanks, *Latvju tautiskā kustība* (Jelgavā, 1927), pp. 33–4.
43. Edvald Uustalu, *The History of the Estonian People* (London, 1952), pp. 123–5.
44. Hans Kruus, *Grundriss der Geschichte des estnischen Volkes* (Tartu, 1932), p. 129.
45. Heinrich Rosenthal, *Kulturbestrebungen des estnischen Volkes während eines Menschenalters (1869–1900)* (Reval, 1912), pp. 74–80, 142–3; Uustalu, pp. 123–4.
46. H. Kruus, *Eesti ajalugu XIX sajandi teisel poolel* (Tallinn, 1957), pp. 228–30. 'Sakala' was the ancient name for the district round Viljandi (Fellin).
47. Kruus, *Grundriss der Geschichte...*, p. 140.
48. Rosenthal, p. 221. 'Virulane' means native of Viru.
49. Ochmański, *Litewski ruch...*, p. 115; B. Genzeli Švietejai ir jų idėjos Lietuvoje (Vilnius, 1972), p. 110.
50. K. Nastopka, *Lietuvių ir latvių literatūrų ryšiai* (Vilnius, 1971), pp. 35, 45.
51. Vincas Kapsukas, 'Iš Aušros archyvų, *Raštai*, vol. X (Vilnius, 1971), pp. 470–9; Ochmanski, *Litewski ruch...*, pp. 148–9; Michał Römer, *Litwa: Studyum o odrodzeniu narodu litewskiego* (Lwow, 1908), pp. 130–2.
52. Ochmański *Litewski ruch...*, p. 144.
53. Z. Angarietis, *Lietuvos revoliucinio judėjimo ir darbininkų kovos istorija* (Smolensk, 1921), pp. 206, 221; Kapsukas, p. 442.
54. *Istoriya Latviyskoy SSR*, vol. II (Riga, 1954), p. 159.

55. V.A. Yatsunsky, 'Znachenie ekonomicheskikh svyazey s Rossiey dlya goro-
    dov Pribaltiki', *Istoricheskie zapiski*, no. 45, 1954, p. 113.
56. L. Truska, 'Lietuvos nezemdirbines burzuazijos skaičius tautinė sudėtis
    ir išsmkslinimas prieš I pasauinį karą', *Lietuvos TSR Mookslų Akademijor
    Darbai*. Serija A 1(50), 1975, pp. 79–91; V. Merkys, *Razvitie promyshlen-
    nosti i formirovanie proletariata Lıtvy v XIX v* (Vilnius, 1969), p. 364.
57. B.V. Tikhonov, *Pereseleniya v Rossii vo vtoroy polovine XIX v* (Moscow,
    1978), pp. 196–202.
58. V. Merkys, *Narodnikai ir pirmieji marksistai Lietuvoje* (Vilnius, 1967),
    pp. 109–15.
59. Z. Angarietis, p. 174; Steponas Kairys, *Lietuva budo* (New York, 1957),
    pp. 270–1.
60. Yu. Martov, *Zapiski sotsial-demokrata* (Berlin, 1922), pp. 187–8.
61. Ibid., pp. 226–7.
62. Ibid., p. 229; *Ob agitatsii* (Geneva, 1896), p. 3.
63. Angarietis, p. 175; Kairys, p. 266; V. Kapsukas, 'Trumpa Lietuvos social-
    demokratų partijos istorija', *Raštai* vol. VII (Vilnius, 1964), p. 548.
64. Kapsukas, 'Trumpa...', p. 553.
65. Kairys, p. 274.
66. N. Michta, Jan Sobczak, 'Stanisław Trusiewicz (Kazimierz Zalewski)', *Z
    pola walki*, no. 1(69), 1975, pp. 111–12.
67. Ibid., p. 114; Walentyna Najdus, *SDKPiL a SDPRR 1893–1907* (Wroclaw,
    1973), pp. 73–7.
68. Kapsukas, 'Trumpa...', pp. 570 ff; Leonas Sabaliunas, *Lithuanian Social
    Democracy in Perspectiive 1893–1914* (Durham, NC and London, 1990).
69. Kapsukas, Trumpa...., p. 557; V. Kapsukas, '1905 Lietuvoje ir Vakarų
    Baltarusijoje', *Raštai*, vol. XII (Vilnius, 1978), p. 537.
70. P. Dauge, *P. Stučkas dzive un darbs* (Riga, 1958), p. 52.
71. Blanks, p. 181.
72. Dauge, p. 51.
73. Ibid, p. 50–1.
74. V. Miske, 'Latvijas revolucionārs kus tī bas izcilais darbinieks Pēteris
    Stučka', *Karogs*, September 1955, pp. 93–4.
75. Ibid., pp. 31–5; Dauge, p. 116–17.
76. K. Lander, 'Ocherki iz istorii latyshskogo naroda', *Russkaya mysl'*, Septem-
    ber 1906, p. 31.
77. S. Isakov, *Skvoz' gody i rasstoyaniya* (Tallinn, 1969), p. 210.
78. Uustalu, p. 146; Kruus, *Grundriss der Geschichte...*, p. 171.
79. Toivo U. Raun, *Estonian and the Estonians* (Stanford, Calif., 1987), p. 82.
80. Kruus. *Grundriss der Geschichte...*, p. 172; Uustalu, p. 147.
81. Piotr Łossowski 'Powstania rewolucyjne w guberniach nadbaltyckich Rosji
    w 1905 roku', *Z pola walki*, no. 2(70), 1975, p. 28; P.P. Girdziyauskene,
    Revolyutsiya 1905–1907 gg. v Litve', *Revolyutsiya 1905–1907 g g. v nat-
    sional 'nykh rayonakh Rossii* (Moscow, 1955), p. 318.
82. Ya. P. Krastyn', 'Revolyutsiya 1905–1907 gg. v Latvii', *Revolyutsia 1905–
    1907 gg. v natsional'nykh rayonakh Rossii*, p. 263.
83. Girdziyauskene, p. 322; Łossowski, p. 29.
84. Römer, p. 317.
85. Ibid., p. 329.

86. Ibid., pp. 386–93; Pranas Čepènas, *Naujųjų laikų Lietuvos istorija*, vol. I (Chicago, 1976), p. 346.
87. T. Karjahärm, R. Pullat, *Eestii revolutsiooni tulles 1905–1907* (Tallinn, 1975), pp. 100–1.
88. Ibid., pp. 113–5; Kruus, *Grundriss der Geschichte...*, p. 185; *Istoriya eston-skoy SSR*, vol II, pp. 443–4.
89. Lander, p. 47.
90. *Istoriya SSSR*, vol. VI (Moscow, 1968), p. 174;; Girdziyauskene, p. 343; Łossowski, p. 33.
91. Karjahärm, Pullat, p. 109.
92. Kapsukas. '1905 Lietuvoje...', p. 556; Bruno Kalnins, 'The Social Democratic Movement in Latvia', A. and J. Rabinowitch (eds) *Revolution and Politics in Russia* (Bloomington, Ind., 1972), p. 140.
93. [Astaf von Transehe-Roseneck], *Die Lettische Revolution*, vol. II, (Berlin, 1907), pp. 335 ff.
94. Łossowski, p. 36; Mosberg, p. 338; B.B. Veselovsky, *Agrarnoe dvizhenie v Rossi v 1905–1906 gg.*, vol. I (St Petersburg, 1908), pp. 357–60.
95. *Aufruf an die zivilisierte Welt über die Bestalitäten in Lettland und Esthland* (Original document held in the British Library, London, catalogue no. 1850. a. 25.)
96. Kruus, *Grundriss der Geschichte...*, p. 189; Kalnins, p. 141; Ochmański, *Historia Litwy*, p. 218.
97. Arnolds Spekke, *History of Latvia* (Stockholm, 1951), pp. 329–36.
98. Adolfs Šilde, *Latvijas vēsture 1914–1940* (Stockholm, 1976), p. 42.
99. Slide, p. 55; Ochmanski, pp. 232–4.
100. Kruus, *Grundriss der Geschichte...*, p. 208; Georg von Rauch, *The Baltic States* (London, 1974), p. 208. 'Maapäev' is an Estonian claque of the German word 'Landtag'.
101. Šilde, p. 100; I. Saat, K. Siylivask, *Velikaya Oktyabr'skaya sotsialisticheskaya revolyutsiya v Estonii* (Tallin, 1977), p. 46.
102. Wilhelm Lieven, *Das rote Russland* (Berlin, 1918), pp. 116–17.
103. Raun, p. 105; Rauch, p. 45; Werner Basler, *Deutschlands Annexionspolitik in Polen und in Baltikum 1914–1918* (Berlin, 1962), pp. 321–2.
104. Basler, p. 322.
105. P. Klimas, 'Lietuvos valstybès kūrimas 1915–1918 metais Vilniuje', *Pirmasis nepriklausomos Lietuvos dēsimtmetsi 1918–1982* (London, 1955), pp. 28–32.
106. Silde, pp. 218–21.
107. Raun, p. 107.
108. V.I. Lenin, *Polnoe sobranie sochineniy*, vol. 37, p. 234.
109. Raun, p. 108.
110. Stanislaw Kamiński, 'Wyparcie wojsk niemieckich z Estonii i Lotwy w latach 1918–1919', Cześć I, *Zapiski historyczne*, vol. XLIII (1978), Zeszyt 1, pp. 64–71.
111. Rüdiger von der Goltz, *Meine Sendung in Finnland und im Baltikum* (Leipzig, 1920), pp. 162, 176, 185.
112. Arveds Schwabe, *Histoire de peuple letton* (Stockholm 1953), pp. 181–5.
113. Von der Goltz, pp. 202, 221–3; Charles L. Sullivan, 'The 1919 German Campaign in the Baltic: The Final Phase', in V. Stanley Vardys, Romuald J. Misi-

unas, *The Baltic States in Peace and War 1917–1945*, (Philadelphia, 1978), pp. 31–40.

114. René Valande, *Avec le général Niessel en Prusse et en Lithuanie* (Paris, 1921), pp. 9–11.

115. Alfred Erich Senn, *The Emergence of Modern Lithuania*, New York, 1959), p. 105.

116. Ibid, pp. 115–225.

117. Rauch, pp. 70–5.

118. W.P. and Z.K. Coates, *Russia, Finland and the Baltic* (London, 1940), p. 28.

2 Interwar Statehood: Symbol and Reality

Nicholas Hope

Some twenty years – between 1920 and 1940 – which mark the lifespan of Estonia, Latvia and Lithuania as independent republics, are not long for a fair assessment. There is a touch of the unreal in the egalitarian colour of democracy which appeared overnight after centuries of feudal servitude, and in constitutional provision of a very generous kind for national minorities and religious denominations. Our view of independent statehood is also influenced by interwar crisis. This caused apparently in these three republics, swift popular rejection of liberal democracy and market economics, and brought to power authoritarian governments of a corporatist stamp, which lasted in substance until formal annexation by the Soviet Union in August 1940. This sudden beginning, mid-term crisis, and abrupt end, can nevertheless mask continuities discussed in the previous chapter, which help to explain why ethnic self-expression and egalitarian democracy have survived all systematic attempts at suppression by Great Powers so far. Without wishing to repeat or change the argument of the previous chapter, or to deny the element of pure chance involved in the new constitutional and social order which emerged between 1918 and 1920 in what was both a war for national independence and a civil war, a slightly different perspective is adopted in this chapter. It might be considered a mild heresy in view of Russian and German rule before 1918, and the continuing influence exerted by these powers before 1940. But the angle of vision changes if one keeps in mind the development of comparatively recent democracies and mixed market economies in Denmark, Norway, Sweden and Finland in the period after c.1860. This is not an argument for a Scandinavian *mare Balticum*, though this opinion was expressed after 1918 by some Scandinavians like the Swedish archbishop Nathan Söderblom, who saw this as part of his Lutheran ecumenism; but an argument which makes sense given a common history, a shared Lutheran religion of the Scandinavian countries with Estonia and Latvia (Lithuania was ninety per cent Roman Catholic), and inevitably close economic and cultural ties in the Baltic region as a whole.[1] The degree of national distinction has been always difficult to assess in a region where so much is interrelated. Finland, the other half of the Swedish dual monarchy until 1809, and Grand Duchy in the Russian empire until 1917, is closer to Estonia and eastern Baltic culture if

41

linguistic self-determination as applied in 1918 is used; but Finland since then has been classified as a Scandinavian state. If the interwar period is placed within this larger perspective (Scandinavian historians also use '*Mellankrigstiden*' to describe Scandinavian interwar crisis) what is striking, is the gradualist path taken on the whole since c.1860 between *laissez-faire* democracy and state interventionism (Norway experienced a particularly rough 1920s in the shape of labour militancy, and the forced sale of farms) by the Scandinavian countries.[2]

To put it very briefly, modern Scandinavian political democracy owes its shape to the emancipation of its Lutheran peasantry and land reform. This took place in the two decades before and after the dissolution of the twin monarchies of Sweden-Finland and Denmark-Norway in 1809 and 1814. Loss of Great-Power status in 1809 and 1814, and financial ability thereafter to muster only token armed forces (the war over the duchies of Schleswig/Slesvig and Holstein/Holsten of 1864 was a reckoning for Denmark), has played a prominent part too in the self-determination of small Scandinavian nation-states. How to to represent politically a rapidly increasing rural population composed of small-scale farmers and a far more numerous population of cottars and day labourers, has provided the colour of Scandinavian left-liberal (*venstre*) politics which appeared in Norway after 1814, in Denmark with the fall of absolutism and Denmark's new democratic constitution of 1849, and in Sweden with the end of the old parliamentary system of four privileged estates in 1865–6. The Scandinevian dilemma, how to defend an existence as nation-states in the shadow of the Great Powers Russia and Germany, has shaped policies of neutrality and, after 1918, produced disarmament policies, humanitarian mission and sponsorship of the rights of little nations. National independence brought the same political issues inevitably to the attention of the three Baltic republics.

However, it is in the following aspects of Scandinavian domestic politics after c.1860, that many similarities with the domestic scene of the three Baltic republics discussed in this chapter lie. Self-education, economic improvement as Western market economies, and the co-operative spirit were the hallmarks of Scandinavian rural liberalism. They were spread by a communications revolution consisting of steamship and railway, manifest in new harbour and railway towns, and in new industries like Swedish and Finnish timber-processing. A sizeable rural and industrial proletariat in 1900 produced a debate about the nature of the traditional state built on hierarchical power relationships. Was its role to be *laissez faiare*, or should it be socially aware, and therefore interventionist? The big 'folk movements' associated with self-education given institutional shape by the Grundtvigian 'High-School' further education movement in Denmark and

Figure 2 The Baltic States, 1918–40

Norway, widespread religious sectarianism and temperance, and the co-operative in agriculture and nascent industry, carried this Scandinavian lay-person's politics beyond 1914. The distinctive feature beneath the modern Scandinavian rhetoric of class was the way social democracy, as it emerged in Sweden, Denmark and Finland, co-operated before and after 1914 on the whole with government, and bridged economic and cultural differences between town and country, even if this only amounted to what Swedes in the 1930s called 'horse-trading' (*kohandeln*) between Social Democrats and Agrarians. The idea of the socially-aware state – what was described in 1936 as Sweden's 'middle way' between capitalism and socialism – was in many ways a sequel to this development and the First World War economy of neutral Scandinavia, which inevitably increased the amount of state control.[3] This mix of market economics and state interventionism was defined typically in the section on financial policy in the Danish Social Democratic Odense programme of 1923 as, 'public works should be curtailed in periods of economic growth, and encouraged in times of economic recession'.[4]

It is as small agrarian nations with growing mixed economies – a process which was well under way after c.1860 despite the hold of the manorial economy in what came to be republican Estonia, Latvia and Lithuania – that one should keep in mind Scandinavian development. Estonia, Latvia and Lithuania were obviously suitable for capitalist agriculture based on arable (rye and wheat), meat (mainly bacon), and dairy farming. On the other hand, Lithuania was different from the Scandinavian countries in sev-eral respects. Her rural population were mostly Roman Catholic. She was the most backward economically of the three Baltic republics. Mediocre estate management, often absentee, of a Russian, Polish, French, and German service nobility, widespread illiteracy, and the lack of any urban manufacture and industry, had prevented economic and constitu-tional progress before 1920. But in size, some 56 000 square kilometres, and with a population of some two million in 1925, Lithuania was in size comparable to Denmark. Over eighty per cent of Lithuania's land was used for the cultivation of rye, wheat, barley, potatoes and flax. After land reform in 1920, Lithuania thus became a country with a potential for suc-cessful small-scale co-operative wheat, dairy, and cattle farming of the Scandinavian type.

Lutheran Latvia and Estonia were much closer to the Scandinavian economies. Latvia, some 66 000 square kilometres in size, with a popula-tion of just under two million in 1925, with fifty per cent of the land divided equally into grass and arable land, and run by individual farmers growing rye, wheat, barley, potatoes, and specializing in dairy farming. Like Estonia, the possibility of a mixed economy of a Scandinavian type seemed promising in Latvia before 1914. The seaports of Riga, Ventspils (Windau), and Liepaja (Libau), had cornered Russian and eastern Baltic trade, and were centres for heavy and light industry. Timber had also become an important growth industry. Estonia, the smallest of the three republics, just 48 000 square kilometres, with a population of just over one million in 1925 and comparable in size to Denmark also had an economy eminently suitable not only for traditional rye, wheat, barley and flax cultivation, but also for cattle and dairy farming. Many rivers provided power, especially the rapids of the river Narva which powered the Narva cotton, flax and woollen mills. As a land of lakes and forests, Estonia was similar to Finland. She possessed like Latvia, important commercial ports like Tallinn, and Baltiski (Baltic Port). On the other hand, Estonia was the only republic with mineral deposits. Oil-shale beds in strata along the north coast from Baltiski to Narva, and its clay and limestone, provided the basis in 1920 for new fuel and cement industries. The Estonian timber industry, like Sweden's and Finland's, was well established before 1914. Paper, cardboard boxes, matches and furniture were already exported from Tallinn to Great Britain, Holland and Belgium.[5] Estonia, among the three republics, thus contained the most promising signs of a developing mixed economy of the Scandinavian type: so much so, that by 1939 it could produce, with the Japanese and British example in mind, the wry Danish comment, 'Estonians have become such expert agriculturalists that they are forcing the Danes out of their own market'.[6] This comparison was most apparent in the flourishing co-operative movement established already in the 1870s to buy farms, and to further the Danish model of dairy and meat marketing. Southern Estonia, and the northern part of 'Livonia' were already covered by a network of co-operatives in 1914. Many were forced to close during the war, but they quickly resumed operation after 1920. Like those in Denmark, Norway, Sweden and Finland, these co-operatives expanded from organizations providing credit and insurance into an established institutional framework for learning the newest methods and technology. Before and after 1920, many Estonians and Latvians also travelled to the Scandinavian countries to learn the latest techniques.

Lutheranism was an important bond linking the Baltic republics to the Scandinavian states, if Roman Catholic Lithuania is excepted. According to the 1925 census 78 per cent of the population of Estonia were Lutheran whereas in Latvia they numbered 57.2 per cent, the latter also including a significant Roman Catholic minority of just under 25 per cent.[7]

Though Weber's argument is tempting, it might be misleading to link capitalism with a rural and nascent urban Protestant ethic in Lutheran Estonia (25.2 per cent lived in towns in 1922) and Lutheran Latvia (23.5

per cent lived in towns in 1920), and backwardness with Lithuania's
Roman Catholic rural population.[8] Towns in Estonia and Latvia were still
defined administratively and legally, and not by size or economic phy-
siognomy. Capitalist smallholding farming became very successful in
Lithuania in the 1930s. Kaunas and Vilnius also contained significant Jewish communities: in 1925, roughly 50 per cent of the population in Kaunas
(120 000), and 36 per cent in Vilnius (130 000) were Jews.[9] As significant
as any widespread Protestant capitalist ethics in Estonia and Latvia was the
strong sense of moral rectitude and mutual help in extended peasant families where oral tradition counted. This was shaped too by a strict moral code
contained in the catechisms of Swedish and German church order which
lasted until 1918, and the brotherly ethics of Moravianism, which experienced a second flowering as an emancipatory lay-person's religion in
Estonia and 'Livonia' after 1820.[10]

Independence after 1918 was of seminal importance for the postwar
religious order of Estonia and Latvia, because land reform in 1919 ended at
a stroke the German manor's patronage, and handed parish government to
Estonia's one hundred and forty-one, and Latvia's two hundred and ninety
parishes. Parochial self-government brought lay and more undenomina-
tional churchmanship. The comparison with Denmark after 1849 springs to
mind, if one excepts the great plurality of religious opinion which characterised the Danish *Folkekirke* thereafter. Church and state were also formally separated in Estonia in 1925, and in 1934 state legislation established
a larger degree of state control over church administration and finance. A
similar development took place in Latvia. In 1934, a new church law put all
religious denominations under the Home Office, and granted full freedom
of religion. Every denomination was given public status, and rights to own
buildings, levy voluntary dues, open seminaries and schools. Any group of
fifty citizens was entitled to register as a religious denomination, and no
single denomination was allowed special rights of protection by the state.
The national principle was also increasingly emphasized in a republic
where nearly a quarter of the population were Roman Catholic. The principle of appointing Latvian Roman Catholic archbishops and bishops was
established in the concordat of 1922, which created the Metropolitan
Archbishopric of Riga, restored monastic orders, and reintroduced Roman
Catholic schools and seminaries. The Latvian Russian Orthodox church,
like its Estonian sister church, also left the Moscow Patriarchate, and was
put under the Patriarch of Constantinople, who came to Riga to consecrate
the first Latvian Metropolitan Archbishop in 1936. Also significant, and
common to both Lutheran Estonia and Latvia, was the tension between
their national congregations and the Lutheran German congregations. This

expressed itself inevitably in popular support for the restoration of the old Lutheran link with Sweden, and for Sweden's postwar Lutheran ecumenism. Söderblom, as Archbishop of Uppsala, was invited to consecrate Estonia's and Latvia's first Lutheran bishops, Jacob Kukk in Tallinn in 1921, and Karlis Irbe in Riga in 1922.[11]

LAND REFORM

If we turn to what happened in the period of independence, of far-reaching constitutional significance was the fact that land reform and parliamentary democracy appeared simultaneously between 1919 and 1922. Finland experienced in a similar pattern of development in the period marked by her 1919 constitution, and land reform enacted by the *Lex Kallio* of 1922.

Land reform amounted to a social revolution in Estonia, Latvia and Lithuania. It dispossessed an ethnically different landed aristocracy, and turned almost overnight a feudal peasantry into 'classless' nations of propertied small farmers. There was indeed a touch of the miraculous in this change, if the failure of emancipation and land reform before 1918 and the outcome of the peace is borne in mind. Travellers noted in towns like Tallinn the embarrassment at questions about origins, and the fact that few people had any sense of direction, so close had the extended peasant family been bound to the soil.[12] Though bitterly contested by former Baltic barons in Estonia and Latvia, and by the former Russian, Polish and German service nobility of Lithuania, land reform was also a remarkably peaceful transition. The creation of smallholder farms was of great political significance, because it sanctioned parliamentary republicanism; even during the so-called authoritarian period in Lithuania after 1926, and in Estonia and Latvia after 1934, in the minds of the rural majority. Smallholdings also strengthened widespread aversion to communism as a secular ideology of moral and social chaos, and to communism as a regime whose terror many peasant families unfortunately experienced in the turbulent and uncertain two to three years between 1918 and the establishment of a settled national framework.

Land reform in Estonia was enforced by its Constituent Assembly in 1919. Of the 1419 German manors which owned 58 per cent of all land, and 30 per cent rented out as 23 023 small farms, 1065 estates or 96.6 per cent were nationalised to create a national land reserve. 55 104 new homestead farms were created. Most were sold; only a few were rented. Of the 23 023 rented from the estates, most were given outright to farmers who had rented the farm for 40 years or more. By 1925, there were already

126 561 farms.[13] This act, given the continuing struggle between Russian Bolshevik, German *Freikorps*, and Estonian nationalist forces between 1918 and 1920, consolidated Estonian parliamentary republicanism. Land reform allowed republican forces to mobilise effectively; it denied Estonian Communist Party support in rural areas where most Estonians lived; and it created a propertied small-farmer class which tenaciously upheld the values of self-education and expression, equal opportunity, and co-operation, which they had striven for in their national movement before 1918. In the longer term, it produced a liberal conservatism suspicious of the competition and secular outlook of new urban business, industry, and labour.[14] Land reform also laid the basis for a mixture of free-market and co-operative farming on Scandinavian lines. The 1920s in both Estonia and Latvia saw laws establishing agricultural schools and co-operatives, and cheap credit from government for seed, fertilisers and farm improvements.

Land reform in Latvia had a similar effect in being implemented by its Constituent Assembly in September 1920, almost two years before its constitution appeared. Out of the 1338 German manors owning 48.1 per cent of the land, a state land fund of almost three and a half million hectares was established. Owners of confiscated estates were, however, allowed to keep 50 hectares.[15] Land reform was favourable to a majority of new farmers owning 10–30 hectares. The implication of this social revolution for the creation of a pro-Western and anti-communist constituency can be seen in the way the figure of 38.8 per cent landowners and 61.2 per cent landless in 1897 was turned around by the census of 1925 to 70.9 per cent with land and 29.1 per cent without. This helps to explain why an active Latvian Communist Party mustered a mere six to seven per cent in the national elections of 1928.[16]

In Lithuania, its Roman Catholic peasantry became smallholders in laws of August 1920, March 1922 and August 1925. Forty per cent of the land in the shape of entailed estates (*majorats*) acquired by 450 mainly Polish and Russian noble families, but also by a few German, French and Italians as a result of service to the Tsar, were turned into farms with a maximum of 25 hectares for mainly landless peasants and demobilised soldiers.[17] But a problem remained in the shape of some 3000 private owners who were allowed to retain the 'centre'; meaning house, outbuildings, and some land. This became politically divisive as part of Lithuania's minority problems.

PARLIAMENTARY DEMOCRACY AND CULTURAL PLURALISM

The extremely egalitarian constitutions of Estonia (21 December 1920), Lithuania (1 August 1922) and Latvia (7 November 1922) reflected the radical break with the past dictated by land reform. There is a distant similarity with Denmark's democratic constitution of 1849 which put an end to absolutism, though it admittedly followed emancipation and land reform enacted some forty years earlier between 1786 and 1800. The two decades of independence thus consisted of a coming to terms with radical constitutional principles symbolised by single-house parliaments (neighbouring Finland had gained one in 1906), which suited egalitarian-minded smallholders who liked the referendum style of Swiss, French, American and contemporaneous Weimar republican democracy.[18]

The Estonian constitution was particularly democratic. Government, like the Lutheran church, was put effectively in the hands of the rural smallholder majority. The constitution provided for popular referendum along Swiss *Eidgenossenshaft* lines, by making constitutional reform impossible without the consent of the majority of those entitled to vote. Popular initiative in legislation ruled. The legislature, the parliament (*Riigikogu*), was elected for three years, and remained constitutionally more important than the executive, since government was seen as a permanent parliamentary commission. The head of state (*Riigivanem* – the eldest in the state) and his government lacked any veto against parliamentary decisions. The Latvian constitution was similar in its insistence on popular sovereignty, and the Swiss idea of popular democracy. It was the only constitution of the three republics to remain in force for the entire period of independence. Parliament, the *Saeima*, was elected also for three years, with the difference that a president was elected by simple majority for three years. Parliament fixed the budget, confirmed the cabinet, and fixed the strength of the armed forces in peace and war. Constitutional amendment needed a two-thirds majority in parliament.[19]

Lithuania was similarly egalitarian. The memory of Lithuania in 1905 as the first nation to demand autonomy from Russia was an agent, as was Lithuanian Socialism and Populism, in radical constitutional colouring similar to the Weimar Republic.[20] This was problematic in a state which was Roman Catholic. Parliament, the *Seimas*, like Estonia's parliament became both legislative and executive authority. The state president was no more than a figurehead. Proportional representation, the case also in Estonia and Latvia, ensured in principle multi-party democracy. But here political resemblance with Estonia and Latvia ended. Postwar anti-Bolshevik and anti-secular Roman Catholic party-politics played an influential role in postwar Lithuanian constitutional development. This has not been properly written up so far, and a cursory treatment can only be given here.[21] At the level of high politics, relations between Vilnius and the Vatican were bad from the start. The new state was recognised on 10 November 1922, but no Lithuanian church province was created, since the Curia preferred to regard Vilnius as a Polish see. Diplomatic relations were even broken off after the Polish concordat of 1925, when Vilnius was assigned as a bishopric to Poland. Things improved somewhat with Pius XI's bull *Lituanorum gente* of 4 April 1926. It created a Lithuanian church province with Kaunas as its archbishopric. Also, after hard bargaining, Lithuania recognised in a concordat of 10 December 1927 the Vatican's designation of the Klaipeda (Memel) areas, annexed in 1923, as *Praelatura nullius Klaipeda.*[22] In party politics, democratic republicanism was put in question by a young clergy, who as supporters of lay politics regarded the choice of any political party as valid so long as it was behind the Roman Catholic church. Catholic Action, it seems, was also very influential in Lithuanian party-political life. The outcome was an inevitable polarisation of party-politics around religious and ideological issues, given the presence of active liberal Populist and Socialist parties. Until 1926, the Roman Catholic political bloc composed of Lithuania's Christian Democratic Party, Peasant Alliance, and Federation of Labour dominated Lithuanian politics and gave the semblance of stability. But it came to an end in May 1926, largely as a result of its failure to do anything about Vilnius, evidence of a corrupt government spoils system, and its poor economic record. The coming to power of a coalition of Socialists and Populists was little short of a catastrophe for the Vatican and Lithuania's church leadership. Allegiance to Lithuania's new democracy was put in question. But Lithuanian nationalism was also questioned by the Vatican's hostility to the new nationalist and authoritarian *Tautininkai* minority government which came to power a week after the concordat on 17 December 1926, because it excluded the Christian Democrats, and began to introduce secular policies. Relations worsened under president Smetona. The papal nuncio was expelled on 5 May 1931, and state control of religion was tightened. The fifth draft constitution, of February 1936, proposed to establish state registry offices planned by Prime Minister Slezevicius in 1926. This would have separated the Lithuanian state from the Roman Catholic church. In this sense, the Roman Catholic church, which questioned Lithuanian democracy, and which criticised presidential national government after 1926, strengthened the secularism of Lithuanian nationalists.

Two further radical constitutional arrangements reflected ideals that could be misused. The Estonian and Latvian constitutions included extensive sections of basic rights. Article 13 of the Estonian constitution guaranteed for instance 'freedom of expression of personal ideas in words, print, letters, pictures and sculpture'. This was symptomatic of the humanitarianism and concern about individual and national self-expression which also typified politics in the Scandinavian countries after 1918. Constitutional provision for minorities with a strong sense of their historical roots was thus likely to prove problematic for all three republics (Figure 3).[23] Though small in numerical terms, the Germans, given extensive minority rights, were able to play an especially and increasingly influential and divisive role in Estonian and Latvian politics, and in religious and economic life.[24] In Lithuania, although more ethnically homogenous, with over four-fifths of its population drawn from the eponymous nation, their Roman Catholic faith soured national allegiance, and made a fair solution of minority and border questions difficult. There was also an influential Jewish minority (7.2 per cent), which in 1920 had already gained constitutional autonomy over its affairs. This provided the blueprint for extensive minority rights in the Lithuanian constitution. Though negligible in percentage terms, its other minorities, Germans, Russians and Poles, became as troublesome in the 1930s, as in Estonia and Latvia.[25] Civil equality, self-determination of each minority, and the use of one's own language in official life (business, courts, local government) and education, thus amounted to a model of cultural autonomy inspired by Estonia, which could easily be misused when the economy took a down-turn, or when Germany and Russia regained their strength as Great Powers in the 1930s.

Proportional representation of the kind which in Latvia in July 1923 granted the right to a group of any five persons to register as a political party, played into the hands of the unscrupulous, and was complicated by over-generous representation given to Latvia's national minorities. Twenty-six political parties contested the Estonian elections of 1923, 14 of which were eventually elected; in Latvia in 1925, 26 parties were elected.[26] Minorities could be influential too. The Lithuanian minority government of Socialists and Populist of May 1926 made concessions like building more private schools to the Polish minority in return for helping to bring it to power.[27] Government became as unstable as that in the Weimar Republic. Estonia and Latvia had 17 and 16 cabinets respectively in 14 years. The average lifespan of a cabinet was eight to ten months. Party machines also became too important. But the weakness of liberal constitutional arangements can be overdrawn. The Scandinavian post-war democracies, with the exception of Denmark's four governments before German occupation in May 1940, were also beset by frequent changes of government. Norway experienced 12 governments, Sweden 15, and Finland 18 between 1920 and 1940.[28]

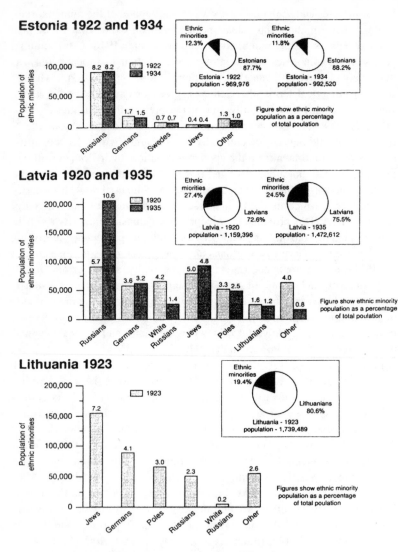

Estonia 1922 and 1934

Latvia 1920 and 1935

Lithuania 1923

Sources : Eesti Statistika Kuukiri, Nr. 24(3), 1924, pp.10-11;
Eesti Bank, *Estonian Economic Yearbook 1937* (Tallinn, 1938), p.115;
Latvijas Statistika Gada Grâmata 1936 (Riga 1936), pp. 8-9;
Latvijas Statistika Gada Grâmata 1930 (Riga 1931), p.3;
Lietuvos Statistikos Metraštis 1934 m. (Kaunas, 1935), p.13.

Figure 3   Ethnic composition of the interwar Baltic States, 1920–35

SOCIAL AND ECONOMIC ACHIEVEMENTS

Before turning to the shift towards authoritarian regimes, it is crucial to stress positive features which continued throughout the entire period of independence. These consisted of continuing enthusiasm for untested egalitarian and humanitarian constitutional arrangements, the rapid extension of efficient national education systems, social welfare provision, economic advance as countries exporting agricultural produce, and in the case of Estonia and Latvia, progress as reasonably successful mixed economies of a Scandinavian type. Baltic democracy was not destroyed by engineered presidential government and a popular vote for Nazi dictatorship as was the case with the Weimar Republic, but by another bout of German and Russian imperialism which could not be stopped by neutral foreign policies and disarmament pursued by both the Scandinavian states and Baltic republics. Nazi occupation of Norway and Denmark in April 1940 was just as much of a trauma as Soviet annexation was for the three Baltic republics in August 1940.

The independence period as a whole witnessed a remarkable expansion of primary, secondary, higher, and adult education: especially in Estonia and Latvia. This built on the advance of literacy, primary and secondary educational provision, and adult self-education in the late nineteenth century. This development was very close to that in the Scandinavian countries. On the other hand, given Russian rule and the hold of the manor, specifically Estonian, Latvian and Lithuanian education systems could not be installed before the constitutions of 1920–2.

In Estonia, compulsory education was introduced in 1920.[29] Illiteracy, some 10 per cent in 1897, was wiped out by 1930, with the exception of a Russian minority population in districts along Estonia's eastern frontier. The Petseri province still showed 35 per cent illiteracy in 1934.[30] There was a massive expansion of free primary schools: in 1927 there were 1398 of them. A School Building Fund was also established by the state in 1922 into which some 8 500 000 crowns were invested between 1922 and 1935. An extensive network of public libraries and well-organised archives also constituted one of the notable achievements of independent Estonia. In 1927, there were 818 public libraries, in contrast to none before independence. These benefited from generous state subsidies and numerous gifts of books from local authorities and private organisations. They were complemented by the efficient Central State Archives in Tartu, the State Archives in Tallinn, several new municipal archives of which Tallinn was the most important, and the splendid and unique folklore archives under the Estonian National Museum of Tartu. These institutions provided the basis for a flourishing interwar ethnographic and social history. The republic finally ensured Estonian access to higher education at Tartu University (1632) which, in its reconstituted form of 1802, had been largely a university training German and Russian students. In 1927, 82 per cent of its 4651 students were Estonian. Similarly, 86.4 per cent of students at the new Technical Institute founded at Tallinn in 1918 were Estonian. New agricultural, industrial and commercial schools complemented higher education. An educational league (*Eesti Haridusliit*) was also established to promote lay education. It organised vocational and general courses, so-called people's universities of the Scandinavian type, evening and Sunday schools, as well as kindergartens. This was distinctly similar to contemporary Finland.

Latvia showed similar enthusiasm. Free compulsory education was introduced in 1920, to a republic where the need to stamp out illiteracy was higher than in Estonia, given a larger Russian population along Latvia's eastern frontier. An illiteracy rate of 22 per cent in 1920 was reduced to 10 per cent (7 per cent if Russian speakers are not included) in 1937.[31] Generous provision was also made for libraries. In 1939, there were 1911 schools and 912 public libraries. In the shape of the Latvian State Printing Office, Riga became once again a centre of printing, as it had been before 1700. Many vocational schools, technical institutes, commercial schools and foreign language schools were also established. Agricultural schooling was actively fostered: in 1937, there were 59 such schools crowned by the new Academy of Agriculture at Jelgava. The entire education system including theological seminaries, drama and music institutes, was financed either by the state or the municipalities. Vocational education received special emphasis. As in Estonia, adult education was represented by 14 people's universities and their branches. Latvians also gained access to higher education with the opening of the State University of Riga in 1919. Like the Estonians, the Latvian authorities and people showed great enthusiasm for their rich folklore. Riga's Historical Museum and its monumental edition of *Dainas* complemented the fame and work of Estonia's National Museum.

Lithuania also showed the same pattern of development.[32] There were already, in 1919, 1036 primary schools, and the number increased to 2292 in 1931–2. But illiteracy was a much greater problem than in Estonia and Latvia. In 1923, 32.6 per cent of the population were unable to read or write. This posed problems for the recruitment of an ethnic officialdom to run the new state.[33] On the other hand, considerable advance was made in education, to such an extent that by the time of the introduction of compulsory education in November 1931, 116 per 1000 were attending school compared with 111 per 1000 in Latvia, and 105 per 1000 in Estonia. Higher and further education were also comparatively successful. The fact that the old Lithuanian university of Vilnius (1579) was run by Poles after October 1921, meant that a new Lithuanian university had to be opened at Kaunas in February 1922. By 1927, it was providing an education for some 68.5 per cent nationals. Adult education spread by co-operatives, and the Agricultural Academy at Kaunas established in 1924, were also popular.

The entire period of independence was notable for significant advances in social provision: particularly in the mixed economies of Estonia and Latvia. The year 1920 marked a beginning in social welfare legislation also, given the rudimentary social provision of the Russian empire and the manorial dependency system hitherto. In this sense, the two decades 1920–40 complemented the qualitative leap forward in social provision in the three Baltic republics noted by Scandinavian social historians in the Scandinavian countries in this period.

In Estonia, the process began with the need to revise the antiquated pensions legislation of the Russian empire. In 1920, a law concerning aid to pensionaries of the Russian empire living in Estonia was passed; this was followed by a law providing pensions to families of dead or disabled soldiers, and in 1924 by a pension for government and municipal officials, which was extended to employees and workers in government enterprises in 1926. In 1936, a comprehensive Army Pension Law and a Civil Service Pension Law replaced this legislation. In 1925, a Public Relief Law was passed similar in purpose to British welfare legislation. It tried to ameliorate poverty and indigence, and help especially the many orphaned children. This was administered by the state and by local government. The eight-hour day was introduced in 1918, supplemented by a special law of 1931, by a law on collective agreements of 1929, and paid vacation of industrial workers in 1934. Compulsory insurance against illness and accident meant two-thirds of sickness insurance being paid by employers, and the rest by the insured themselves; accident insurance was paid by the employer, except in the case of agricultural labour, where a part of the insurance was paid by government.[34]

In Latvia, similar continuous advance was made before 1940. Labour remained peaceful under governments which tried, after the establishment of the eight-hour day for industrial workers and six-hour day for white-collar employees in 1922 (the latter causing much comment in Europe), to establish favourable working conditions. Trade unions were protected within the framework of the International Labour Organization, and special emphasis was put on developing a comprehensive social security system, which included legal entitlement to antenatal care in 1931. The Latvian republic also followed the British and Estonian system, which entitled all citizens who were indigent or incapacitated to assistance either from the state or from local government. A keynote of this social legislation was its continued advance under authoritarian government after 1934. This development reflected a growing public concern for adequate social welfare. Many private organisations also co-operated with the Ministry of Public Welfare and the municipal health departments in what amounted in the mid-thirties to a more or less comprehensive security system which included regular inspection and controls by state medical officers of markets, restaurants, industrial concerns and schools, and a widespread network of hospitals, health resorts and rest homes.[35]

Economic advance in the three republics throughout the independence period was dictated by the new smallholding agriculture. Estonia's agricultural census of 1929 estimated 3.1 million hectares as being owned by smallholder farmers.[36] This was an economic environment where towns were relegated almost to a service role, if one excepts the industry and commerce of Riga, Tallinn, Narva, and the smaller seaports of Estonia and Latvia.

The chief features of economic advance in these smallholding agricultural economies was a steady increase of the area under cultivation, and the success of wheat, dairy and bacon exports before 1940. There was a continuous demand for new land. Marshes were drained and kilometres of canals dug. Independence was also a success story for rye and wheat. The 1930s saw an export surplus of the principal food crops for the first time since the 1880s in all three republics. Rye, the chief Estonian crop, was also protected by a State Rye Monopoly Law of 1930. The Estonian Government purchased the surplus in the autumn for storage at fixed prices. A remarkable increase in average yield was also engineered by the introduction of modern techniques and fertilisers.

Estonia was particularly successful. Estonia switched status from being a food importing country in 1923–33, to being an important European agricultural exporter after 1934. Some 500 dairies in 1930, the majority of which were run on the Danish co-operative basis, provided the main source of income for the Estonian farmer. In 1936, central distribution was organised by the Central Association of Co-operative Dairies (*Piimahüingute Keskliit "Voieksport"*). Estonian butter and bacon became the most important export: mainly to Germany and Great Britain. It was a success story which seemed to produce an almost continuously favourable agricultural balance of trade before the outbreak of war in 1939.

Estonian rural economic development, like that in Latvia and Lithuania, owed its success to a widespread agricultural co-operative movement, rather than to the new corporatist ideology of the 1930s.[37] In Estonia, in 1928, two-thirds of all farmers were members of co-operative societies.

Co-operatives had increased from 763 to 1909 between 1925 and 1930. These were part of the Estonian Co-operative League which had been founded as long ago as 1919 to promote and develop the Estonian co-operative movement. It acted as an intermediary between individual co-operative societies and government, and as a source of loans and advice for farmers. The Estonian People's Bank, founded in 1920, and a network of co-operative banks (175 in 1932) also worked closely with this Co-operative League. Co-operative retail organisations were also very popular with a membership of some 40 000 in 1936. The commercial centre of the co-operative retail system was the central organisation of consumer's so-cieties known as the Estonian Co-operative Wholesale Society (*Eesti Tarvitajate Keskühisus*), established in 1917, which acted as a purchasing and selling agent for its membership.

Estonia alone among the three new republics was lucky in possessing a reasonably developed industrial infrastructure based on textile, metal and timber industries. But the changeover to a national market was difficult in the 1920s. The Kreenholm cotton mills at Narva, the biggest in Europe in 1914, and the Baltic cotton mills at Tallinn, had supplied yarns for the cotton-spinning industry of central Russia until 1918. After 1918, unfin-ished cotton was temporarily sent to Germany for bleaching and printing. An Estonian finishing process really started for the first time in the mid-1920s. Estonian heavy industry prospered during the First World War in much the same way as Finland's in work for the Russian war effort. The huge naval yards at Tallinn (formerly Reval) had provided the Russian Baltic navy with battleships and cruisers up to 40 000 tons. The Tallinn freight-works had also supplied rolling-stock for Russian railways. The changeover to peace was therefore as catastrophic as it was in Latvian Riga. Progress within a national market really took place in timber and paper, cement, and the new oil shale industry. Foreign capital was attracted for the first time in the mid-1920s; notably by the already important export–import timber and wood trade of firms like A.M. Luther, and the old Dundee family shipping firm (established in the 1630s) of Messrs Thomas Clayhills and Son in Tallinn; the new State Timber Industry of Tallinn and Tartu controlled by the Ministry of Agriculture; several private oil shale companies, and the Government Oil Shale Works established in 1918 at Kohtla-Järve. This new fuel technology, given its use as the cheapest form of industrial power, proved particularly successful. The neighbouring Estonian oil shale and cement industries complemented each other. Com-mercial and industrial advance was, however, chequered compared with agriculture. The foreign trade balance remained adverse until 1925. A bal-ance of exports and imports in 1925 and 1926 was soon countered by adverse trade balances in 1928 and 1929. On the other hand, Estonian industry did demonstrate that it was no longer dependent on the Russian market. In 1930, Russian trade amounted to 10.5 per cent. Paper was the only permanent commodity to secure a place in the Soviet Union.[38]

Latvia's economy, also, was dominated by smallholder co-operative agriculture. In 1935, some 60 per cent of the Latvian population were still classified as engaged in some form of rural occupation; only 15 per cent were engaged in industry. There was also an increase in the area of arable land and in production. The amount of land under cultivation grew from 1 729 628 hectares in 1914, to 2 113 684 in 1935.[39] Latvia also changed from imports to exports in the main cereal crops rye and wheat after 1933. Dairy farming, particularly butter and bacon for export, became almost as successful as that in Estonia. This was due to the way the co-operative, which included some 70 per cent of Latvian farmers as early as 1914, had became the centre of Latvian economic and social life. The co-operative flourished because it provided, as was the case in Estonia, the necessary credit and advice. A People's Bank of Latvia, *Latvijas Tautas Banka,* was established, like its Estonian counterpart, in 1920. By 1937, the movement included 532 credit and savings organizations with 130 000 members. This development was supported from July 1938 by a state fund, which guaranteed deposits with credit and savings co-operatives. Co-operative insurance, notably against fire, was extremely popular. In 1937, there were 401 branches with membership of 103 055.[40] The Latvian co-operative dairy industry, established on Danish lines before 1914, leapt forward after 1920. In 1937 there were some 268 co-operative dairies. Rural consumer co-operatives also played as important a role as those in Estonia. This were amalgamated by a Latvian central co-operative organization (*Turiba*) in December 1936. It is worth mentioning that Latvia's pre-war rural co-operative movement also produced several of the Latvian Republic's leading politicians.

Latvian industry was much less successful than Estonia's, given the picture of devastation in 1918. Industry in Riga incurred losses through evacuation and requisitions which amounted in 1915 to some 500 million gold rubels. The Latvian Government thus decided in 1920 to promote agriculture and turn manufacture and industry to production for the home market. What industrial advance there was really belonged to the 1930s.[41] State support of a new national timber industry and its by-products climbed to some 40 per cent of Latvia exports, and thus became an important source of income for a state which in 1939 owned almost 80 per cent of Latvia's forests. Technical specialisation like the development of water power appeared just before the end of independence when Swedish expertise was used for the construction of a new power station and dam at Kegums on the Daugava river, and smaller hydroelectric plants between 1936 and 1940.

Lithuania, given the lack of an urban infrastructure, developed also a relatively successful agricultural economy run by small farms. Manufacture and industry remained undeveloped before 1940. In 1939, both employed less than eight per cent of the labour force. After land reform in 1922, an indigenous co-operative movement which had appeared during the First World War became also very successful in dairy and meat production in the decade 1920–30. It was one of the factors which led authoritarian government after 1926 to support dairy and meat production rather than wheat for an export market directed chiefly at Germany. The state became an active supporter of the Lithuanian co-operative movement, and this ensured that Lithuanian dairy and meat production became the main source of national income in the 1930s. This success was curtailed only by Hitler's decision after 1933 to limit Lithuanian imports as punishment for Lithuania's claim to the Klaipeda (Memel) area.[42]

THE ESTABLISHMENT OF AUTHORITARIAN REGIMES

The three Baltic republics did, however, produce presidential regimes of a nationalist stamp. The fact that they lasted more or less until annexation by the Soviet Union in August 1940 has made it difficult for historians to assess the direction in which these republics were going. Several points can be made. The preservation of cultural identity, seen for example in generous constitutional provision for minority rights, has always been more important to Estonians, Latvians and Lithuanians than an aggressive national mission. In a negative sense, this made a common foreign policy before 1940 as difficult as did the antipathy of Danes to Swedes, or Norwegians to Danes, in the formulation of a common Scandinavian foreign policy, and it strengthened the argument of nationalists who disliked the constitutional freedoms granted to minorities in the three republics. Land reform, in creating propertied smallholder farmers, produced a powerful patriotic political interest of a liberal nationalist hue, which became increasingly 'conservative' as time passed by. This was put into relief by the slogans 'Latvianisation' and 'Lithuanisation' directed at the politically vocal minorities – notably the German – after 1930. Some commentators have emphasised the lack of a civic culture as hastening authoritarian government.[43] Certainly, many suddenly enfranchised smallholders, who had to get used to constitutions with powerful parliaments and weak governments, had little idea of how parliamentary government worked. Arthur

Ransome even noted, that in Tallinn, top hats worn by the British consul
and vice-consul on state occasions, produced 'special awe and astonish-
ment' and startled 'ministers into ordering at least two from England for
the use of the Cabinet'.[44] However, more importantly, political extremism
was frowned upon in republics in which many rural people had experienced political terror during the period 1918–20. An abortive communist
coup in Tallinn in 1924 worried many. Urban secular socialism became
increasingly suspect (the case also in Finland), and in all of the three republics active Socialist parties lost ground by 1930. Non-socialist parties had
always a clear majority in parliament. This was different to Socialist
Sweden, Denmark, and even Norway in the 1930s, where Socialist parties
had been able to bridge the urban–rural gap with programmes of national
unity. Lutheranism and Roman Catholicism also remained very influential
in shaping conservative smallholder politics. Many Estonian, Latvian and
Lithuanian farmers, like their Finnish contemporaries, disliked the advance
of postwar secularism, since they lived in a countryside where sanctifica-
tion of life's rites of passage was still felt necessary. On the other hand, one
should not take the degree of popular support for presidential government
in any of the three republics after 1930 too seriously. Statistics can be misleading. Popular democratic behaviour remained strong; the co-operative
remained a guiding institution and principle; and a liberal education for all
was enthusiastically supported. Many, given the nature of the still sparsely
populated and isolated countryside, and the unhurried life of a very traditional church year, did not take political twists and turns too seriously
either. Getting on with improving one's own life was regarded as more
important than national politics. In this sense, popular belief in the benefits
of the new republican constitutions continued under presidential government, regardless of the emasculation of parliamentary power and the
creation of corporatist institutions.

Political development in the second half of the 1920s drifted towards
propertied 'middle-class' order. There was also disenchantment with the
many tiny parties. The creation of a more clearly defined party structure
became an object of government and the political parties themselves. In
Estonia, Kaarel Eenpalu, president of parliament in 1926, pursued a conscious policy of reducing the number of political parties. Political organisations putting up new candidates were made to pay deposits which were
forfeited if they won less than two seats. He also tried to unite the smallholder interest as an Agrarian Union Party in 1931/32. It was to win 42 out
of the 100 seats in the 1932 parliament, although it lasted for only a few
months thereafter. Party politicans also saw the benefits of amalgamation
for the formulation of policy. In 1932, the National Centre Party was

formed out of the Labour, National, Christian National, and Landlords parties. This change in political behaviour was accompanied by the realisation, as the Depression began to take effect in falling farm prices and unemployment, that constitutional provision of weak executives made it impossible to manage economic recession. This was distinctly similar to political argument in Scandinavia for what has been described as the demand for 'crisis management': namely programmes of national unity built on public works programmes which allowed the market to continue in a more subordinate role.[45] The difference was that Social Democracy had already become important as governing parties in Sweden and Denmark by 1930, and in Norway after 1935. On the other hand, Finland was more similar in political complexion. Social Democracy had been extremely successful until 1918, but it had to fight for its life in the late 1920s in a state where rural smallholders created by the *Lex Kallio* had become politically vocal as a national liberal constituency interested in firm patriotic government which upheld Lutheran moral and social values. But this shift from parliamentary to presidential government was far from easy. A second Estonian referendum of June 1933 on a proposal to increase executive power was thrown out by a majority of 330 000 to 160 000.[46] It took much agitation, expecially by the new nationalist paramilitary Association of Estonian Freedom Fighters (*Vabadussojalaste Keskliit*) founded in 1929, to turn a third referendum of October 1933 into a massive majority in favour of presidential government: 416 879 for, and 156 000 against. A president was installed for the first time, who was elected by popular vote for five years, and was given powers to issue decrees, declare states of emergency, appoint and dismiss governments and dissolve parliament.

Extra-parliamentary politics in the shape of a paramilitary fringe, though numerically unimportant and destined to swift oblivion in Estonia and Latvia, strengthened the case for strong government. The Estonian Freedom Fighters, veterans from the struggle for independence between 1918 and 1920, devoted their organisation, built on the *Führer* principle and linked to the Finnish *Lapua* movement, solely to agitation for authoritarian government.[47] In Lithuania and Latvia, paramilitary groups took on a more overtly Nazi colouring, while being thoroughly hostile to the German minorities. This was true of Voldemaras's Iron Wolf *Gelezinis Vilkas* organisation of 1926, and several Nazi-type Latvian organisations which modelled themselves on the Iron Wolf and became vocal in the crisis years 1930–3. Celmins's youthful Fire Cross *Ugunkrusts* of 1933, renamed Thunder Cross *Perkonkrusts* after its prompt ban, was like the other Latvian groupings, with its slogan 'Latvia for the Latvians', a curious mixture of *Führer* principle, *Volksgemeinschaft* corporatist ideology, more anti-Semitic than its Lithuanian counterpart, and blatantly Germanophobic. These organisations served to consolidate to a certain extent a new nationalist mood, but more significantly strengthened the case for presidential government, given the threat of a coup they posed. This was the case with the sacking of Voldermaras by President Smetona, and his subsequent banning of the Iron Wolf in September 1929. It was also true of the disbandment of the Estonian Freedom Fighters by Päts and his commander-in-chief, General Laidoner, in March 1934, as a 'threat to the security of the state' after its success in winning the three largest towns, Tallinn, Tartu and Narva in the January presidential elections.

Presidential government differed in timing and character in each of the three republics.[48] The earliest and most sudden change took place in Lithuania with the military coup by army officers on the birthday of President Grinius on 17 December 1926. It brought the nationalists and Christian Democrats under Voldermaras as prime minister to power until 1927, when its president, Smetona, ended the 1922 constitution by promulgating a new one providing for an independent election of a strong president, and by dissolving parliament. Lithuanian presidential government was the outcome of the political climate already mentioned, which was shaped by the conflict between the religious and secular, the latter being identified with the implementation of an egalitarian and secular national constitution. The minority government of Populists and Social Democrats under Prime Minister Slezevicius of May 1926 which used the support of Lithuania's ethnic minorities, soon became very unpopular as a result of socialist and secular policies which resembled a *Kulturkampf*. It had refused to acknowledge the new church province of Lithuania, and its socialist Home Office minister had spited the new diocesen authorities by refusing to honour their baptismal certificates (the Roman Catholic baptismal rite was the most important family event in Lithuania); had rejected diocesan appointment of schoolmasters who taught religion; and had cut the school budget for religious instruction. The new government had also proposed state rather than diocesan payment of clergy stipends. Moreover, it was showing a tolerant attitude to Lithuania's Roman Catholic Polish minority. As repayment for support in the elections which brought it to power, this government allowed further expansion of Polish private schools acknowledged in Lithuania's minority constitutional provision. In an immediate sense, government proposals to reorganise the army and its officer corps produced this coup in the interests of Lithuanian retrenchment.

In Estonia and Latvia, presidents came to power without military support seven years later, largely as a result of the new mood for better national order; financial crisis which was destroying the new status of the small-holder rural majority; and urban white-collar and labour unemployment. Estonian and Latvian presidential government was more of a nationalist and rural response to crisis management of the kind which was being implemented by admittedly socialist governments in Denmark and Norway between 1930 and 1935. The Estonian Social Democrats even accommodated themselves to Päts's political programme. The Latvian Socialists were, however, more vociferous in their struggle with both the Nazi-style paramilitary groups (they had founded their own Socialist Workers' Sport League in 1927), and government anti-Left politics like the supreme court's conviction in 1933 of seven Communist deputies for treasonable activity. The outcome was a brief period of emergency government in Estonia and Latvia in March 1934, which paved the way for presidential power. In Estonia, parliament was prorogued by president Päts, in effect dissolved, except for two short sessions in the autumn of 1934. In Latvia, Ulmanis was still prime minister, but as a self-styled *Führer* (*Tautas Vadonis*) assumed powers which already amounted to absolute control implied by the fusion of premiership with presidency which he finally carried out on 14 April 1936.

The authoritarian regimes of Smetona in Lithuania, Päts in Estonia and Ulmanis in Latvia, can be classified as benign rather than malignant, if one approves of such definition. All three men were of the same generation – Smetona was born in 1874, Päts in the same year, Ulmanis in 1877 – who had played a leading role in national liberation, and who identified themselves with rural smallholder politics. Ulmanis had risen through the ranks of the Latvian rural co-operative movement. Firm national government of the kind expressed by Päts '*Peremees maja*' (a master is needed in the house), which was extremely hostile to Nazi and Communist extremism and paramilitary violence, typified this undramatic new order. These men tried to a greater or lesser extent to implement a corporatist 'reconstruction of public and social life', based on the curious mixture of a belief (in Päts's case) that corporations survived better than politicians in the new climate of the 1930s, and support of local government as the way to develop a sense of community and the democratic ideals of 1920–2.[49] This meant, of course, banning the Communist parties, and subjecting trade unions to corporatist control. On the other hand, limited freedom was still given to the socialist press, which made full use of this; the courts of the three republics remained independent; municipal self-government and education were actively supported; and in economic affairs the market economy and private and co-operative enterprises were allowed to coexist with increasing government management. Presidential government did mean, however, separation of church and state, and increasing state control over church affairs, which presented a problem of crisis proportions in Lithuania. Generous constitutional provision for national minorities was revised particularly in Latvia and Lithuania with view to emasculating the growing economic and cultural power of the Germans. On the other hand, minority language instruction in schools remained untouched in Latvia; minority language schools remained partly or entirely subsidised by Smetona, and his government actively supported the influential Lithuanian Jewish community which flourished in contrast to those of the Poles and Russians. Also all religious denominations in Lithuania continued to receive annual state subsidies.

Annexation in August 1940 and recent history make it impossible to say how these three republics might have developed. Ulmanis governed according to the Latvian constitution of 1922, although he had subverted its powers; Smetona and Päts moved in the direction of a return to limited parliamentarism. Smetona installed a cabinet of national unity with Christian Democrats and Populists in February 1938, which also began to ease relations with the Roman Catholic church. Päts allowed, in his new constitution of January 1938, direct presidential election in parliamentary elections in which individuals were allowed to compete with his Patriotic Front. Many unofficial candidates campaigned in most electoral districts. As a result, the Patriotic Front gained only a two-thirds majority. On the other hand, the presidential period after 1933–4 showed a powerful economic upswing, and advances in local government, education and social provision of the kind we have seen. These suggest, leaving aside the totally different political nature of these Baltic presidential governments to government in the Scandinavian countries, that 'crisis management' did mark, nevertheless, a similar political experiment. Presidential government in the three Baltic republics by presidents who had an extremely unclear idea of what corporatism meant in practice, was a mix of circumscribed constitutional freedoms, municipal self-government, and the free market, with increasing state economic and social management. On the other hand, the available evidence suggests that a new cultural identity born politically in the 1860s, and the new political democracy of 1920–2, continued to shape the political beliefs and actions of Estonians, Latvians and Lithuanians in a way undreamt of in Germany after 1933. This accounts in part for the egalitarian and stubborn defence of their separate identities in and since 1940.

ACKNOWLEDGEMENTS

This chapter is based on a series of lectures 'Northern Europe 1800–1945', which I gave at Mainz University in the winter term 1990/91 during the first Erasmus staff-exchange between the history departments of Mainz and Glasgow universities. I would also like to acknowledge my debt to the oral history taught me by my Estonian mother (1910–90), and rare printed material in her personal estate. In addition, I have used material which I collected during a summer spent with my Estonian relatives in Tallinn in 1973.

NOTES

1. Söderblom wrote, for instance, in a letter of July 1922, of the 'Lutheran ring established around the Baltic, *mare Lutheranum*', quoted in, B. Sundkler, *Nathan Söderblom. His Life and Work* (London, 1968), p. 277. See note 11.
2. S.A. Nilsson, K.G. Hildebrand, B. Öhngren (eds.) *Kriser och krispolitik i Norden under mellankrigstiden, Nordiska Historikermötet i Uppsala 1974* (Uppsala, 1974); S.U. Larsen and I. Montgomery (eds) *Kirken, Krisen og Krigen* (Bergen, 1982). One of the few assessments which treats the interwar Baltic region as a whole is the 'Braudelian': Louis Tissot, *La Baltique, situation des pays riverains de la Baltique. Importance économique et stratégique de la "Méditerranée" du Nord* (Paris, 1940). This should be supplemented by: G. Smith, 'Soziale und geographische Veränderungen in der Bevölkerungsstruktur von Estland, Lettland und Litauen 1918–1940', in, *Acta Baltica* 19/20 (1981), pp. 118–81.

   Independent statehood is discussed in: G. von Rauch, *The Baltic States. The Years of Independence, Estonia, Latvia, Lithuania 1917–1940* (London, 1974), and the two collections of essays: V.S. Vardys and R.J. Misiunas (eds) *The Baltic States in Peace and War 1917–1945* (Pennsylvania and London, 1978), and B. Meissner (ed.) *Die Baltischen Nationen: Estland, Lettland, Litauen* (Cologne, 1990), which includes a survey of current research in western Europe.
3. Title of the influential book written by the American journalist Marquis W. Childs, *Sweden: the Middle Way* (London, 1936); latest edition, *Sweden: the Middle Way on Trial* (New Haven and London, 1980).
4. *Norden under mellankrigstiden*, pp. 87–8.
5. Notably '*Luterma*' plywood chair-seats; plywood boxes for the British empire's carrying trade in Indian and African tea, rubber and tobacco; 'Kave' boxes for chocolates and sweets, etc., manufactured by the wood and timber import–export business of A.M. Luther Ltd (1897), established in Tallinn in 1841. Estonian cardboard boxes were particularly popular in London's Bond Street and Brompton Road: 'Ah, yes, Estonia ... what a funny thing. That's where my wife's hat-boxes come from', quoted in, Owen Rutter, *The New Baltic States and their Future. An Account of Lithuania, Latvia and Estonia* (London, 1925), p. 224.
6. Ronald Seth, *Baltic Corner. Travel in Estonia* (London, 1939), p. 157.
7. L. Arbusow, '*Baltisches Gebiet*' in, *Die Religion in Geschichte und Gegenwart*, 2nd edn (Tübingen, 1927), vol. 1, col. 747. Arbusow's article, cols. 744–50, leaves out rather typically Roman Catholic Lithuania. There is a

more up-to-date account, 'Baltikum II' by P. Hauptmann in, *Theologisches Realenzyklopädie* (Berlin and New York, 1980), vol. 5, pp. 154–7.

8. See R. Beerman's stimulating: 'Max Weber, Friedrich Engels and the Soviet Baltic Republics', *Co-existence* 12, no. 2 (1975), pp. 158–74. Urban population in Estonia and Latvia: A. Pullerits (ed.) Estonia, Population, Cultural and Economic Life (Tallinn, 1937), p. 3. *League of Nations European Conference on Rural Life 1939 (Latvia)* (Geneva, 1939), p. 11.

9. The Jewish community, 7.6 per cent of the Lithuanian population, was the largest minority.

10. This is discussed in my forthcoming book, *German and Scandinavian Protestantism, 1700–1918* (Oxford). By 1850, Moravian membership and conversion to Russian Orthodoxy accounted for some 20 per cent of Estonians and Letts.

11. Discussion in, Sundkler, *Söderblom*, pp. 274–87. Typical of Söderblom's ecumenism and sense of history, was his handing over of the pectoral cross belonging to the murdered Orthodox bishop Platon (14 January 1919) to the Estonian bishop Kukk in his consecration ceremony, and his gift at this consecration ceremony of a contemporary portrait of Gustavus Adolphus to the Latvian congregation of the Jacobi church to remind them of former Swedish and Latvian common church order. Söderblom had, however, to consecrate the first Latvian bishop in St Jacobi in the morning, and a German Lutheran bishop in St Peter's in the evening of the same day, *ibid.*, p. 284.

12. Seth, *Baltic Corner*, p. 12. 'In all the years of my acquaintance with (Estonians) I have never met one who knew how to tell me the way', Arthur Ransome, *Racundra's First Cruise* (London, 1923), *Mariner's Library Reprint* no. 38, (London, 1958), p. 110.

13. T. Parming, 'The Collapse of Liberal Democracy and the Rise of Authoritarianism in Estonia', *Sage Professional Papers in Contemporary Political Sociology*, series/number 06/010 (1975), p. 24.

14. *Ibid.* p. 23.

15. A. Bilmanis, *A History of Latvia* (Princeton, 1951),, p. 335.

16. A. Spekke, *History of Latvia. An Outline* (Stockholm, 1951), p. 364; A. Silde, 'Die Entwicklung der Republik Lettland', in Meissner (ed.), *Die Baltischen Nationen*, p. 66.

17. V.S. Vardys, 'Die Entwicklung der Republik Litauen', in *ibid.* pp. 82–3; W. Schlau, 'Der Wandel in der sozialen Struktur der baltischen Länder', *ibid.* pp. 226–7.

18. Finland's parliament of 1906 was the most democratic in Europe: *viz.*, a single house (200 members) elected by universal suffrage (minimum age twenty-four) based on a proportional system, and the requirement of a qualified majority for the most important leglisation.

19. Bilmanis, *Latvia*, p. 337.

20. Populists and Socialists held 29 and 14 seats respectively in the constituent assembly 1920–2, and 19 and 11 in the first *Seimas* 1922–3; the bloc of Christian Democrats, Farmers' Union, and Federation of Labour, 59 and 38 seats in these two parliaments. After coming to power in May 1926, Populists and Socialists held 37 seats; the Christian Democrat bloc 30 seats. Appendix A in, L. Sabaliunas, *Lithuania in Crisis. Nationalism to Communism 1939–1940* (Bloomington and London, 1972).

21. Brief discussion: *ibid.* pp. 3–7.
22. 'Litauen' by M. Hellmann in, *Lexikon für Theologie und Kirche* 2nd edn (Freiburg, 1961), cols. 1078–80. Von Rauch, *Baltic States*, p. 163. Relations with the Vatican were normalised with the creation of a Roman Catholic theology faculty at Kaunas University in 1937. It was dissolved in 1940.
23. Minorities: M. Garleff, 'Ethnic Minorities in the Estonian and Latvian Parliaments: the Politics of Coalition', in, V.S. Vardys and R.J. Misiunas (eds), *The Baltic States*, pp. 81–94; M. Garleff, 'Die kulturelle Seltbstverwaltung der nationalen Minderheiten in den baltischen Staaten', in Meissner (ed.), *Die Baltischen Nationen*, pp. 87–107. A sense of their living tradition can be seen for example in C. Russwurm, *Eibofolks, oder die Schweden an den Küsten Ehstlands und auf Rüno* (Reval, 1855), 2 vols, and in Arthur Ransome's comments, that Rüno's Swedes lived in the 1920s in 'an odd kind of Middle Ages, centuries removed from the modern competitive struggle of the continent', and that they were 'as uniform as a procession of nuns' when they came out of church on Sundays, *Racundra's First Cruise*, pp. 29, 31, 144.
24. Garleff, 'Ethnic Minorities', in, V.S. Vardys and R.J. Misiunas, (eds), *The Baltic States*, p. 81.
25. Garleff, 'Die kulturelle Selbstverwaltung', in, Meissner (ed.), *Die baltischen Nationen*, pp. 89–91.
26. Summary: V.S. Vardys, 'The Rise of Authoritarian Rule in the Baltic States', in, V.S. Vardys and R.J. Misiunas, (eds) The Baltic States, pp. 66–9.
27. See below, p. 62.
28. *Kriser och Krispolitik* (see note 2) provides excellent statistical tables.
29. A.R. Cederberg, S. Csekey, J.G. Granö (eds) *Eesti* (Handbook) 2nd rev. edn (Tallinn, 1930), p. 52 *passim*. The importance of Estonian self-education at village level after c.1860 is discussed by O. Loorits, 'The Renascence of the Estonian Nation', *The Slavonic and East European Review* 33 (1954–5), 25–43.
30. Pullerits, *Estonia*, p. 48.
31. Bilmanis, *Latvia*, pp. 371–3.
32. Von Rauch, *The Baltic States*, pp. 133–4.
33. In 1923, 83.9 per cent of the Lithuanian population were autochthon; but only 63 per cent compared to 20.4 per cent of Lithuania's Jewish population (7.6 per cent) were employed as civil servants. See, V.S. Vardys, 'Die Entwicklung der Republik Litauen', in Meissner (ed.) *Die Baltischen Nationen*, p. 76.
34. Pullerits, *Estonia*, pp. 20–4.
35. Bilmanis, *Latvia*, p. 370; Silde, 'Die Entwicklung der Republik Lettland', in, Meissner (ed.), *Die Baltischen Nationen*, p. 70. In Denmark in January 1933, Thorwald Stauning's social-democratic government replaced over fifty older public welfare laws by a code of social welfare worked out by the Minister for Social Affairs, Karl Steincke. This code consisted of four acts, which introduced a comprehensive system of social insurance, and guaranteed every Dane the right to a reasonable standard of living.
36. Pullerits, *Estonia*, p. 74.
37. Useful discussion in *ibid.*, pp. 131–40; *Eesti* (1930), p. 58.
38. *Eesti*, pp. 59–60.
39. Bilmanis, *Latvia*, p. 364; *Conference on Rural Life 1939* (*Latvia*), p. 26.

40. *Ibid.*, pp. 48–53.
41. Silde, 'Die Entwicklung der Republik Lettland', in, Meissner (ed.), *Die Baltischen Nationen*, p. 69; Ulmanis, *Latvia*, p. 362 *passim*.
42. Vardys, 'Die Entwicklung der Republik Litauen', in, Meissner (ed.), *Die Baltischen Nationen*, pp. 82–3.
43. R. Taagepera, 'Civic Culture and Authoritarianism in the Baltic States 1918–1940', *East European Quarterly* 7, no. 4 (1973), pp. 407–12.
44. Ransome, *Racundra's First Cruise*, p. 55.
45. See note 4. '*Solidarisk samfunnspolitik*' was used to describe this policy by the new Norwegian Labour coalition government of 1935.
46. Von Rauch, *The Baltic States*, p. 148.
47. Parming, 'The Collapse of Liberal Democracy', p. 39.
48. See Vardys: 'The Rise of Authoritarian Rule in the Baltic States' in, Vardys and Misiunas (eds), *The Baltic States*, pp. 65 80.
49. Päts, 'the community will have to rely increasingly on these corporate organizations rather than on the gifts or powers of any individual, for men pass away, but the corporations abide', quoted in Pullerits, *Estonia*, p. 183.

3 Incorporation:
The Molotov–Ribbentrop Pact
David Kirby

One of the most difficult problems encountered by the small new states of Europe during the interwar years was how to acquire a decent mantle of security without unduly compromising their political independence. In this regard, the three Baltic countries of Estonia, Latvia and Lithuania were particularly ill-favoured. The great powers were by and large indifferent to their survival as independent countries, and they possessed no vital resource which might have persuaded one or more of those powers to extend a protective arm. In spite of efforts to coordinate foreign and defence policies, the three conspicuously failed to pull together in the manner of the Scandinavian countries.[1] Lithuania was wholly absorbed in its quarrel with Poland over the Vilna question, and its occupation of the Memel region in 1923 also brought it into potential conflict with Germany. These were compelling reasons enough for Latvia and Estonia to be wary of entanglement in the affairs of their southern neighbour, whose religious, cultural and historical traditions were in any case very different. The Estonians and Latvians did share a degree of common history in that both had suffered for centuries under the yoke of serfdom imposed by German colonists, but their main desire on escaping from that bondage was to stress their own national uniqueness; in consequence, they tended to pay little attention to each other, separated as they were by mutually incomprehensible languages. Worried about German resurgence, the two countries signed an agreement for closer co-operation in 1934, and extended this to include Lithuania at the end of the year. Although the treaty made provision for regular meetings of foreign ministers, it did not cover military co-operation. The French and Soviet governments intimated at the end of 1934 that they would look favourably upon a Baltic military alliance, but the Estonians refused to consider such an idea, and continued to oppose it on subsequent occasions when the issue was raised by Lithuania. There was a degree of friction and mutual suspicion between the three countries throughout the years of independence which made close co-operation unlikely.[2]

Such differences might have been of little consequence had not the trio been wedged between Russia and Germany during a period when, in the delicate language of a British Foreign Office official, 'both these great neighbours had succumbed to unprincipled regimes'.[3] Although recent history and the continued presence of a German minority in Latvia and Estonia placed the *Baltikum* within the ambit of a German sphere of influence, it was never high on the list of the Führer's priorities. For Stalin, on the other hand, the *Pribaltiki* was of great importance as a potentially vulnerable frontier zone. The unwavering commitment of the Soviet Union to peaceful and good relations with its neighbours was carefully qualified by the party secretary, in a speech to the eighteenth party congress on 10 March 1939: 'We stand and we will stand on that position insofar as these countries will maintain such relations with the Soviet Union and insofar as they do not attempt to infringe directly or indirectly the interests, integrity and inviolability of the frontiers of the Soviet state...'.[4] And at the end of March, less than a week after the Germans had compelled the Lithuanian government to surrender the Memel (Klaipèda) area, the ministers of Latvia and Estonia were handed a note by Maxim Litvinov warning their governments that any agreement with outsiders which infringed upon their independence would be regarded as intolerable by the Soviet Union.[5]

Litvinov's note – one of his last acts as commissar for foreign affairs before being replaced by Molotov – underlined the basic Soviet mistrust of their small neighbours' ability (or willingness) to resist pressure from a third party hostile to the Soviet Union. The Finnish government had received similar intimations in 1938, for example.[6] The reaction of the neighbours was predictable: annoyance, suspicion of Soviet motives and an unwillingness to perceive the anxiety which lay behind these crude advances. The Estonians, already nervous that some kind of deal was being planned between Britain and the USSR which would give Moscow a free hand in the Baltic, turned to Germany in order to counteract such a move.[7] The Germans for their part were more than willing to flatter the Baltic states, and there was a flurry of top-brass military visits during the early summer months. Non-aggression treaties were also signed by Germany with Estonia and Latvia on 7 June 1938. These treaties were worth no more than the paper they were written on – contingency plans 'to occupy the Baltic states up to the border of the former Kurland and to incorporate them into the Reich' had been proposed (but soon shelved) by Hitler in April – and they aroused opposition in the states concerned.[8] More seriously, they gave the Soviet leadership further grounds for suspicion of the pro-German leanings of their neighbours.[9] Even the British complained that the attitude of the Baltic states was creating difficulties in the tripartite talks between Moscow, London and Paris. The British representative in Tallinn, for example, tore a strip off the Estonian foreign minister during a walk in the woods in July, telling him that the Estonians were being ungrateful and foolish:

> They were attacking Great Britain for having 'sold' them to the Bolsheviks, although we had not yet done anything to imperil their sovereignty and in fact had been fighting their battles for nearly three months. They openly showed their mistrust and dislike to Soviet Russia, and by their bitter reproaches that Great Britain was giving them up to destruction, they were making it more difficult for His Majesty's Government and they were doing much to justify the Soviet contention that the Baltic states could not be trusted to ask for help before it was too late. Prominent Estonian statesmen had told me at various times during the past few years that they would accept German help to repel any Soviet aggression, but would refuse Soviet help to repel German aggression. This, I said, was not impartial neutrality and might give the Soviet government grounds for insisting that Estonia was not competent to decide when help was necessary.[10]

In the opening round of these tripartite talks, the British ambassador to Moscow had voiced Britain's objections to the Soviet terms for guarantees for the Baltic states, saying that none of those states wished to be associated with a Soviet guarantee. By the end of June, however, the British had begun to consider shifting their ground. In Cabinet on 26 June, the Foreign Secretary Lord Halifax cited, as evidence that the Baltic states were perhaps not so adamantly opposed to the Russian proposal of a tripartite guarantee as they made out, an interview with the Latvian minister to Brussels, who had claimed that it was only fear of offending Germany that had prompted Latvia to object to a guarantee, which it would otherwise welcome. Prime Minister Chamberlain on the other hand was strongly opposed to naming the Baltic states in any guarantee, and wanted the first article of any agreement to include the words 'maintaining its independence and neutrality against aggression' as a means of reassuring the states to be assisted. Holland and Switzerland should also be included in any list if the Soviet side insisted on naming the three Baltic states.[11]

The Soviet side not only insisted upon a list of named states to be guaranteed: it also demanded the inclusion of 'indirect' as well as direct aggression into the draft treaty. Lord Halifax regarded this proposal as 'completely unacceptable... The use of the term "indirect aggression" would confirm the worst suspicions of the Baltic states whose objection to the proposed treaty rests largely on the fear of Russian interference in their internal affairs'.[12] The British were nevertheless still prepared to go some way towards meeting Soviet demands. The Cabinet committee on foreign policy agreed on 19 July that the British and French would be prepared to add a general formula providing for consultation in the event of aggressive action against the Baltic states which did not fall within the definition of indirect aggression contained in Article One of the draft treaty 'which the Russians wanted to do something about'.[13] On this rather vague note, the military mission departed for Moscow. Its members were instructed not to discuss the defence of the Baltic states, since neither Britain nor France had guaranteed them. The talks soon become bogged down, and were rendered superfluous with the signing of the Nazi–Soviet non-aggression pact on 23 August, concluded with a speed and ruthlessness which contrasted sharply with the crabbed and slow progress made by the British and French in their talks.

In his final report to the British government on 28 August, the head of the military mission opined that 'it is highly probable that the pact contains secret clauses regarding the dividing up of the spoil (Poland and the Baltic states)... Russia's aim would probably be to acquire part of Poland, part of Romania and certain ports and islands in the Baltic'.[14] The Russians had made it pretty clear that they expected Britain to assist them in acquiring these strategic bases, and they demanded German recognition that the ports of Libau (Liepāja) and Windau (Ventspils) should fall within the Soviet sphere of interest on 23 August. That the Führer consented to this concession may be an indication of the price he was willing to pay, albeit temporarily, to secure Soviet acquiescence towards German aggression against Poland.

The first clause of the secret protocol of 23 August defined the northern border of Lithuania as the frontier of the spheres of interest of Germany and the Soviet Union; both parties moreover recognised the interest of Lithuania in the Vilna (Vilnius) territory, taken by Poland in 1920. As the German plans for war against Poland came to a head at the end of August, several attempts were made to encourage the Lithuanian government to stage some kind of military demonstration against the Polish frontier.[15] Although the Lithuanian government resolved on 5 September to remain neutral, the Germans continued to drop hints about the occupation of Vilna until mid-September, when the whole idea was suddenly abandoned. There is evidence to suggest that the Russians were worried about German activities concerning Lithuania, and Soviet intervention in Poland may well have been spurred on by this anxiety.[16] The rapid advance of Soviet troops into eastern Poland disconcerted the Germans, and Stalin was not slow to take advantage of the situation. On 25 September, he suggested to the German ambassador that Germany might be given additional territory in the final partition of Poland in return for conceding Lithuania to the Soviet sphere of interest. If Germany consented, 'the Soviet Union would immediately take up the solution of the problem of the Baltic countries in accordance with the protocol of 23 August and expected the unstinting support of the German government'.[17]

Stalin had in fact already begun the process of resolving the Baltic question. The Estonian foreign minister Kaarel Selter had arrived in Moscow the previous day, ostensibly to sign a wartime trade agreement. When he met his Soviet counterpart at nine o' clock in the evening, he was soon left in no doubt about the true purpose of his visit. Trade relations between the two countries were satisfactory, declared Mr Molotov, but political relations were not. The case of the *Orzeł*, a Polish submarine which had escaped from internment in Tallinn on 18 September, was cited as an argument that Estonia was incapable of defending its neutrality. The Soviet Union had to have effective guarantees for its security, and for this reason demanded a military pact and mutual assistance treaty which would allow it to station troops on Estonian territory. Estonian assurances of uncompromising commitment to neutrality cut no ice with Molotov, though he assured Mr Selter that the Soviet Union had no intention of impairing Estonian sovereignty or of forcing communism upon the country. He reluctantly agreed to suspend the talks in order that Mr Selter might contact his government, but on their resumption at midnight, a draft mutual assistance treaty was presented to the Estonians. Molotov once more voiced his annoyance at what he took to be the delaying tactics of the Estonians but finally agreed to Mr Selter's return to Tallinn for further instructions.[18]

After a series of hurried meetings and consultations on the afternoon of 26 September, the Estonian government decided to bow to the inevitable.[19] The delegation returned to Moscow with instructions to accept the Soviet demands in principle and to try and soften the terms. Instead they had to face new demands. Using as an excuse the reported sinking of a Soviet vessel by an unidentified submarine, Molotov insisted upon the right to station 35 000 troops on Estonian soil for the duration of the war. After much wrangling, at which Stalin was present, the Soviet side agreed to lower the figure to 25 000, and to locate the naval base at Paltiski instead of Tallinn. The Estonians also insisted that the assistance clause of the treaty would be valid only in the event of an attack by a great power. When the treaty was signed late in the evening of 28 September, Stalin gave his assurances that the Soviet Union would respect Estonian sovereignty. The Estonian government had acted wisely, he told the delegation, in signing the treaty; they could easily have gone the way of Poland.[20]

At the end of the afternoon session of negotiations, the Estonian delegation encountered the German foreign minister and his advisers in the ante-room. As Estonia's fate was being decided, Lithuania was also being transferred from the German to the Soviet sphere of influence. The Reich government also secured Russian agreement for the evacuation of the Baltic German minority. Meanwhile, in Riga the Latvian foreign minister Vilhelms Munters assured the British minister that 'he has no special reason at present for fearing difficulties with the Soviet government', though he did admit to being anxious because he had no news of the Soviet–Estonian negotiations.[21] He was to be rudely disabused a few days later, when it was his turn to be subjected to the bargaining tactics of Molotov and Stalin. The Soviet leader told him bluntly that 'as far as Germany is concerned, we could occupy you'. As in the Estonian case, the Soviet side scaled down its initial demands regarding the size of the garrison and the location of naval bases, though Stalin ominously added that if the war were to spread, the treaty would have to be supplemented.[22] The Lithuanians were treated somewhat differently, since the Soviet Union proposed to restore the Vilna region to Lithuania in return for a mutual assistance pact. Molotov's revelation that the Germans expected the Lithuanian government to cede to them the Suwałki strip caused embarrassment in Berlin and gave added weight to Stalin's assurances that in accepting the benevolent protection of the Soviet Union, Lithuania had avoided becoming a German protectorate.[23]

These events were generally perceived by the outside world as spelling the end of independence for the Baltic states. Diplomatic reports also spoke of a deep sense of gloom and pessimism prevalent among the populace at large. The governments and press of the three states however strove to put the best possible gloss on the treaties, declaring that they provided a firm assurance of their continued neutrality.[24] The Soviet invasion of Finland at the end of November, and the establishment of a puppet government headed by the Finnish communist O.W. Kuusinen in the occupied town of Terijoki on 1 December 1939, was a further blow to the Baltic states. In private, politicians and military leaders confided that their only hope lay in a quick resolution to the conflict in the West, which would ensure that the victorious side took measures to restore their influence in the Baltic region.[25] In order to keep these hopes alive, and to counter the impression that the Baltic states had already lost their independence, the three countries strove to coordinate their policies and gave their support to the *Revue Baltique*, whose first number appeared in February 1940. Other options were few indeed. There were increased military contacts, and the period of military service was increased in Latvia and Estonia; but it is highly unlikely that the leadership was seriously considering armed resistance. President Antanas Smetona of Lithuania was willing to accept the establishment of a German protectorate over his country, and entered into secret discussion with the Germans to sound out the possibility of realising this.

As the spring drew on, rumours of a possible German attack on Russia in the autumn began to circulate widely.[26]

Relations between the Soviet garrison forces and their involuntary hosts were cool but correct, though there were a number of incidents, and frequent alarms. On 2 February, for example, Soviet anti-aircraft guns fired on an Estonian aircraft flying above the harbour in Tallinn, mistaking it for a Finnish raider. This provoked quite sharp press comment, which the British minister reported to London: 'This same hostility has existed amongst the majority of the Estonian populace for weeks past and it is even more open today.... Soviet soldiers and sailors walking about Tallinn are ostracised by the populace.'[27] Soviet planes frequently violated the terms of the treaty by flying outside the prescribed air corridors. Demands were also made for additional facilities and territory beyond the terms of the autumn agreements. The activities of local communists also gave some cause for worry to the Baltic governments, in spite of Stalin having assured Mr Munters in October 1939 that: 'There are no Communists outside of Russia. What you have in Latvia are Trotskyists; if they cause you trouble, shoot them.'[28] There were numerous reports of increased communist activity in April 1940. In Latvia, the number of persons arrested for anti-government activities rose significantly, though not a few were arrested with the tacit assistance of the Soviet military authorities, prompting the suspicion that the eagerness of the Latvian comrades for action was not yet in the interests of Soviet policy towards the Baltic states.[29]

The ground began to shift under the feet of the hapless Baltic governments in the spring of 1940, as the German war machine began to roll in the West. An article published in *Izvestiya* on 16 May dismissed small-state neutrality as 'mere fantasy'. The Soviet press also began a campaign against the Baltic states, accusing them of harbouring pro-Allied sympathies. In the autumn of 1939 it had been the northernmost republic which had first experienced Soviet pressure; in May 1940, it was to be the turn of Lithuania.[30] Significant numbers of tanks and tracked artillery were moved from the Vilna region to the vicinity of Kaunas during the third week of May, and at the end of the month the Lithuanian foreign minister went to Moscow to discuss Soviet complaints about the treatment of its troops. Molotov refused to see him and insisted that the prime minister visit Moscow. When prime minister Merkys met Molotov on 7 June, he was presented with demands for the dismissal of the minister of the interior and the head of the security forces in Lithuania. At a later meeting, Molotov accused the Baltic states of conspiring to create an anti-Soviet military pact. The Lithuanian government desperately sought to comply with Soviet demands, but to no avail. On the evening of 14 June, Molotov delivered an ultimatum to the Lithuanian government. This repeated all the previous accusations of bad faith and anti-Soviet activities, and demanded that the minister of the interior and head of security be put on trial for organising 'provocations' against Red Army troops. A new government committed to fulfilling the terms of the mutual assistance pact was to be formed immediately, and an unspecified number of Soviet forces were to be freely allowed to enter Lithuania to ensure that these conditions were met. The Lithuanians were given until 10 o'clock the following morning to reply. President Smetona urged resistance, but, unable to win over the majority of his government, he declared his intention of going abroad and vested temporary powers in the prime minister. The government, its confidence already shattered by the disastrous events of the last two years, decided to accept the ultimatum and empowered general Raštikis to form a new government. This was not however acceptable to Moscow, which announced that deputy foreign minister V.G. Dekanozov would arrive in Kaunas to supervise the formation of the government. Soviet troops began occupying strategic points in Lithuania on the evening of 15 June, as president Smetona crossed the frontier into Germany. Ultimatums calling for the immediate creation of new governments and the admission of Soviet troops were delivered to the Latvian and Estonian governments on 16 June, demanding an answer the same day. Aware of the large numbers of troops massing on the frontiers, with no hope of support from outside, the governments agreed to the Soviet demands, and troops began to pour in early the following day.[31]

In all three cases, high-ranking Soviet emissaries were sent to the Baltic capitals to ensure that the terms of the ultimatums were fully carried out. In order to smooth the way, they employed emollient phrases and even hinted at some form of continued independence or at least autonomy.[32] They were also concerned to ensure that the new governments were created as far as possible in accordance with the constitutional practices of the countries. For this reason, Dekanozov sent a delegation to try and persuade Smetona to return from East Prussia. When that failed, he was obliged to dictate the names of the people deemed reliable for government office by Moscow to the man to whom Smetona had entrusted provisional authority, prime minister Merkys. The new prime minister was Justas Paleckis, a left-wing journalist who soon joined the communist party. The government was a mixture of fellow-travellers and liberal democrats such as the deputy prime minister and acting foreign minister Vincas Krėvė-Mickevičius, with the addition of several communists at the end of June, including Mečys Gedvilas to the key post of minister of the interior. The new Latvian government was presented to president Ulmanis on 20 June. It was headed by

Professor Augusts Kirchenšteins, 'a worn-out, uncertain old man, who clearly lacks self-confidence, assurance, expertise and a will of his own' according to the Finnish minister to Riga, and contained a similar mixture of left-wingers and communists in key positions.[33]

The last government to be formed was that of the country doctor and minor literary figure, Johannes Vares. Andrey Zhdanov was unwilling to accept the suggestions of president Päts when the two men met on 19 June, though he promised to consult Moscow. In the meantime, the local communists began to organise demonstrations in close liaison with the Soviet legation. Maxim Unt, who had been involved in underground activities during the thirties, claimed in a memoir that he was asked by an official of the legation on the evening of 18 June if he would agree to enter government as minister of the interior. It was at the Soviet legation that detailed discussions as to the composition of the Vares ministry took place on 20 June, and it would also seem that plans for massive workers' demonstrations for the following day were also hatched at this meeting.[34] 'In the morning workers were summoned to demonstrate in the main square', reported the British representative. 'Workers were forced to attend but did so half-heartedly. The police were ordered not to interfere and Soviet armoured cars surrounded the demonstration.'[35] The demonstrators then proceeded up the hill to the seat of government on Toompea, and demanded the resignation of prime minister Uluots and a new ministry which would maintain good relations with the Soviet Union. Having been told that this decision was now in the hands of Zhdanov and Vares, the demonstrators, accompanied by several light armoured vehicles, set off to the other side of town to the presidential palace. The president was shouted down when he attempted to address the crowd of between one and three thousand, but he was able to calm the situation by meeting a three-man delegation. The demonstrators then went off to the central prison, where a few men jailed for spying for the Soviet Union were released. There can be little doubt that Zhdanov used these demonstrations as an additional means of putting pressure on Päts to accept the list of ministers presented to him by Vares, though it should be added that similar demonstrations were staged in the other two republics at the same time. Although Vares had succeeded in persuading Zhdanov to accept the left-wing historian Hans Kruus as deputy prime minister, Päts was unable to push through any more changes on the evening of 21 June, and finally agreed to accept the list.[36]

For over four decades, the official Soviet line on these events had been that rotten fascistic regimes hostile to the USSR were toppled by a popular revolution, and the role played by Zhdanov, Vyshinsky and Dekanozov (and sinister agents such as the Estonian Karl Säre) deliberately downplayed. The tide has now turned with a vengeance, and it is the back-stairs machinations and the dominant role of the occupying Soviet forces which are at the centre of attention. For the Baltic peoples struggling to break free of the coils of Soviet empire, the regimes which perished in the summer of 1940 evoke a rather more positive image than perhaps was the case at the time. All three had begun to run into serious difficulties before the outbreak of war. Lacking any real political dynamism, their claims to speak for and defend the interests of the nation had been badly dented in autumn of 1939. Those most closely associated with the regime appear to have been the most pessimistic, while the optimism of oppositional moderates such as Ants Piip (who took over the foreign office portfolio in the Uluots government formed in October 1939) proved ill-founded and naive. The accusations of secret military preparations and collusion with Britain and France which Molotov levelled against the Baltic governments in May–June 1940 were merely excuses to intervene. There was a greater awareness of the need to cooperate, and the three states were quietly trying to build up their armed forces, but they were sufficiently sanguine to realise the hopelessness of any attempt to rid themselves of the Soviet presence. Far from 'intriguing' with the Allies, as Molotov alleged, the governments of the three states probably still hoped that a rift in German–Soviet relations might be their salvation.[37]

Undoubtedly, the old regimes had lost much of their remaining credibility among the people at large, and there were many – especially those who had suffered for their opposition in the past – who were prepared to welcome and work with the new governments. This honeymoon period proved to be short-lived. Professor Krėvė-Mickevičius, the new Lithuanian foreign minister, was bluntly told by Molotov at the end of June that his country, together with the other Baltic states and Finland would have to join the glorious family of the Soviet Union, and 'speaking with great emotion' he informed the British representative in Kaunas that incorporation of his country into the Soviet Union had already been decided upon.[38] Although Vyshinsky, addressing a crowd in Riga on 21 June, spoke several times of the independence of the Latvian republic, rumours were already circulating a fortnight later of the forthcoming elections paving the way for communist-dominated assemblies which would probably vote for incorporation.[39]

These rumours proved all too true. Less than a fortnight was allowed between the calling and the holding of the elections, in mid-July. In all three countries, the committees in charge of the elections were controlled by the communists. Numerous obstacles were placed in the way of parties wishing to register. Opposition candidates had to produce at short notice their programmes for inspection; most were rejected by the electoral committees. In Lithuania, some 2000 were arrested on the night of 11–12 July, including many leading political figures, and the now acting president Paleckis issued a stern warning that only the enemies of the new Lithuania would stay at home on election day. The communists as such were hardly in a position fully to control the situation. All three parties had been severely weakened by repression at home and the purges in the Soviet Union, which had scythed down the most able leaders. Contacts with Moscow were even broken off for a time in 1938 when the foreign bureaux of the Latvian and Estonian communist parties were dissolved. The weakest of the three was the Estonian communist party, which could only claim some 150 members when the party was legalised in June 1940. The Latvian party had some 800 members at the end of 1939, but arrests at the end of the year and in April 1940 deprived the party of most of its central committee. The Lithuanian party had some 1500 members, of whom at least one-third were Jewish.[40] The number of sympathisers in pro-communist organisations was much higher, and in Latvia and Lithuania especially, there were numerous left-wing groups and parties willing to make common cause with the communists in the workers' blocs which contested the elections.[41]

Those organisations which did not align themselves with the new forces soon found themselves disbanded. The institutions upon which the old regimes had rested were dissolved; policemen, army officers and civil servants were dismissed and prominent figures arrested. On the other hand, new posts were created and hefty wage increases (soon swallowed up by price inflation) were given. As Dov Levin has pointed out, substantial numbers of Jews benefited from the new order, in terms of greater access to higher education and to jobs hitherto denied them. On the other hand, the new order had no time for Zionism or Jewish cultural and religious observances, nor did it grant any favours to Jewish property owners.[42] Jews were not spared either in the mass deportations which were carried out on the eve of the German invasion in 1941. In the eyes of many Lithuanians and Latvians, however, the Jews were identified with the communist regime, and as the Germans rapidly advanced into the Baltic region in the summer of 1941, there were several vicious pogroms in Latvian and Lithuanian towns.

Minorities, some of whose members prominently identify themselves with the new regime, are easily tarred with the same brush, and can of course be used as scapegoats. It is much less easy to identify other elements of the indigenous populations which rallied to the new order. It would seem that a substantial section of the liberal and left-wing intelligentsia were prepared to give the new governments their support for a programme of progressive reforms, but that goodwill rapidly evaporated. A number of measures designed to secure working-class support were passed by the new governments, and one should not suppose that all demonstrations were carefully stage-managed by the occupying forces, using unwilling workers. The ridiculously high vote for the workers' blocs in the July elections and the dutiful proceedings of the assemblies (described by one eye-witness as 'a theatrical affair... the deputies voted like sheep in unanimity') reveal nothing other than the neuroses and intellectual bankruptcy of Stalinism.[43] In a situation of great fluidity and change, both at home and abroad, and one which moreover was transformed once more in the summer of 1941, it is highly unlikely that people had the time to consolidate their views. For the vast majority, making shift and adapting in order to survive was probably the only option. An official of the British embassy in Moscow, paying a visit to Tallinn in September 1940, noted that the town still seemed tidy and attractive, the people well-dressed and prosperous-looking, in contrast to the citizens of Lwów which 'had already had the benefit of six months' Soviet administration when I saw it last January'. 'The feelings of the Estonian people', Mr Russell reported, 'are at present a mixture of apathetic resignation to their fate, forlorn hope for an ultimate delivery by Great Britain or Germany, fear of the OGPU, contempt for their conquerors, and bitter regret that they did not, like the Finns, make a bid for freedom'.[44]

Although all three small countries shared the same fate in an operation which has all the appearances of being timetabled in Moscow, their perceptions of that fate differed, as the above extract may indicate. For the Estonians, linked by linguistic and cultural ties, Finland and the Finnish people have offered hope and an example to be emulated since the mid-nineteenth century.[45] Such an ideal model has not been available so readily to the peoples of Latvia and Lithuania. Russians and Jews may have had personal, cultural or even emotional connections with the Soviet Union, Catholicism and perhaps a common history linked Lithuanians and Poles, but there were also powerful circumstances (a history of religious persecution, linguistic nationalism) which prevented any closer ties being made. As we have seen, the three countries were divided over foreign and defence policies and objectives, and when they did make a belated attempt to co-ordinate their actions in 1939–40, this helped provide a pretext for the Soviet Union to complete its occupation.

In the circumstances, it would have been folly to resist, but it might be argued that the governments of Päts, Ulmanis and Smetona need not have collaborated to the extent which they did. By agreeing to mutual assistance pacts in the autumn of 1939, they clearly compromised their countries' future existence. With hindsight, no doubt, they might have wished that they had endorsed the idea of guarantees from the tripartite powers in the spring–summer of 1939, though it would also be rash to assume that this might have led to the conclusion of any firm alliance between the Western powers and the Soviet Union. A Lithuanian force despatched to the Vilna region in the first fortnight of September might also have opened up a rather different scenario in which the Baltic countries could have played a more active role in the defence of their own interests, but once again, this can only be a tentative speculation. The Finnish government which refused to accept the Soviet terms during negotiations in the autumn of 1939 rested firmly upon majority support in the democratically-elected parliament; this cannot be said of any of the Baltic regimes which bowed to Soviet pressure. Finland's gallant resistance against overwhelming odds during the Winter War of 1939–40 earned the plaudits of the West, but did not guarantee unconditional support in the postwar years, when Finland seemed on the brink of being drawn completely into the Soviet sphere of influence. The demise of the independent Baltic states was felt to be regrettable, but not a matter of high priority for the governments of the United Kingdom or the United States. Indeed, in the spring of 1942, the hard-pressed British government was prepared to concede the Soviet claim to *de jure* sovereignty over the three states, but was persuaded to think otherwise by the Americans.[46]

NOTES

1. On the failed efforts to create the semblance of unity, see the chapter by Edgar Anderson, 'The Baltic Entente: Phantom or Reality?' in V. Vardys and R. Misiunas, eds, *The Baltic States in Peace and War 1917–1945* (Pennsylvania, 1978), pp. 126–35. It might also be remembered that the creation of a Scandinavian bloc in the 1930s did not spare any of the northern European countries from the rigours of war: even Sweden was forced seriously to compromise her neutrality before German pressure.

2. The view expressed by the deputy foreign minister of Estonia to the German chargé d'affaires in April 1939 'that Estonia continued to regard [Latvia's attitude] with the deepest mistrust, as far as the Soviet Union was concerned' is an indication of the poor state of the relationship: *Documents of German Foreign Policy 1918–1945* [*DGFP*] Series D (1937–1945) vol. 6, London, 1956, p. 246.

3. Marginal note by O'Malley to a despatch from the British minister in Riga (Orde), 8 October 1939: Public Record Office, London: Foreign Office archive: FO 371/23689: N 5326/518/38.

4. McNeal R, ed., 1967 *I.V. Stalin. Sochineniya* vol. 1(14), Stanford, p. 344.

5. Litvinov to Estonian minister, 28 March 1939, in: *Documents of British Foreign Policy 1919–1939* [*DBFP*]. Third Series vol. 5 (London, 1952), pp. 350–1, and H. Arumäe, ed., *Molotovi-Ribbentropi paktist baaside lepinguni. Dokumente ja materjale* (Tallinn, 1989), pp. 16–17.

6. This episode is dealt with in detail by J. Suomi, *Talvisodan tausta. Neuvostoliitto Suomen ulkopolitiikassa 1937–1939. Holstista Erkkoon* (Helsinki, 1973) p. 204ff. See also D. Kirby, *Finland in the Twentieth Century* (London, 1979), pp. 117–19.

7. Frohwein (German minister to Tallinn) to Foreign Office, Berlin, 24 April 1939: *DGFP* vol. 6, pp. 316–17.

8. See details of 'Operation White' in *DGFP*, vol. 6, pp. 224–8. For opposition voiced by Estonian politicians, see the minutes of the meeting of the commission for national defence of the Riigivolikogu in Arumäe 1989, pp. 61–4. The non-aggression pacts have been studied most recently by Rolf Ahmann, who concludes that they were 'part of German efforts to secure, economically and militarily, the localization of an attack on Poland without an understanding with the USSR'. R. Ahmann, 'The German Treaties with Estonia and Latvia of June 1939 – Bargaining Ploy or an Alternative for German–Soviet Understanding?', *Journal of Baltic Studies* 20/4, 1989, p. 338 *et seq.*

9. See for example, the report of the German ambassador to Moscow, Count Schulenburg, on 7 August in *DGFP*, vol. 6, p. 1076. The Finnish minister reported similar suspicions amongst Soviet officials: S. Myllyniemi *Baltian kriisi 1938–1941* (Helsinki, 1977), p. 50.

10. Gallienne to Foreign Office, London, 11 July 1939: *DBFP*, vol. 6, pp. 325–7.

11. Cabinet Committee on Foreign Policy minutes, 26 June 1939: FO 371/23067: C 9315/3356/18. The report of the Latvian minister was swiftly rebutted in Tallinn and Riga.

12. Halifax to Seeds, Moscow, 6 July 1939: *DBFP*, vol. 6, pp. 277–8.

13. Cabinet Committee on Foreign Policy Minutes, 19 July 1939: FO 371/23071: C10267/3356/18.

14. Admiral Drax's report, 28 August 1939: *DBFP*, vol. 7, pp. 608–9. The Estonia minister to London reported on 22 August that there were rumours of Germany being prepared to acknowledge that Finland, Estonia and Latvia fell within the Soviet sphere of influence. Arumäe 1989, p. 90.

15. Weizsäcker to Zechlin, Kaunas, 29, 30 August 1939: *DGFP*, vol. 7, p. 423, 450. The Estonian army command was also informed of German pressure on Lithuania to attack Poland: Arumäe 1989, p. 114.

16. See Wiley (Riga) to State Department, 17 September 1939, reporting a conversation with the Soviet military attaché, in *Foreign Relations of the United States. Diplomatic Papers. The Soviet Union 1933–1939* [*FRUS*] (Washington, 1952), pp. 938–9. A draft German–Lithuanian defence treaty, dated 20 September (the day after the Red Army occupied Vilna), would have established a German protectorate over Lithuania: *DGFP*, vol. 8, p. 112.

17. Schulenburg to German Foreign Office, 25 September 1939: *DGFP*, vol. 8, p. 130.

18. The minutes of the Selter–Molotov talks are in Arumäe 1989, pp. 122–30.

19. The Estonian army command had been in touch with their German counterparts and had been told unequivocally that no help could be expected from

that quarter. See the extract from the memoirs of Colonel Maasing in Arumäe 1989, p. 133, and the minutes of a session of the defence and foreign affairs commissions of the Estonian parliament, ibid., pp. 137–45.

20. Details of the talks in Arumäe 1989, pp. 151–71. See also Selter's account of his negotiations in *Eesti riik ja rahvas teises maailmasôjas* vol. 2 (Stockholm, 1955), pp. 39–42, and appendices 10, 11, pp. 195–6.
21. Orde to Foreign Office, 28 September 1939: FO 371/23689: N4829/518/38. The head of the Northern Department at the Foreign Office thought it astonishing – if true – that as late as 30 September, the Latvian government had no special information about Soviet–Estonian relations (N4901/518/38): but there is little evidence of contacts between Selter and Munters during these crucial days. According to the Latvian minister to London, Selter's successor 'more or less apologised for the failure of his predecessor' to consult the Latvian government before accepting the Soviet terms: memorandum by Collier, 4 January 1940, FO 371/24758: N206/165/59.
22. Munters's report on negotiations in Moscow, 2–3 October 1939, is printed as an appendix in *Report of the Select Committee to Investigate Communist Aggression and the Forced Incorporation of the Baltic States into the USSR. Third Interim Report of the Select Committe on Communist Aggression, House of Representatives. Eighty-Third Congress. Second Session* (Washington, 1954), p. 428f.
23. Myllyniemi 1977, pp. 72–5. B. Kaslas, ed., *The USSR–German Aggression against Lithuania* (New York, 1973), pp. 146–7, contains the account of the Moscow negotiations on 7–8 October by the Lithuanian foreign minister.
24. See for example the extracts from *Rahvaleht* (30.9), *Päevaleht* (2.10) and *Briva Zeme* (9.10) in *Review of the Foreign Press 1939–1945* Series B, vol. 1 (Munich, 1980). A markedly different tone to that of the official government line was struck at the meeting of the foreign affairs and defence commissions of the Estonian parliament on 2 October: Arumäe, pp. 184–91. There is a detailed survey of opinion within the Baltic countries in Myllyniemi 1977, pp. 75–86.
25. For example, Gallienne to the Foreign Office, 5 October 1939: FO 371/23689; N5327/518/38, reporting on a conversation with Colonel Saarsen of Estonian Intelligence. Myllyniemi 1977, pp. 114–15.
26. Myllyniemi 1977, pp. 113–21.
27. Gallienne to Foreign Office, 3 February 1940: FO 371/24758; N2042/169/59.
28. Preston to Foreign Office, 19 April 1940: FO 419/35; N4794/1803/59. Stalin gave similar robust assurances to the Lithuanian foreign minister: *Third Interim Report,* pp. 315–16.
29. Myllyniemi 1977, pp. 129–33.
30. The fact that Lithuania shared a common border with Germany may well have put it first in line to be dealt with. When Sir Hugh Dalton asked the Soviet ambassador to London, Ivan Maisky, why his government was acting in such a way in Lithuania, Maisky reportedly replied: 'Your troops were twenty-four hours too late in reaching the Albert canal. We do not want to be twenty-four hours too late on the East Prussian frontier.' Dalton's memorandum of conversation with Maisky, 18 June 1940: FO 371/24844; N5877/30/38.
31. L. Sabaliunas *Lithuania in Crisis: Nationalism to Communism 1939–1940* (Bloomington, Ind., 1972), pp. 177–88. *Third Interim Report,* pp. 243–50,

290–7, 321–38. See also the documents detailing troop movements in Estonia in the early hours of 17 June in: *1940 god v Estonii. Dokumentyi i materialyi* (Tallinn, 1989), pp. 103–6.

32. For details, see my chapter on 'The Baltic States 1940–1950' in: M. McCauley, ed., *Communist Power in Europe 1944–1950* (London, 1977), p. 27.

33. Myllyniemi 1977, p. 146. The British minister to Riga described Kirchensteins as 'a mild-mannered man of science, whose lack of knowledge of foreign affairs is self-confessed and complete', and his government as composed mainly 'of middle-class intellectuals of democratic views'. Orde to Foreign Office, 5 July 1940: FO 371/24761; N6510/1224/59.

34. *1940 god v Estonii*, p. 111–20 for a series of memoirs by communist activists.

35. Gallienne to Foreign Office, 26 June 1940: FO Printed Papers 419/35; N6484/1224/59. Gallienne's report is largely substantiated by other evidence; see *Eesti riik ja rahvas*, vol. 3, pp. 7–31.

36. *1940 god v Estonii*, pp. 121–32 for memoirs of participants. A. Isberg, *Med demokratin som insats. Politiskt-konstitutionellt maktspel i 1930-talets Estland* Studia Baltica Stockholmensia 4 (Stockholm 1988), pp. 122–30 gives a detailed account of events and an assessment of Päts's actions. According to the Finnish minister to Tallinn, leading Estonians were still optimistic about the situation, and even Päts thought things could have been worse. Myllyniemi 1977, p. 149.

37. A. Seidl, ed., *Die Beziehungen zwischen Deutschland und der Sowjetunion 1939–1941* (Tübingen, 1949), p. 181. Germany was in fact about to embark on a policy which would lead to the invasion of the Soviet Union one year later. Already in July 1940, the former Lithuanian minister in Berlin, Kazys Škirpa, claimed he could detect the beginnings of the breach, and the conclusion in August of a secret transit agreement for German troops en route to northern Norway enabled Finnish army officers to believe that their country had been aligned with Germany.

38. *Third Interim Report*, pp. 341–4. Preston to Foreign Office, 5 July 1940: FO 371/24761; N5943/1224/59.

39. Orde to Foreign Office, 21 June 1940: FO 371/24761; N5833/1224/59, and 27 June 1940: N5889/1224/59. Gallienne to Foreign Office, 5 July 1940: FO 371/24761; N5943/1224/59.

40. *Ocherki istorii kommunisticheskoy partii Latvii*, vol. 2. Riga, 1966, p. 365ff. for details of the Latvian CP, which, according to the journal *Kommunist* (12/1964, p. 68), was 'decapitated' by the purges. For the Estonian CP, see *Ocherki istorii kommunisticheskoy partii Estonii*, vol. 2. (Tallinn, 1963), p. 386. Sabaliunas, 1972, p. 54. For Jewish CP membership, see D. Levin, 1980 'The Jews in the Soviet Lithuanian Establishment, 1940–1', *Soviet Jewish Affairs* 10/2, p. 24. The pre-war Jewish population of the republic of Lithuania was about 150 000, and an additional 100 000 was added with the inclusion of the Vilna region. There were about 95 000 Jews in Latvia, and 5000 in Estonia.

41. There is a detailed account of Jewish involvement in the elections in Lithuania and Latvia in: D. Levin, 'The Jews and the Election Campaigns in Lithuania, 1940–1, *Soviet Jewish Studies* 10, 1980, pp. 39–51, and D. Levin, 'The Jews and the Sovietisation of Latvia, 1940–1', *Soviet Jewish Affairs* 5, 1975, pp. 42–46. For the role of the Latvian social democrats, see B. Kalniņš

De baltiska staternas frihetskamp (Stockholm, 1950), pp. 227–9. As Dr Kalniņš pointed out in a private communication (25 December 1974), the social democratic party was also crushed by the Ulmanis regime, but was not allowed to reorganise after 17 June: the small left socialist party joined forces with the communists.

42. Levin 1975, p. 49. See also D. Levin, 'The Jews in the Soviet Lithuanian Establishment, 1940–41' *Soviet Jewish Affairs* 10, 1980, pp. 21–37.

43. The witness was Gallienne, reporting to the Foreign Office on 24 July 1940: FO 371/24761; N 6045/1224/59.

44. Memorandum by J.W. Russell of the Moscow embassy, September 1940: FO 371/24762; N6939/1224/59. Mr Preston, reporting from Kaunas, spoke of a rapid deterioraton in living standards, with the Lithuanians soon learning the trick of dressing badly in order to avoid the eagle eye of OGPU. N7288/1224/59.

45. See for example the article on the nineteenth-century nationalist C.R. Jakobson's thoughts of Finland, published in 1939 by Hans Kruus, the man who was to be appointed foreign minister of the Vares' government in June 1940, in *Jäämerestä Emäjoen rannoille* (Helsinki, 1939), pp. 183–92.

46. See my chapter, 'Morality or Expediency? The Baltic Question in British–Soviet Relations 1941–1942', in Vardys and Misiunas 1978, pp. 159–72, and A. Kochavi, 'Britain, the Soviet Union and the Question of the Baltic States in 1943' *Journal of Baltic Studies* 22, 1991, pp. 173–82.

4 The Baltic States as Soviet Republics: Tensions and Contradictions

Aleksandras Shtromas

REPRESSION AND RESISTANCE 1941–45

The incorporation of the Baltic states into the USSR was met by their peoples with almost total dismay but very little, if any, outward resistance. The process was handled by the legitimate Baltic governments which decided against 'senseless' armed resistance and gave in to Soviet pressure allowing the Red Army 'peacefully' to occupy their countries. The people were thus caught unawares and reluctantly submitted to Soviet rule.

The Soviets and the local Baltic communists knew, however, only too well how insignificant and marginal their support in the Baltic countries was and how strongly the nations of these countries were in principle committed to resisting them. Therefore they planned well in advance a series of repressive measures aimed at breaking any resistance to Soviet rule in the area. To this effect Order No. 001223 of the NKVD (the People's Commissariat of Internal Affairs) of the USSR, 'On the Operative Accounting of the Anti-Soviet and Socially Alien Elements', was issued as early as 11 October 1939, that is, the day after the conclusion of the Pact of Mutual Assistance between the USSR and Lithuania (the last such pact in the series of three) and more than eight months before the Baltic states were in any real terms taken over by the Soviet Union.[1] The only purpose such an order could have had was preparation for purging the Baltic states from all those who had the potential for organising and carrying out resistance to Soviet rule.

This indeed proved to be the case. Deportations from the Baltic states were ordered by the USSR's People's Commissar of State Security, Merkulov, on 19 May 1941,[2] and the notorious, strictly secret, and extremely detailed 'Instructions Regarding the Manner of Conducting the Deportation of the Anti-Soviet Elements from Lithuania, Latvia, and Estonia' were issued by Merkulov's deputy, Serov, sometime between February and 7 June 1941.[3] The ordered deportations started in all three republics simultaneously, on the night of 13–14 June 1941. During the one week that was left before the outbreak of the war (22 June 1941), 34 260 persons were deported from Lithuania, 15 081 from Latvia, and 10 205 from Estonia.[4] This massive purge marked the peak of the constant wave of repression that, albeit on a much smaller scale, had taken place in the Baltic states throughout the entire period of Soviet rule in 1940–1. These repressions were directed against political, public, and religious figures of the independence period and, more selectively, against people suspected of resistance or oppositional activities, making anti-Soviet pronouncements, or simply refusing to co-operate with the Soviet regime. It is estimated that Soviet repression and evacuations to the USSR in 1940–1 cost Lithuania 39 000, Latvia 35 000, and Estonia (where Soviet forces stayed the longest and some conscription into the Red Army was effected) 61 000 citizens.[5] (These numbers do not include many thousands of people imprisoned by the Soviet authorities but neither killed nor deported before the Soviets retreated from the territories of the Baltic states.)

It is interesting, though, to note that these ferocious repressions totally failed to achieve their goal. If anything, they were counterproductive. These measures demonstrated the brutality and deviousness of the Soviet regime to many unsuspecting and, in the beginning phase of Soviet rule, entirely neutral people. In so doing, the repression contributed to the growth of resistance in terms of both the numbers of resisters and the determination to resist. The massive and indiscriminate character of Soviet repression hit many innocent people, but failed, in fact, to destroy the bulk of the organised resistance forces, whose preparations for an armed insurrection continued unabated. Indeed, the day after the German attack on the USSR an armed insurrection of the Baltic peoples against Soviet rule broke out, and it was so well co-ordinated and organised, so massive and determined to win, that the retreating Soviet troops were unable to quench it.

Of course, the spirit of Baltic resistance to Soviet rule was greatly increased by the precarious international situation and the almost unanimous conviction of the Baltic peoples that the imminent war between Germany and the USSR would spell a rapid end to Soviet rule in the area. This conviction was strengthened and substantiated by the fact that Baltic political emigrés in Germany successfully took on the task of organising and co-ordinating the activities of resistance groups within their respective countries. Without explicit German approval and direct support, they certainly would not have been able even to start such activity. The Germans were indeed extremely helpful to these emigrés, providing them with everything they needed to achieve success (including arms supplies, logistics and the means to transport supplies to the Soviet-controlled Baltic territories). The Germans were keen to ensure that, on the day of the attack against the Soviet Union, insurrection behind Soviet lines would flare as widely and powerfully as possible.

The full story of the organisation of resistance and the insurrection against Soviet rule at the outbreak of the German–Soviet war in June 1941 is best documented in the Lithuanian case. The Lithuanian ambassador to Germany, Colonel Kazys Škirpa, who organised and led the resistance from Berlin, published a book of memoirs in which he included all the relevant documents about the organisation of that resistance and insurrection. It clearly transpires from these documents that as early as July 1940 Škirpa was busy forming in Berlin the Lithuanian Activist Front (LAF), an anti-Soviet resistance organisation uniting all non-communist segments of the Lithuanian political spectrum. These activities of Škirpa and his associates were supervised and, in a way, guided by the German Foreign Office via its liaison man with the Lithuanians, Dr P. Kleist. The LAF was formally inaugurated on 17 November 1940, and, when ready to start combat activities behind Soviet lines, was transferred to the supervision and guidance of the Abwehr Amt (Intelligence Office) of the OKW (High Command of the Armed Forces). The OKW's liaison man with the Lithuanians, Colonel-Lieutenant Dr Graebe, replaced Dr Kleist. Very soon four special Lithuanian posts were established within the Abwehr system on the German–Lithuanian (now Soviet) border for constant maintenance of links and supply lines between the LAF centre in Berlin and its branches in the country. As Škirpa emphasised, these posts played a crucial role in assuring the success of resistance organisation in general and of the insurrection of 23 June 1941, in particular.[6]

What was true for Lithuania must have been true also for Latvia and Estonia, although corroborating documents are less readily available. Undoubtedly German support played a significant role in the successful organisation of resistance and insurrection in all three Baltic countries, although one should not overestimate this factor. For without the genuine determination of the masses of indigenous peoples to join the resistance forces, without the faithfulness to the cause of liberation that assured the survival of the widespread organisational network of the resistance movements despite some 'successful' arrests and disclosures made by the Soviets, the whole enterprise, with or without German support, could not have got off the ground and, even if it had, the result would have been nothing but a great flop.

Only part of the organised resistance forces were directly connected to the co-ordinating and supply centres in Berlin. Some such forces sprang up and operated independently without ever establishing any links with these centres or, perhaps, without even suspecting their existence, For example, the Berlin-based LAF's local Lithuanian network in 1941 numbered about 36 000 members organised in combat units and ready to strike, whereas the total force of organised combatants who participated in the Lithuanian insurrection of June 1941, was about 100 000, that is, 'about three times the size of the members of underground organizations under the leadership of LAF'.[7] Hence, without denying the significance of German support in making the resistance movements in the Baltic organisationally and logistically viable, one has to conclude that the German role was secondary and supplementary in nature, unable to determine or even to affect significantly the emergence and scope of these movements.

Popular uprisings on a massive scale took place in all three Baltic republics in June 1941. The Lithuanian insurrection started on 23 June 1941, the day after the German invasion, and it took the insurgents the next three days to free the whole of Lithuania from Soviet rule. Some places in Lithuania were freed more than a week before the advancing German armies marched in. The Lithuanian Provisional Government installed in power by the insurrections on 23 June immediately declared the restoration of Lithuania's sovereignty and effectively took charge of the country's affairs. Indeed, when German troops occupied Lithuania they found a country that, to their surprise and to the displeasure of the Reich's leadership, was effectively ruled by a legitimate national government. It took the Nazi authorities six weeks to dismantle this government (it was dissolved on 5 August 1941) and to put Lithuania under the control of their own occupational administration. The Provisional Government (except for three of its members) refused to be a part of the Nazi-installed local administration.

The Latvian insurrection, in which about 60 000 resistance fighters took part, followed almost immediately. On 26 June 1941, an official Soviet broadcast from Riga was forced to admit the fact that 'Latvia was in open revolt'.[8] On 28 June, the insurgents expelled the Red Army from Riga and announced the formation of a Latvian government. Soviet forces, however, regained control of Riga the next day, and they crushed the Latvian government. Nevertheless, the Latvian armed struggle against the Soviets continued until the Germans took Riga on 1 July 1941.[9]

A similar uprising took place in Estonia, with about 50 000 participants. Here it was a more protracted and a less spectacular affair; most of the time the insurgents were involved in guerrilla-style warfare rather than in a direct frontline confrontation with the superior forces of the Red Army. The Estonian guerrillas, however, fared quite well in this warfare: in its course they killed 4800 Red Army men and took 14 000 prisoners.[10] They themselves lost only 541 fighters on the battlefield.[11] On 7 July 1941, when the Germans crossed the Estonian border, they 'found on their arrival the national flags flying everywhere' – an indication of how effective the Estonian guerrillas were.[12] Indeed, in major parts of southern Estonia, the guerrillas had replaced Soviet local administrations with Estonian ones days and even weeks before the arrival of the Germans. 'Tartu was under full or partial Estonian control from 10 to 28 July.' The Estonian capital of Tallinn, as well as the whole northern part of the country, was under much firmer Soviet military and administrative control, which partly explains why there was no attempt to create an Estonian government.[13] An Estonian National Council for co-ordination of the activities of resistance forces, however, with the last pre-occupation prime minister, Jüri Uluots, at its head, was formed at the very start of hostilities.

These national insurrections made absolutely obvious the illegitimate, antipopular nature of Soviet rule over the Baltic states. Soviet claims that the establishment of their regime was in accordance with the 'unanimous popular will', and the masquerades of elections and other gimmicks that were supposed to substantiate these claims were blatantly exposed as fakes within hours. In other words, the mass insurrections of June 1941 indicated an explicit and total rejection of the Soviet regime by the overwhelming majority of the Baltic populations. The genuine collective will of these nations – to restore their non-Soviet, pre-1940 sovereign statehoods – had thus been actively expressed. In 1941 this will, however, was brushed aside and trampled upon by the new masters, the Nazis, as brutally and unequivocally as by the Soviets in 1940 (and, where they managed, in 1941).

During the German–Soviet war the Baltic nations found themselves in the most peculiar and unenviable situation of being unable to pursue their national aspirations by siding with either of the warring parties; as R. Silde-Karklins succinctly pointed out, 'they had to resist equally the imperialist plans of both, the Germans and Soviets, thereby running the risk of being ground between the two'.[14] The task of resisting both was indeed formidable. On the one hand, the Baltic peoples were reluctant to be used by the Germans as cannon fodder and tried to sabotage all efforts to this end; but, on the other hand, they were tempted to exploit for their own national ends the acute need of Hitler's embattled Reich to recruit them to military service. The idea was to establish under German auspices (but, if necessary, even by defying the Germans) an independent military force that, after an eventual German retreat, could engage in a struggle against the advancing Soviets. By enlisting Western support for this struggle, it was hoped that such forces would prevent the USSR from re-establishing its rule over the Baltic states and that these states would thus be put back on the map.

The attempts to implement this plan can be illustrated by the example of events in Lithuania. After the dissolution of the Lithuanian Provisional Government, German attempts to mobilise the Lithuanians for either German military service or industrial work in the Reich were so effectively sabotaged that, as E. J. Harrison pointed out, by the end of 1943 the Lithuanians had successfully wrecked almost all plans directed at using them for serving German needs.[15] Indeed, the initial plan to recruit people for work in Germany was fulfilled only by 5 per cent, and the later (March 1943) attempt at creating a Lithuanian national SS legion (which was supposed to be not less than 150 000 men strong) was a complete failure, which the ensuing severe German repressions against the Lithuanians were unable to correct.[16]

Faced with such massive passive resistance, the Germans decided to change gear and get what they wanted by applying 'co-operative' tactics. They allowed the Lithuanians to form an independent Territorial Defence Force and promised that this force would be used only within the Baltic area (along the Narva–Vilnius line). The Germans also agreed to accept the appointment as commander of this force of the highly popular nationalist general, Povilas Plechavičius. The response to the appeal calling on Lithuanian youth to join this force, which General Plechavičius issued on 16 February 1944 (the day of Lithuanian independence), surpassed all expectations. In a few days, more than 30 000 volunteers signed up, and an even greater number had to be turned down. As soon as the force was formed and acquired a militarily viable shape, however, the Germans broke all their promises. They ordered the incorporation of this force into the SS and thus put it under direct German command.

This turn of events outraged Plechavičius, who bluntly refused to bow to these orders and issued his own, disbanding the force altogether. As a result, the Gestapo arrested the general together with the members of his staff, imprisoned them all in a concentration camp, and indiscriminately executed 100 soldiers from among the few the Germans had managed to capture before the force disbanded. (The rest of the captured troops, 3500 of them, were integrated into the German Luftwaffe and sent to service airports in western Germany.) The main contingent of the force, more than thirty thousand men in full uniform and with all their weapons, successfully went into hiding, thus forming the bulk of the Lithuanian guerrilla army later known as the LLA (Lithuanian Freedom Army), which was to fight against the Soviets for more than eight years.

Similar developments took place in Estonia where, in February 1944, Uluots, the last pre-Soviet prime minister of the country, issued an appeal along the same lines as that of Plechavičius and got the same tremendous response. Even those Estonians who had previously fled to Finland to avoid German conscription voluntarily returned home (after a German pardon for their desertion was granted) to join the newly formed Estonian Territorial Defence Force, assigned to defend Estonia against the Soviet advance. In

Latvia, events took a somewhat different turn (because of Germany's extended hold over Courland), but the results were approximately the same.

This is how all three Baltic nations acquired, during 1944–5, a token military force that, however ill-equipped and weak by any other standards, was sufficient for mounting a protracted guerrilla war. It was hoped that by engaging in such a war the Baltic nations would be able to attract Western support for the cause of Baltic independence from the USSR and thus ultimately succeed in achieving independence.

RESISTANCE AND REPRESSION, 1944–52

It has been estimated that the initial (1945) strength of these guerrilla armies was 30 000 fighters in Lithuania, 15 000 in Latvia, and between 10 000 and 15 000 in Estonia.[17] The number of active supporters, liaison men, and other 'part-time' guerrillas in each case was several times as large. From 1945 onward, the number of guerrilla fighters was steadily rising. The original nuclei of the guerrilla armies were joined by forces that had been clandestinely organised to fight the Germans, and after the Germans' retreat continued to fight against the Soviets.[18] Later, great numbers started to flee to the forests to join the guerrilla forces. These individuals consisted of several categories, which Misiunas and Taagepera have divided as follows:

1. 'willing and unwilling German collaborators and draftees';
2. 'men avoiding Soviet draft and Red Army deserters';
3. the victims of 'Soviet land distribution and other social restructuring measures';
4. actual and/or potential victims of 'Soviet screening and deportation campaigns';
5. peasants fleeing from or threatened by the farm collectivisation process (and the deportations connected with this process), which was activated in 1949;
6. other individuals 'when they could no longer take the insecurity of civilian life'.[19]

The absolute number of active guerrilla fighters never grew much over the initial numbers. As Misiunas and Taagepera convincingly explained, this was because 'the average life span of a forest brotherhood career has been estimated to be two years due to casualties, disease, and return to civilian life'. Hence, 'over the 8 years of intensive guerrilla activity (1945–52), about 100 000 people may have been involved in Lithuania ... The Latvian and Estonian forest brotherhood may have involved a total of about 40 000 and 30 000 respectively, at one time or another'.[20] This assessment is directly substantiated by a statement made by the director of the LCP Central Committee's Institute of the History of the Party, Romas Šarmaitis. In an interview with American journalist George Weller, Šarmaitis stated that, during the eight years of guerrilla war in Lithuania, 20 000 guerrillas and a similar number of Soviet troops perished on the battlefield.[21]

The last great influx of civilians (peasants fleeing from collectivisation and deportation) into the guerrilla forces occurred in 1949. That year the guerrilla movements reached their peak, but they started declining sharply soon afterward. In 1950 they were practically over as nationwide movements in both Estonia and Latvia.[22] By 1951-2 only about 5000 guerrillas operated in Lithuania and by the end of 1952, the Unified Command of the Lithuanian Freedom Army (LLA) issued the order to end the armed struggle and proclaimed self-demobilisation of the army.[23] In this order, however, the LLA issued a call to all its members and to all Lithuanians to continue the struggle for freedom by peaceful means.

After eight years of incessant and desperate fighting, the guerrilla war in the Baltic thus came to an end; the Baltic nations entered a period of peaceful coexistence with their Soviet rulers.

There is no doubt that in the beginning the guerrillas had commanded almost total popular support. The overwhelming majorities of the Baltic nations were involved in guerrilla activities, carrying out certain duties on behalf of the guerrillas, assisting in hiding and feeding them, and helpful them in varying ways. Thus, for most of the time during the guerrilla war, the Soviets in the Baltic area controlled firmly only the larger towns and roads, whereas the countryside belonged to the guerrillas almost entirely.

In their struggle against the guerrillas the Soviets used a variety of means, of which straightforward armed combat was the least prominent and successful. From time to time the Soviets 'combed' the forests, but their main repressive emphasis was placed on the destruction of the civilian environment that was conducive to guerrilla activities. To this end, annual mass deportations of native Baltic people to Siberia were carried out between 1945 and 1951. Relatives of the guerrillas and families friendly to them, as well as members of the 'dispossessed bourgeoisie of towns and villages', were the first affected.[24] The biggest mass deportation took place in 1949, when all the 'kulaks' and other peasants 'barring the way to the collectivisation of agriculture' were affected.[25] Overall, during 1945-51, not less than 600 000 natives (or about 9 per cent of the total native population) were deported from the Baltic area to Siberia and similar inhospitable (or even uninhabitable) places of the USSR; about half of the deportees came from Lithuania.[26]

For any contact with the guerrillas a civilian was liable to face the charge of treason and sentencing to twenty-five years in the labour camps. Aiding guerrillas under duress or the threat of death was no excuse; a Soviet citizen was supposed to die rather than help the enemy. In September 1944 instructions were issued to the NKVD troops to shoot any suspect on the spot and to burn down any house, farm, or village suspected of harbouring 'bandits'.[27] These instructions were carried out throughout the following years. These unprecedentedly harsh, indeed genocidal, measures which initially boosted the guerrilla forces, resulted in the long run in their demise.

Parallel to the mass repressions, the Soviets made every effort to enlarge the base of their indigenous popular support. They managed to retain as champions of their cause the tiny groups that had supported them initially – among them a certain segment of the national intelligentsia that had been anti-establishment during the years of independence. It would perhaps be wrong to suggest, as many people do, that such prominent national figures as Petras Cvirka or Antanas Venclova (Lithuania), Vilis Lacis or Augusts Kirchenšteins (Latvia), and Johannes Vares-Barbarus, Johannes Semper, and Artur and Eugen Kapps (Estonia), chose to support the Soviet regime so unequivocally merely out of opportunism or careerist motivations. At the beginning, their motives were most likely sincere and, indeed, idealistic. And later? Then it was in any case too late: perhaps temptingly comfortable to stay in, too frightening to quit, or both. Having been incorrigible romantics during the years of independence, these progressive intellectuals learned only too well how to be even more incorrigible pragmatists under the incomparably harsher conditions of Soviet reality.

The ability to rely on these people and to use them for the consolidation and representation of the Soviet regime, though an important asset, was far from sufficient to make the Soviet authorities secure in their running of the Baltic countries. Therefore, in order to secure a firmer grip on power in the area, the Soviets urgently needed to sway to their side much larger, truly grass-roots segments of the Baltic population. Their interpretation of events in terms of class rather than national struggle was quite effective for this purpose. Indeed, some natives, especially among those whose position in traditional Baltic societies was at the lower end of the scale and whose prospects for upward mobility were extremely limited, let themselves be convinced by Soviet official propaganda that the ongoing struggle in their countries had nothing to do with national liberty, which was only being used as a cover by the former ruling classes, who sought the restoration of their lost privileges.

Of course, under the 'second Russians' (the regime established after the Soviets returned to the Baltic at the end of the war) the ranks of Soviet supporters were joined, in the first place, by great numbers of conformists and careerists, people who would have supported any ruling power either out of respect for its sheer might or, as the Lithuanian poet, Vincas Kudirka, once wrote, 'for a nugget of gold, for a spoonful of tastier food'. But there were also quite a few people who went over to the Soviet side because they were genuinely converted to its 'truth'. The fact that the Soviet regime generously offered to young and ambitious people of humble origins ample opportunities for promotion and thus for leading positions within their respective societies – something that most had not even dreamed of under pre-Soviet conditions – was perceived by some as nothing less than the embodiment of social justice. Hence, by taking such opportunities, individuals were under the impression that they had taken up a great cause – the cause of the construction of communism, of a truly just and affluent society. They were genuinely unable to discern that, in fact, they had fallen for an old trick that newly established dictatorial regimes have used throughout history to compensate for their lack of legitimacy – the trick of recruiting a fraction of the lowest classes in the population to form a new establishment, an uprooted 'praetorian guard'. Such a group is easily manipulated because of its complete dependence on the regime not only for positions of power and privilege but for sheer physical survival.

Many different methods for the recruitment of that praetorian guard (or, as the official propaganda put it, the winning of the 'children of Baltic workers and working peasants for the service to their own working people's state') were employed in the Baltic area as soon as the Soviet regime was re-established there during 1944–5 by the advancing Red Army. Newly set up educational facilities figured most prominently among them. So-called *rabfaks* (accelerated full-time high school graduation courses that paid their students quite generous stipends) were established in major cities for the most zealous adherents. A wide network of evening high schools for working youths (where one could graduate from high school without interrupting work) was evolved for those who were ambitious enough to attend. The graduates of these educational establishments were given a great deal of preference in getting places in the universities and other institutions of higher learning, whose first task now was to breed 'in-house specialists' regardless of their academic qualifications.

For deserving activities – those who joined the Soviet militia forces, agreed to serve in the 'extermination battalions' (semi-military units of native people specially formed to fight against the guerrillas later renamed

'people's defenders' squads'), otherwise expressed their unswerving willingness to serve the Soviet system – special 'educational shortcuts' were
arranged. These took the form of either different 'academies' preparing
barely literate people in a few months to serve as judges, procurators,
security and militia officers, economic managers, and so on, or party
schools for people specially selected to enter the key apparatuses of party
and governmental administration.

Through such means the Soviet regime within a few years managed to
build up its Baltic cohorts of faithful and dedicated native cadres. This process was more prominent in Lithuania and Latvia than in Estonia, where
the 'native cadres' were primarily 'Yestonians', that is, people of Estonian
origin living in Russia, where they had been assimilated. These 'Yestonians'
were imported into Estonia in 1940–1 and 1944–6 to occupy leading positions and to assure the country's smooth sovietisation. Such people were
also imported into Latvia and Lithuania, but there, especially in Lithuania,
they were more equally mixed with genuine natives.

The relative success of this policy of promoting indigenous people who
decided to rise via Soviet offices 'from filth to wealth', apart from assuring
the regime the necessary numbers of native workers for its cause, also produced a genuine ideological split within the Baltic societies. What was formerly a straightforward confrontation between occupied Baltic nations and
the occupying foreign power thus was extended into a genuine confrontation between a tangible minority (several thousand) of the Baltic population, who for idealistic or opportunistic reasons embraced communist
ideology and goals, and the great majority of the people, who refused to
accept the Soviet regime and remained faithful to the ideology and goals of
national independence.

In this sense, one could say that the guerrilla war acquired the dimensions of a genuine civil war. Indeed, as long as the open battle between the
regime and the guerrilla (or partisan) armies went on, it provided a con-
necting link and a rallying point for the active expression of genuinely
popular views and goals. The whole spectrum of the contradictory political
orientation of the Baltic nations was manifested in this battle. There was
little doubt that only a small minority converted to the new masters; the
overwhelming majority was still committed to resisting them.[28]

The mood of resistance, so overwhelming in the beginning, started to
flounder as years went by. With no support, let alone help, from the West
(which preferred to turn a blind eye to the Baltic struggle for freedom),
more and more Baltic people started to perceive their lonely struggle
against the huge Soviet state machine as not only futile but nationally
suicidal. They became keen to end it by any means. Among such people were

several leading figures of the resistance movement, for example, the Lithuanians Jonas Deksnys, Juozas Markuliś, and Kostas Kubilinskas. Knowing that they would not be able to persuade their colleagues in the resistance leadership to stop the armed struggle, they went so far as to become secret agents of the KGB, actively helping it (mainly by providing vital intelligence) to destroy the resistance movement from within. As a result of their collaboration, many thousands of their former friends and colleagues, together with their families, were killed or imprisoned for long years in Soviet labour camps. But they remained unrepentant, saying that if that was the price for assuring the nation's physical survival, it was worth paying.[29]

Thus, after eight years of desperate armed struggle, the period of open resistance started to come to an end. It did not finally stop because of a decisive Soviet military victory against the resisters. After all, the Baltic guerrillas had been defeated many times before and many times new volunteers had come to restore their ranks. In the 1950s, however, largely for the reasons explained above, no more recruits were available to continue this hopeless struggle. The fact that at a certain point fresh forces for further open resistance did not emerge and that the whole open resistance movement was slowly dying out does not at all mean that the Baltic nations had internally surrendered to the Soviet regime or had decided to accept it wholeheartedly. Rather, they had realised that direct opposition to the occupation, under the continuing circumstances of East–West peaceful coexistence, was not simply doomed to fail but was fraught with consequences that could be literally fatal. Hence, the Baltic peoples ceased their war against the Soviet occupier not out of acquiescence but because of their newly and very painfully acquired realistic perception of their political situation in the world. It was neither the Soviets nor the Baltic nations but political realism that triumphed. And therefore the war was far from over. As the subsequent chapter shows, the Baltic nations simply delayed the final act of their struggle with the occupier until better times, knowing by then quite well that these better times could not be brought by their efforts alone.

COMPLIANCE AND PROTEST, 1952–82

When armed resistance broke down and compliance became the order of the day, the voice for the ideals of national independence vanished together with the identifiable organisational framework of opposition to Soviet rule. These ideals, removed from the visible social surface to take refuge in an atomised shape within the inner consciousness of individual Balts, yielded the social scene to the monopolistic dominance of Soviet official ideology and values. As a result, the latter, though never 'interiorized' by the vast majority of people, assumed the position of the only moral and ideological bond holding the Baltic societies together. Needless to say, this situation caused the profound alienation of most individual Balts from the official societies in which they had to live. The hope that in time this alienation would soften and finally be replaced by genuine integration proved futile; in fact, as time went by, it only deepened. Moreover, and this was the most striking development, over time the alienation acquired an absolute and universal dimension that it had never had before.

Indeed, the limited ideological support the Soviet regime had initially achieved in the Baltic countries and had maintained (even increased) during the time of terror was gradually but irretrievably lost after 1952, during the time of peaceful coexistence of the people and the regime. It is paradoxical but nevertheless true: the apparently total victory of Soviet communism over Baltic societies gradually brought an equally total rejection of it within the moral and political consciousness of the Baltic peoples.

The ideals and expectations that Baltic people with communist convictions (or, at least, aspirations) had attached to the new regime completely failed to materialise. There was now less freedom and more injustice; poverty, instead of disappearing, sharply increased and, because of the collectivization of agriculture, became clearly irredeemable for all except a handful of top communist bureaucrats. The rivers of blood that had flowed so amply accomplished only one task: the seating of the new élite, the old-time communist apparatchiks and their newly recruited 'praetorian guards', in positions of power and privilege. The continuing denial of national and individual rights could no longer be justified by either war or class struggle. In this respect, the new circumstances had a particularly strong, sobering effect on erstwhile communist idealists, who saw in them the betrayal of everything they had believed in and hoped for. It was a shocking discovery that appeared with such blatant clarity that communist sympathisers found it impossible to ignore it.

Despite this realisation by the new élite (or the 'new class', as Milovan Djilas put it), almost all of its members decided to soldier on. The majority continued out of purely selfish and careerist motivations such as fear and greed; a few had mixed motives, including the determination to use their newly acquired positions of influence for the benefit of their countries and people. Some, probably the most naive and idealistic, failed to adjust to reality as it was and, by entering into conflict with its rigorous demands, were crushed or dropped by the system.[30]

The 'realistically minded' native apparatchiks who learned how to avoid risks and continued to serve the regime obediently were perhaps more bitter about the situation in which they found themselves than anyone else. After all, it was they who, in their day-to-day activities, constantly experienced the stifling power of Moscow's directing hand and the humiliation of being deprived of any independent will and reduced to the status of robots blindly implementing whatever arbitrary and repressive decisions were handed down. Whatever their motivations for continuing in the positions of the new élite, their ambitions were deeply frustrated and their inner discontent and disappointment were rather overwhelming. This is how the Soviet regime lost among the indigenous Balts its last genuine, ideologically motivated, support. By the mid-1950s, it had gone completely, and sheer opportunism took its place.

The 'breakdown of ideology' inevitably produced certain clashes that at least partially came into the open. The first such manifestations took place in Estonia. They started in 1946 with the suicide of Johannes Vares-Barbarus, the chairman of the Estonian Soviet government (and, before that the head of the 'people's' government). There is strong evidence suggesting that the cause of Vares's suicide was the blatant contrast between his expectations for Estonia's future, which motivated him to become one of the main architects of her Sovietisation, and the reality of the Soviet Estonia over which he presided.[31] Many, if not all, indigenous Estonian Communists had similar feelings. They tried to preserve Estonia's nationhood by whatever modest means were in their power. Alerted to these attitudes by Vares's suicide, the Kremlin closely watched the Estonian Communist Party and in 1950 decided to launch a purge of its indigenous leadership and membership. A great number of leading Estonian Communists, including the first secretary of the Central Committee of the Estonian Communist Party, Nikolai Karotamm; the chairman of Estonia's Council of Ministers, Arnold Veimer; and the chairman of the Presidium of the Estonian Supreme Soviet, E. Päll were accused of bourgeois nationalism, narrow localism, ostentatious isolationism from the rest of the USSR, and immersion in narrowly conceived and essentially nonsocialist national traditionalism.[32] As a result, the leadership of the Estonian party, as well as the whole apparatus of Estonian administration were 'Yestonianized' and Russified more than ever before. The first secretaryship was handed over to Johannes Käbin, another 'Yestonian' who hardly even understood the Estonian language; his duty was to assure that no more 'deviations' would occur in the future, and he did his best to fulfil that duty.

A similar crackdown took place in 1958–9 in Latvia. The main culprit there was Eduards Berklavs, the vice-chairman of the Latvian Council of Ministers and former first secretary of Riga's party committee. Together with him, the chairman of the Latvian Trade Union Council, A. Pinskis; the first secretary of the Latvian Communist Youth League, A. Ruskulis; and scores of other leading Latvian Communists were purged – charged with 'Latvian bourgeois-nationalist deviation'.[33] The chairman of the Presidium of Latvia's Supreme Soviet, K. Ozolins, also lost his job in the purge. He was replaced by Janis Kalnberzins, who had been removed from the post of first secretary of the CC of the Latvian Communist Party, which he had held from 1940 until the purge in 1959 (as the man with overall responsibility for the party he was found guilty by association). A Russian communist of Latvian origin, Arvids Pelše, became the first secretary of the CC of the Latvian Communist Party and vigorously pursued into the early 1960s the task of removing every indigenous Latvian from a position of higher responsibility. (Even Vilis Lacis, the veteran chairman of the Council of Ministers, who publicly dissociated himself from the 'deviationists' and was active in denouncing them, was dismissed from his post.) Nevertheless, a 1971 letter from 17 Latvian old communists (who preferred to remain anonymous), addressed to several of the world's communist parties, not only openly defended Berklavs's line but went much further by vigorously denouncing Soviet policies in Latvia. The letter demanded that the 'fraternal parties' take up with the CPSU the gross breaches of 'Leninist national policy' perpetrated in Latvia. This letter manifested with all clarity that, although suppressed, the national ideals of the native Latvian communist establishment were as much alive as ever.[34]

Matters in Lithuania were different in appearance but not in essence. There were no party purges in Lithuania and no accusations of dissent or deviation against any party members. This was largely due to the fact that, unlike his counterparts in Latvia and Estonia, the first secretary of the CC of the Lithuanian Communist Party, A. Sniečkus, was an outstandingly strong, inveterate and autocratic leader who, without interruption from the end of 1926, had practically been in sole charge of the Lithuanian Communist Party and in full control of everybody in it. There was no question of anyone in the Lithuanian party speaking out or doing anything at all without Sniečkus's prior consent. He had total authority over his companions and also managed to carry this authority in his relations with Stalin and the whole Kremlin leadership. Sniečkus's ruthlessness and implacability were legendary. During the time of deportations and repressions he would not spare even his closest relatives, let alone anyone else. Stalin personally was extremely impressed with Sniečkus's performance and even used to say that the two of them were then the only real communists left in the whole of the Soviet Union.[35] Mikhail Suslov, who in 1944 was dispatched from Moscow to Vilnius as chairman of the Lithuanian Bureau of the CC of the All-Union Communist Party and whose job was to supervise

Lithuanian communists in their fight against the 'class enemy' and to 'help' them to build a socialist society, was not only full of admiration for Snieckus, but fell heavily under his influence. Snieckus carried this influence until his death in 1974, which explains how he was able to get away with so many things that would have spelled the end of a party career for anyone else.

In the end, however, the disappointment with Soviet reality affected the fanatical Snieckus as much as it did other indigenous Baltic communists. But he was too experienced a politician to deviate openly from Moscow's line; he knew how to succeed and survive where Karotamm or Berklavs had failed.

A Lithuanian samizdat author writing under the pseudonym of T. Ženklys, who had known Snieckus quite intimately for a number of years, testified in his obituary on Snieckus that during his last twenty or so years in power (from the late 1940s or early 1950s) Snieckus changed beyond recognition. 'At the beginning, Moscow could not even dream of a more assiduous servant of its will in Lithuania,' wrote Ženklys. But 'increasingly from year to year, one could perceive in Snieckus's activity a national orientation, a defence of the specific interests of Lithuania, an effort first of all to see to the country's proper development, to the rise of its prosperity'.[36] So we see that a spiritual evolution, leading to disillusionment with the Soviet order and an understanding that false gods had been served, affected even the most dedicated and Stalinist Baltic communists, to say nothing of the others. True, some remained convinced communists and Marxists, but they stopped identifying their beliefs with the 'real socialism' of the Soviet regime.

By the first half of the 1950s there were no more indigenous Baltic people who continued to support the Soviet regime out of idealism or conviction. Nor did any of the indigenous Balts still believe in communism as represented and implemented by this regime. Hence, the enforced situation of total outward compliance had been complemented by an equally total inward dissent. It goes without saying that inward dissent tends to find some forms of expression in social action and thus partially reduces the totality of compliance. This, however, does not change the peculiar combination of basic compliance with total dissent that has been the characteristic feature of the relationship between the Baltic peoples and the sociopolitical system in which they lived. To understand how this combination worked practically, it is necessary to distinguish between the then Baltic peoples' *teleological* and *practical-pragmatic* political orientations.

The teleological political consciousness coincides with the people's positive vision of the desirable political future for themselves, their nations,

and the world around them. It therefore also implies a certain plan for political change, without which these future-oriented goals would remain
unachievable. As I have argued elsewhere, the teleological political consciousness of the Baltic peoples was cohesive, lent itself to a proper definition, and was universal in the sense that it was shared by every native
Balt, including even the most active collaborators with the regime.[37] It
could be defined by the following five-trait cluster:

1. Re-establishment within its ethnic boundaries, for each Baltic nation,
   of a free and truly independent nation-state;
2. Transformation of the present political, social, and economic order
   into one that would be: (a) consistent with national traditions; (b)
   committed to putting national interests first; and (c) able to provide
   sufficient room for individuals and their freely formed associations to
   exercise independent initiative, defend their legitimate interests, and
   otherwise realise their potential in all spheres of life, first of all
   asserting their true national-cultural identity.
3. Establishment of direct, tight and durable political, economic,
   cultural, and person-to-person links with the Western world,
   accompanied by the removal of all restrictions on foreign travel and
   aimed in the end at the integration of the Baltic states into the
   community of Western nations;
4. Restoration on the territory of each Baltic state of an ethnically,
   linguistically, and culturally compact – if not entirely homogenous –
   national society (this aim was considered to be the highest priority in
   all three Baltic republics but was more acute in Latvia and Estonia,
   where the Russians and other minorities constitute nearly one half
   and two-fifths of their respective populations; in Lithuania the non-
   Lithuanians made up only about 20 per cent, of whom the immigrant
   Russians are less than half);
5. Promotion within the framework of a nationally compact society of
   complete religious and cultural freedom for all.

How was this teleological orientation translated into the pragmatic attitudes towards social reality that determined everyday political behaviour
characterised by basic compliance with Soviet rule? Compliance required
all Baltic people to accept a certain degree of conformism, which varied
from one person to another. One could draw a certain continuum between
total conformism and total nonconformism, within which one could place
the practical-pragmatic political orientation of the great majority of the
Balts. Indeed, very few were total conformists who built their whole lives
and careers on unquestioning subservience to the regime and thus

completely sold out their natural teleological orientation for the sake of security, power and comfort. The majority of Balts who invested their lives in rendering political service to the regime managed to combine conformism with what one could call the conservationist orientation, or simply *conservationism*. This orientation expressed itself in the use of official position to do whatever was deemed possible for the preservation of the nation's identity, integrity and its natural and spiritual resources – as well as for the enhancement of its relative welfare. The degree to which this conservationist attitude expressed itself delineated the limits of one's compliance with the regime. In certain cases, conservationists trespassed the limits of official toleration and, sometimes inadvertently, found themselves in a position of activist dissent.

Outbursts of extrastructural activist dissent (opposing certain policies of the regime or demanding change) started in the Baltic as early as 1956 (four years after the end of armed resistance) and continued unabated.[38] It is in these outbursts that the genuine teleological political orientation of the Baltic nations clearly manifested itself. But, even more important, ever-increasing coincidence between the people's practical-pragmatic and teleological political orientations had been marked. In other words, during the years 1956–82, a diminution of compliance with official ideological and political demands and a growing assertion of the people's national selves (through protests, demands, samizdat publications, and various other forms of independent activity) slowly but steadily developed in all the Baltic republics.

Overt dissident activities in the Baltic states during the last decades, especially since the late 1960s, are sufficiently well documented in various publications.[39] What should be said, however, is that, spontaneous mass manifestations apart,[40] systematic protest activities that at first were sporadic and focused on specific issues (religious rights, creative freedom, and freedom of information)[41] gradually began to centre on more general issues of national and individual rights. Dissent acquired a more regular organisational pattern in the form of various groups and committees, as well as periodical samizdat publications.

In Lithuania, two such committees were formed in open defiance of the regime: the so-called Lithuanian Helsinki Group (1976), which was one of several such groups formed in the Soviet Union in that year, and the Committee for the Defence of the Rights of Catholics (1980). The Helsinki Group, in spite of having lost by 1982 through governmental repression (or death) most of its active members, recruited new ones and kept itself alive throughout the 1980s. From the beginning of 1983, the Committee for the Defence of the Rights of Catholics has been submitted to a repressive onslaught by the authorities, which culminated in the trials of its leaders, Father Alfonsas Svarinskas, in May 1983 (sentenced to seven years of internment and three years of internal exile for anti-Soviet propaganda) and Father Sigitas Tamkevičius, in December 1983 (sentenced, under the same indictment, to six years of internment and four years of internal exile). Nevertheless, the committee has survived and continued its activities. A significant boost for the continuation of these activities was the protest letter in defence of Svarinskas and Tamkevičius signed by the unprecedented number of 46 905 people from 71 parishes in May–June 1983. There were a few other organised dissident bodies in Lithuania that did not operate publicly and were known mainly because of their samizdat output. One of such 'invisible' bodies was the Lithuanian Liberation League (LLL) which assumed the leading role in organising mass protest activities during 1987–8. (It was in response to these LLL activities that Lithuania's Party-state authorities agreed to the organisation on 3 June 1988, by 'loyal intelligentsia', of the Sąjudis movement.)

In Latvia, three such groups came into existence in 1975: the Latvian Independence Movement, Latvia's Democratic Youth Committee, and Latvia's Christian Democratic Organisation. By 1976 they started to co-ordinate their activities and issued joint statements addressed to the government of the Latvian SSR, the Australian prime minister (Malcolm Fraser), and others. Another, more activist body, the Organisation for Latvia's Independence, organised throughout the 1970s and the 1980s various protest actions, petitions, and demands. In 1987–8, this dissident body played a role analogous to that of Lithuania's LLL.

In Estonia, two such groups acquired prominence by 1972: the Estonian Democratic Movement and the Estonian National Front. In 1974 another group, Estonian Patriots, came into existence, and the Association of Concerned Estonians was formed in 1976 after the government crushed earlier oppositional bodies. In 1978 two new groups, the White Key Brotherhood and Maarjamaa, mostly concerned with problems of cultural freedom, were formed in addition to the ones mentioned above. All these groups took a lead in organising the mass demonstrations of 1987–8 and thus precipitated the creation of the officially accepted Estonian National Front in spring 1988.

Lithuania was richest for samizdat periodicals not only in the whole of the USSR but also in Eastern Europe. Apart from the *Chronicle of the Catholic Church,* which in 1982 celebrated the tenth anniversary of its uninterrupted appearance, at least twelve other unofficial periodicals circulated in this republic. *Aušra* [The Dawn], the secular samizdat periodical, has appeared regularly since 1975. Between 1976 and 1979 a wide variety of different religious and secular samizdat magazines sprang up. Among the religious ones, *Dievas ir Tėvynė* [God and Fatherland] and *Rūpintojėlis* [Sorrowing Christ] are worth mentioning; among the secular, *Varpas* [The Bell], which appeared since 1977, upheld the Lithuanian liberal tradition; *Alma Mater* (1979) tackled the problems of higher education; *Pastogė* [The Shelter] and *Perspektyvos* [Perspectives] discussed literature, philosophy, and the arts; a few others, such as *Tiesos Kelias* [The Way of Truth] and *Laisvės Šauklys* [The Clarion of Freedom], both started in 1976, had no special profile but represented the nationalist orientation of the Lithuanians by dealing with a variety of different subjects. Several of these periodicals were stopped by the authorities, who discovered and severely punished their editors. However, *Perspektyvos* and *Dievas ir Tėynė* reappeared after a short interval in 1981, and in the same year *Tautos Kelias* [The Nation's Way], an entirely new samizdat periodical publication, was started.

In Estonia the periodical *Eesti Democraat* [Estonian Democrat] has been published since 1971, and *Eesti Rahvuslik Hääl* [The Voice of the Estonian Nation] appeared soon afterwards. What is interesting and specific about Estonia's samizdat periodicals was the fact that some of them were published in Russian; thus the *Estonian Democrat* was published in Russian translation and there was also a special Russian-language samizdat periodical, *Luch Svobody* [The Beam of Freedom]. Another Estonian samizdat periodical, *Poolpäevaleht* [The Semi-Daily], was started in 1978, but it was crushed by the authorities a year later (only six issues were published and circulated).

In spite of the ferocious repressions that the authorities applied to break down organised Baltic dissent, it not only persisted but also developed new forms of organised activities. It is significant that by the end of the 1970s dissident groups in all three Baltic republics had started to coordinate their activities and launched joint ventures. For example, on 23 August 1979 (the 40th anniversary of the infamous Molotov–Ribbentrop Pact), a joint petition bearing 45 signatures of representatives of all three Baltic republics was issued in Moscow. The petition demanded that the USSR and the two German states declare null and void the Molotov–Ribbentrop Pact, which assigned the Baltic states to the Soviet Union. This document must be singled out not only because it was one of the first exercises in Baltic unity of action but also because it marked a totally new departure in Baltic dissident politics. For the first time since armed resistance to Soviet rule stopped, the demand for full restoration of the national independence of the three Baltic states was forcefully made in clear and unequivocal terms by people prepared to risk the full consequences of such an act.[42] In fact the Baltic dissidents of the late 1970s had thus taken up, in a unified manner, the banner of their predecessors, the guerrilla fighters, and had committed themselves to carry it on, this time, however, exclusively by means of peaceful struggle. Thus the resistance movement of the Baltic states, in terms of publicly proclaimed goals, in 1979 returned to its 1940 starting point, in spite of the fact that in 1952 it had seemingly been smashed irreversibly. 1979 was thus a departure point at which the Baltic dissident movements overtly committed themselves to the cause of the restoration of their respective nation-states' independence. What the world saw in 1987–91 as a sudden upsurge in the Baltics of independence-seeking national movements, sprang in fact from that 23 August 1979 petition and gradually developed into a potentially massive popular movement which erupted onto the social surface as soon as glasnost finally ended in people the fear, the belief in the effective mercilessness of Soviet persecution. With that the mood of hopelessness about effective resistance to Soviet rule, about engaging into a fight for the hitherto thoroughly hidden goals constituting the Baltic nations' teleological political consciousness, was dispelled.

The growing co-operation of activist Baltic dissenters with the dissident movement in Russia was extremely significant, too. A unity of purpose was established, whereby the Balts joined the struggle of the Russians for the democratisation of the Soviet Union, and democratically minded Russians made the cause of Baltic independence a part of their own programme for democratic change in the USSR as a whole. The most symbolic expression of this unity was the fact that the petition of 23 August 1979, signed by 45 representatives of the Baltic republics and demanding the restoration of the sovereignty of the Baltic states, was amended by a petition of support for it signed by five representatives of Russian democratic dissent: Mal'va Landa, Viktor Nekipelov, Tatyana Velikanova, Andrei Sakharov and Arina Ginzburg.

The history of the co-operation between Baltic and Russian dissenters goes, however, much further back. In July 1968, a document written and signed on behalf of 'Numerous Members of the Estonian Technical Intelligentsia', entitled 'To Hope or to Act' gave a sympathetic but critical assessment of Sakharov's *Thoughts on Progress, Coexistence, and Intellectual Freedom* and formulated a programme for democratic change in the USSR as a whole, which was conceived by the authors of this document as the prerequisite for the attainment of the freedom of both Russia and Estonia.[43] A similar document, 'Programme of the Democrats of Russia, the Ukraine, and the Baltic Lands', was circulated by samizdat channels approximately at the same time.[44]

In Latvia in 1968, Ivan Yakhimovichs protested against the Moscow trial of Aleksander Ginzburg and Yuri Galanskov, as well as against other convictions and persecutions of Russian dissidents.[45] Together with Petro Grigorenko and others, Yakhimovichs was active in protest activities concerning the Soviet invasion of Czechoslovakia and other issues. In a statement on the eve of his arrest (25 March 1969), Yakhimovichs made an appeal addressed to Bertrand Russell, Alexander Solzhenitsyn, Andrei Sakharov, Petro Grigorenko, Alexander Dubček, and others, expressing his commitment to the struggle for freedom and human rights not only in Latvia but in Russia, the Ukraine, Czechoslovakia, Poland and elsewhere.[46]

In their turn, Sakharov and other Russian dissidents from the late 1960s onward campaigned for the release of Baltic political prisoners and regularly expressed their solidarity with the cause of Baltic freedom. The publicity that the Baltic appeals and samizdat publications received in Western media was possible only because Moscow dissidents transmitted them to Western correspondents accredited in Moscow. (One should note that the petition of 23 August 1979 was launched in Moscow and the Lithuanian Helsinki Group was formed there in 1976.) Baltic emigré literature also found its ways into the Baltic republics via 'transmission points' in Moscow. Moscow's *Chronicle of Current Events* was regularly reporting on events in the Baltic and published extracts from Baltic samizdat documents giving special prominence to the reports from the *Chronicle of the Lithuanian Catholic Church.* The trial of the leading Muscovite dissident, Sergey Kovalev, took place in December 1975 in Vilnius (Lithuania), and one of the charges against him was the dissemination of the *Chronicle of the Lithuanian Catholic Church* via the *Chronicle of Current Events* and other means.[47] Accusations of assisting to propagate the *Chronicle of the Lithuanian Catholic Church* were also raised by the KGB against another prominent Russian dissident, Andrei Tverdokhlebov.[48] The Lithuanian Helsinki Group established in 1976 worked in close co-operation with the analogous group in Moscow. Even closer links between Baltic and other Soviet dissidents were forged in the labour camps where they served their sentences together.[49]

Through all these channels Baltic dissent firmly established itself as a constituent part of the wider USSR's democratic movement and also convinced this movement to embrace the cause of Baltic independence and freedom. As the *Chronicle of the Lithuanian Catholic Church* stated, the work of Russian dissenters for Lithuania 'compelled the Lithuanian Catholics to take another look at the Russian nation. Their sacrifice is necessary for all persecuted Soviet people, it is also necessary for the Lithuanian Catholics'.[50]

During the 1970s to the late 1980s, Baltic activist dissent, although firmly entrenched and ever present as an important element in Baltic social and political life, was practised only by a tiny minority of the Baltic people. Significant were, however, not so much the numbers of Baltic dissidents as the impact they made on the Baltic societies. Under their influence conservationism became much bolder and daring and it gradually embraced almost all native Balts. This process of totalisation of 'intrastructural' dissent was apparently overlooked by the Party and Soviet authorities. When in 1987–8, the activist dissidents started to attract to their protest activities a truly mass following, the Soviet Baltic officialdoms decided to neutralise them by encouraging the loyal members of the cultural and scientific establishments to take the lead in anti-Stalinist and similar mass manifestations expressing real grievances of the people with regard to the regime. The Baltic partocrats thought that by so doing they would isolate the dissidents, relegate them back to nothingness without direct repression, and then, through their traditionally obedient intellectual underlings, maintain effective control over the mass exercise of the liberties permitted by glasnost. This plan, as the next chapter shows, failed to materialise. The National Fronts of Latvia and Estonia as well as the Lithuanian Sąjudis, although initially created by outwardly loyal Soviet intellectuals, soon acquired their own momentum and by 1989 had started to challenge the ruling communist parties and the Soviet regime. History was thus to prove that dissent in the Baltic states was total indeed and that the difference between conservationist and activist dissent was not of substance but only of method.[51] When, because of glasnost, the difference in methods became irrelevant, nothing was left to draw a dividing line between the few activist dissidents and the rest of the people – they organically and naturally merged into one cohesive entity committed to shedding their artificial Soviet identity and wholeheartedly to embrace the cause of restoration of their national independence and freedom.

NOTES

1. The text of Order no. 001223, issued by the NKVD of the USSR on 11 October 1939, is not available. Our knowledge of this order springs from explicit references made to it (invoking both the number and the date) in the 'follow-up' orders of the people's commissariats of internal affairs and state security of the Baltic republics. Full texts of these orders are available and were published in English translation in the *Third Interim Report of the Select Committee on Communist Aggression* (House of Representatives, Eighty-Third Congress, Second Session, under authority of H.R. 346 and

H.R. 438) (Washington, DC, 1954) [hereafter referred to as *Third Interim Report*]. Among such orders the following ones should be mentioned: no. 0054 of 28 November 1940, 'On the Negligence in Accounting of Anti-Soviet and Socially Alien Elements', issued by the Lithuanian SSR's People's Commissar of Internal Affairs, Guzevičius (pp. 470–2); and no. 023 of April 25, 1941, 'On the Organization of the Operative Accounting in the County [*uezd*] Branches of the People's Commissariat of State Security' (pp. 495–7). The second of these refers twice to NKVD Order no. 001223. See also no. 0037 of 23 May 1941, 'On Preparation for the Operation Ordered by the Directive No. 77 of May 19, 1941, of the People's Commissar of State Security of the USSR' (pp. 515–20). Both no. 0023 and no. 0037 were issued by the Lithuanian SSR's People's Commissar of State Security, Gladkov.

2. The 'Merkulov Directive', no. 77 of 19 May 1941, is referred to in Order no. 0037 of 23 May 1941, issued by Gladkov as the basis for 'the direction, preparation and execution of the operation of purging the Lithuanian SSR from the hostile anti-Soviet and criminal and socially-dangerous element' (*Third Interim Report*, p. 515). The text of this directive is not available.

3. The text of the notorious 'Serov Instructions', which does not bear either a number or a date of issue, is published in the *Third Interim Report* under a misleading heading: '1. Moscow Instructions on Deportations, Order no. 001223'. In fact, the 'Serov Instructions' and the NKVD's Order no. 001223 are two entirely separate documents. Not only are their subjects different (accounting of the people to be purged in Order no. 001223, and the execution of deportation in the 'Serov Instructions'), but so are their issuing organs. (Order no. 001223 is consistently referred to as a document issued by the People's Commissariat of Internal Affairs, the NKVD, whereas Serov signed his instructions in his capacity as deputy people's commissar of state security [of the NKGB].) The attribution of a date 'between February and June 7, 1941' to the 'Serov Instructions' is based on the fact that: (1) the NKGB was only created, by its separation from the NKVD, in February 1941 (hence, it could not have issued any documents earlier than that); and, (2) the original text of the document was stamped as received in the NKGB office of the city of Šiauliai on 7 June 1941. (For a detailed elaboration on the subject of the dating of the 'Serov Instructions', see Dr Constantine R. Jurgela, 'Review of Bronis J. Kaslas, ed., *The USSR–German Aggression Against Lithuania*', *Ukranian Quarterly* 29, no. 4 [Winter 1973]: 407–11, esp. pp. 409–11.)

4. For these figures see 'Pirmoji sovietinė okupacija (1940–1941)' [The First Soviet Occupation, 1940–1941], in *Lietuvių Enciklopedija* [Lithuanian Encyclopedia], vol. 15 (Boston, Mass., 1968), p. 369 (on Lithuania); *Latvju Enciklopedija* [Latvian Encyclopedia] (Stockholm, 1950), p. 477 (on Latvia); and E. Uustalu, 'Events After 1940', in A. Rei, ed., *The Drama of the Baltic Peoples* (Stockholm, 1970), p. 320 (on Estonia).

5. This estimate is convincingly elaborated in R. Misiunas and R. Taagepera, *The Baltic States: The Years of Dependence* (1940–1980) (London, 1982), p. 41.

6. See K. Škirpa, *Sukilimas Lietuvos suverenumui atstatyti: Dokumentinė apžvalga* (Uprising for the Restoration of Lithuania's Sovereignty: A

110 · *Aleksandras Shtromas*

Documentary Survey) (Washington, DC, 1973), pp. 26–33, 37–8, 115–16. For an extensive study of these events in English, see A.M. Budreckis, *The Lithuanian National Revolt of 1941* (Boston, Mass., 1968). An account of the LAF's inauguration, together with the texts of the minutes of its inaugural meeting and the Inaugural Act itself, is given in Škirpa, *Sukilimas*, pp. 90–100.

7.   Z. Ivinskis, 'Lithuania During the War: Resistance Against the Soviet and the Nazi Occupants', in V.S. Vardys, ed., *Lithuania Under the Soviets: Portrait of a Nation,* 1940–65 (New York, 1965), pp. 65, 67. The 100 000 is a conservative estimate; in most other sources the figure given is 'at least 125,000 men' (see J.A. Swettenham, *The Tragedy of the Baltic States: A Report Compiled from Official Documents and Eyewitnesses' Stories* [London, 1952], p. 143).

8.   Swettenham, *Tragedy of the Baltic States,* p. 143.

9.   See Misiunas and Taagepera, *The Baltic States: The Years of Dependence,* p. 47.

10. Swettenham, *Tragedy of the Baltic States,* p. 143.

11. See Misiunas and Taagepera, *The Baltic States: The Years of Dependence,* p. 47.

12. *The Baltic States, 1940–1972: Documentary Background and Survey of Developments* (Stockholm, 1972), p. 55.

13. Misiunas and Taagepera, *The Baltic States: The Years of Dependence,* p. 47. According to them, only 5000 fighters were active in northern Estonia, mainly in forests and in the countryside.

14. R. Silde-Karklins, 'Formen des Widerstands im Baltikum, 1940–1968', in T. Ebert, ed., *Ziviler Widerstand: Fallstudien aus der Innenpolitischen Friedens- und Konfliktforschung* (Düsseldorf, 1970), p. 215.

15. E.J. Harrison, *Lithuania's Fight for Freedom* (New York, 1945), p. 46. For a detailed and well-documented treatment of the German failure to use the Lithuanians for their ends, see A. Dallin, *German Rule in Russia, 1941–1945: A Study of Occupation Policies,* 2nd rev. edn (London and New York, 1981), pp. 182–98.

16. Z. Ivinskis, 'Lithuania During the War', pp. 75, 78–81.

17. The Lithuanian estimate, first given by V.S. Vardys ('The Partisan Movement in Postwar Lithuania', in Vardys, *Lithuania under the Soviets,* p. 85) on the basis of a thorough analysis of a number of documents, is shared by all other authors who write about this subject. On Latvia, see R. Silde-Karklins, 'Formen des Widerstands', p. 216. The Estonian figure follows from the analysis given in Misiunas and Taagepera, *The Baltic States: The Years of Dependence,* p. 81.

18. For example, in Lithuania it was the Legion of Samogitia, which 'was formed in 1942 for anti-German purposes' (T. Remeikis, *Opposition to Soviet Rule in Lithuania, 1945–1980* [Chicago, 1980], p. 60); in Latvia it was the army of General Kurelis, which from December 1944 operated in Courland against the Germans. For more details on Kurelis, see sources as different as the publication of the Baltic Committee in Stockholm, *The Baltic States, 1940–1972,* p. 68; and, from the Academy of Sciences of the Latvian SSR, *Istoriia Latviiskoi SSR* [History of the Latvian SSR], vol. 3, 1917–1950, ed. K.J. Strazdin (Riga, 1958), p. 581.

19. Misiunas and Taagepera, *The Baltic States: The Years of Dependence*, p. 82.
20. Ibid., pp. 83–4. The facts on life span are referred to Vardys, "The Partisan Movement", in Vardys, *Lithuania under the Soviets*.
21. *Chicago Daily News*, 17 August 1961. This is a conservative estimate for the guerrillas' death toll. The more generally accepted one, given by the guerrilla sources themselves, is 30 000 (Vardys, 'The Partisan Movement', p. 86; and J. Pajaujis, *The Soviet Genocide in Lithuania* [New York, 1980], p. 108). Some outside estimates deem even this figure too conservative. Since the exact battlefield death toll cannot be established, Misiunas and Taagepera (*The Baltic States: The Years of Dependence*, p. 84) reasonably suggest a compromise solution between 20 000 and 50 000. As for the Soviet casualties, there is overall agreement that they must have been much heavier than those of the guerrillas. The guerrilla sources claim that they killed not 20 000 but 80 000 Soviet troops on the battlefield (see Pajaujis, *Soviet Genocide*, p. 108).
22. On Estonia, see J. Pennar, 'Soviet Nationality Policy and the Estonian Communist Elite', in T. Parming and E. Järvesoo, eds, *A Case Study of a Soviet Republic: The Estonian SSR* (Boulder, Colo., 1978), p. 116. Nevertheless, fighting in Estonia continued well into 1953 when, according to the chairman of the Estonian KGB, Ado Pork, it was largely crushed (A. Pork, 'Na strazhe zavoevaniy Oktiabria', *Kommunist Estonii*, no. 12 [1967]:11). Separate guerrillas continued to operate in Estonia even in the 1970s, as A. Küng reports, referring to information about the execution in 1976 of a guerrilla fighter, Kalev Arro, published in the Soviet Estonian Press (A. Küng, *A Dream of Freedom* [Cardiff, 1981], p. 202). On the decline of guerrilla resistance in Latvia, see J. Rutkis, ed., *Latvia*: Country and People (Stockholm, 1967), p. 260. The last known major battle between the guerrillas and Soviet forces in Latvia took place in February 1950 (ibid., p. 275).
23. Misiunas and Taagepera, *The Baltic States: The Year of Dependence*, p. 90; and K.V. Tauras, *Guerrilla Warfare on the Amber Coast* (New York, 1962), p. 95. The actual warfare in Lithuania did not stop even after 1952, since several large guerrilla units disregarded the order and continued to operate well into 1954. Thus one of the guerrilla leaders, A. Jonušas, when interrogated by the KGB, declared: 'In December 1952 I was appointed commander of the 'Darius' region. Three units – *Pilis* (Castle), *Jūra* (Sea), and *Geležinis Vilkas* (Iron Wolf) – belonged to this region and were subordinated to me. I continued in this post until June 21, 1954, i.e. until the day of my arrest' (Lithuanian Academy of Sciences, *Archyviniai Dokumentai: IX Rinkinys* [Archival Documents: Ninth Collection], ed. Z. Vasiliauskas [Vilnius: 'Mintis', 1968], p. 116). It is also indicative that the 'extermination battalions', formed to fight the guerrillas 'on the spot' in 1944, were finally disbanded only in 1954. Separate Lithuanian guerrillas remained active in the 1960s and 1970s. In 1965, *Tiesa* [Truth], the LCP daily newspaper, solemnly announced that the last Lithuanian guerrilla, Antanas Kraujelis, had been discovered by security forces and was shot in the battle that ensued, but five years later, in 1971, another such 'last guerrilla', Henrikas Kajotas, was found.
24. Each administrative-territorial unit was given a quota for the number of people to be deported from its territory. Then a special commission consisting of the leading party, KGB, and Soviet officials of this unit would prepare a list

of people to be deported. Since the deportations were usually performed in one or, at the most, two consecutive days, people on the list could avoid deportation if on these days they happened to be absent from home. However, the quota had to be met regardless of circumstances, and it always was, by deporting an equal number of the neighbours of the absentees, people who originally were not on the list at all.

25. Conservative estimates suggest that in 1949 alone about 200 000 Baltic natives were deported to Siberia and Kazakhstan. Of the 200 000, 60 000 were from Estonia. This is carefully calculated in R. Taagepera, 'Soviet Collectivization of Estonian Agriculture: The Deportation Phase', *Soviet Studies* 32, no. 3 (July 1980): 379–97, esp. p. 393. In my view, Taagepera's data allow us to put the estimated number much higher, up to 70 000–75 000. T. Parming, in 'Population Changes and Processes' (Parming and Järvesoo, *A Case Study of a Soviet Republic,* p. 27), actually puts it to 'at least 80 000'. Conservative estimates cite 50 000 from Latvia (calculated in G. King, *Economic Policies in Occupied Latvia* [Tacoma, Wash., 1965], p. 83). Again, a conclusion that a higher number, at least 60 000–65 000, was involved, seems to me more justified by the data used. Misiunas and Taagepera arrived at the conclusion that at the least 80 000 were deported from Lithuania in 1949 (*The Baltic States: The Years of Dependence,* p. 96). Other, less conservative, estimates arrive at a joint figure more than twice as high, namely 456 000 Baltic deportees (see Silde-Karklins, 'Formen des Widerstands', p. 222). The truth must be, as it usually is, somewhere in the middle.

26. According to Remeikis (*Opposition to Soviet Rule,* p. 42), not less than 300 000 were deported from Lithuania during these six years. The estimates for Estonia and Latvia are 145 000 (Parming, 'Population Changes and Processes', p. 27) and 144 000 (*The Baltic States, 1940–1972,* p. 82), respectively.

27. In testimony before the US Congress (*Fourth Interim Report of the Select Committee on Communist Aggression,* House of Representatives, Eighty-Third Congress, Second Session [Washington, DC, 1954], pp. 1368–74), a former Soviet border guard, Lt.-Col. Grigori Stepanovich Burlitski, stated: 'against these people firearms are to be used and they are to be killed without any further ado. No court is necessary for them. If these people happen to take refuge or run into a house or into a farm or into a village, then this particular house or farm or village is to be considered a bandit farm, a bandit house or a bandit village and those houses or farms or villages are to be destroyed by fire'. The facts about guerrilla warfare in Afghanistan show that Soviet instructions on how to fight guerrillas remained more or less unchanged since 1944.

28. The growth of party membership was slow but steady. Although in Estonia only 56 new party members enrolled in 1944, hundreds followed suit in 1945, so that by January 1946, 1900 members – or 27 per cent of the total membership – were already indigenous Estonians (see Pennar, 'Soviet Nationality Policy', p. 118; and Misiunas and Taagepera, *The Baltic States: The Years of Dependence,* p. 77). In Latvia, by 1 January 1946, about one-half of the 10 987 members of the party were ethnic Latvians, of whom about 3000 or 4000 were indigenous (see King, *Economic Policies,* p. 183). In Lithuania, by June 1946, there were 11 354 party members, of whom about a third were indigenous Lithuanians. Not less than 1500 were admitted after

the war (calculated on the basis of data provided in the *Mažoji Lietuviškoji Tarybinė Enciklopedija* [The Short Lithuanian Soviet Encyclopedia], vol. 2 [Vilnius, 1968], pp. 384–6). However, one can assume that the growth of the Communist Youth League was much more spectacular, since most of those who genuinely went over to the Soviet side were young people. Unfortunately, no precise statistical data are available on this, except that in Lithuania, in 1945, the Communist Youth League counted 3800 members, of whom 1600 belonged to the 'extermination battalions' or 'people's defenders' squads (their total number at the time is estimated at about 7000, a figure that is indicative of genuine Soviet support in Lithuania, since membership of these squads was voluntary). It is also known that in 1946 6000 members of this organisation actively participated in the USSR's Supreme Soviet election campaign, and that by 1950 it counted about 34 000 members, of whom not less than 20 000 are supposed to have been indigenous Lithuanians (see 'Lietuvos Lenino Komunistinė Jaunimo Sajunga' [Lithuanian Leninist Young Communist League], in *Mažoji Lietuviškoji Tarybinė Enciklopedija,* vol. 2, p. 391). The steady growth in the number of Soviet supporters is also demonstrated by the fact that the number of people executed by the guerrillas for collaboration increased throughout 1945–9; according to Soviet sources, 13 000 people were thus executed in Lithuania alone (see Misiunas and Taagepera, *The Baltic States: The Years of Dependence,* p. 86, n24). One should note that only natives were liable to stand trial by the guerrilla tribunals for collaboration. Newcomers – Russians et al. – were not touched. These figures are more or less precise in showing the real extent of genuine Soviet support in the Baltic. As stated before, this support can be measured in thousands of people, whereas the remaining millions either opposed the regime or supported those who opposed it.

29.   J. Deksnys, who, after braving the Iron Curtain three times lost all hope of Western support or help, described his experience and feelings in a series of articles published in the Soviet Lithuanian tabloid, *Švyturys* [Lighthouse] ('*Iliuzijų sudužimas*' [The Collapse of Illusions], *Švyturys,* no. 9 [May 1962]: 10–11, no. 10 [May 1962]: 10–12, no. 11 [June 1962]: 16–17, and no. 12 [June 1962]: 10–11). Although there is no doubt that the series was heavily doctored by Soviet editors, an attentive reader can discern in the articles some useful and persuasive pieces of genuine information. On the activities of J. Markulis, see Pajaujis, *Soviet Genocide,* pp. 106–7. Remeikis (*Opposition to Soviet Rule,* p. 56n and p. 269n) is doubtful about the extent to which Markulis's treachery affected the partisan movement and assumes that in his role as one of its leaders Markulis was representative of genuine resistance thinking and action. This is advertently but not very convincingly denied by K.K. Girnius in his review article on Remeikis's book ('The Opposition Movement in Postwar Lithuania', *Journal of Baltic Studies* 12, no. 1 [Spring 1982]: 66–73, esp. pp. 67–8). There are also eyewitness accounts of Markulis's pronouncements, in which he boasted about his treachery and presented it as an act of patriotic heroism. It seems that K. Kubilinskas, a talented poet, had the hardest lot in trying to reconcile himself with what he had done. He became an alcoholic and died in 1962, before his 39th birthday.

30.   Cases of dissent among the native members of the apparat and the party were the earliest ones. Even later 'extrastructural' and overtly dissident

pronouncements and acts came first from those Balts who held genuinely communist views and criticised the policies of the regime from the standpoint of anti-Stalinist Marxism and communism. It was natural for the naive and idealistic (i.e., those who considered the Soviet regime their own and wanted to adjust it to their idealistic vision rather than to adjust themselves to its oppressive practices) to voice their genuine opinions and protests publicly and in the most simple-minded and straightforward manner. Some of them, like Ivan Yakhimovichs in Latvia or Viktoras Sevrukas in Lithuania, directly founded their petitions and protests on the principles of communist ideology and morality. But it should be noted also that many of those dissidents who did not invoke Marxist-Leninist or communist principles explicitly started their lives as convinced believers in communism and genuine partisans of the Soviet regime and were actually driven into dissent upon finding their convictions inconsistent with the Soviet social and political reality. Such prominent Baltic dissenters as Jüri Kukk (an Estonian scientist and party member who perished in the Gulag in 1981; for a most perceptive study on Jüri Kukk and the Baltic dissent generally, see: R. Taagepera, *Softening Without Liberalization in the Soviet Union: The Case of Jüri Kukk,* [Lanham, Md; New York and London, 1984]), Lidija Doronina-Lasmanis and Maija Silmale (both Latvian cultural figures), Tomas Venclova and Jonas Jurašas (both Lithuanian cultural figures), and many others belong to this category.

These facts corroborate the thesis that the first and most outspoken Baltic dissidents were former communist idealists. People of the traditional nationalist orientation were much more cautious and realistic in their fearfulness of the Soviet regime and thoroughly avoided any open confrontations or disputes with it. Only much later (in the mid-1970s) did some of them – such as Viktoras Petkus and Balys Gajauskas (Lithuanians) and others – start to join the overt dissident ventures already well on the move.

31. See A. Küng, *A Dream of Freedom,* p. 167.
32. Although N. Karotamm came from Leningrad, it would be wrong to consider him a 'Yestonian' since he left Estonia in the 1930s as a political refugee and, like many other refugees from different countries, resided in the USSR for several years as an emigré. The same, to a certain degree, applies to E. Päll, who lived in Russia for many years but whose roots were nevertheless in Estonia.
33. For more details on the so-called Berklavs Affair and the purge in general, see A. Berzins, *The Unpunished Crime* (New York, 1963), pp. 182–4, 255–62.
34. For the English text of that very revealing letter, see *Congressional Record,* 21 February 1972, pp. E1426–30.
35. This story was told to me by a person who witnessed a few conversations between Stalin and Sniečkus.
36. T. Ženklys, 'Pasibaigusi Lietuvos gyvenimo epocha' [The End of an Epoch in Lithuania's Life], *Akiračiai* [The Horizons], no. 3 (57), 1974, p. 7. A shortened version of this extremely interesting article is available in Russian; see A. Shtromas, 'Dve stat'i T. Zhenklisa' [Two Articles by T. Zenklys], *Kontinent,* no. 14 (1977): 229–41.
37. See A. Shtromas, 'Baltic Problem and Peace Studies', *Journal of Baltic Studies* 9, no. 1 (Spring 1978): 3–4. The thesis about the universality of the teleological political consciousness of the Baltic people is elaborated in some

detail and corroborated by existing evidence in Štromas, *Politinė są̇monė Lietuvoje* (Political Consciousness in Lithuania), (London, 1980), pp. 50–3.

38. In November 1956, on All Saints Day, spontaneous mass demonstrations and meetings broke out in Kaunas and Vilnius (Lithuania). The demands were for 'Freedom for Lithuania', 'Solidarity with the heroic peoples of Hungary and Israel', 'Russians out of Lithuania', and so on.

39. Major dissident activities in and documents from the Baltic were regularly reported in the *Chronicle of Current Events*, clandestinely published in Moscow since 1968 and available in English translation from the publications of Amnesty International. The United Baltic Appeal regularly published *UBA Information Services*, a news-release series in which such information was given wide coverage with full texts of major documents made available. The same applies to the ELTA (Lithuanian News Agency in the USA) monthly *Bulletin*, the *Latvian Information Bulletin* (published by the Latvian Legation in Washington), *Estonian/Baltic Events* (published by R. Taagepera), and *Lituanus*. Good collections of Baltic dissident documents are included in P. Reddaway, ed., *Uncensored Russia: The Human Rights Movement in the Soviet Union* (London, 1972); *Documents from Estonia on the Violation of Human Rights* (Stockholm, 1977); V.S. Vardys, *The Catholic Church, Dissent, and Nationality in Soviet Lithuania* (New York, 1978); and Remeikis, *Opposition to Soviet Rule. The Chronicle of the Lithuanian Catholic Church* was regularly published in English by the Lithuanian Roman Catholic Priests' League of America in New York.

40. Mass demonstrations, spontaneous protest meetings, and other similar events were regular in the Baltic republics after November 1956. Another mass manifestation that developed into a full-scale riot took place in Kaunas in 1960, during the festivities devoted to the 20th anniversary of Lithuania's sovietisation. On that occasion militia forces started shooting on the demonstrators, killing and wounding several people, which outraged the crowds to such as extent that they attacked and smashed the forces of law and order present in the city. Two more such mass demonstrations that developed into riots took place in Lithuania. One, in May 1972, was the result of the self-immolation in the central square of the city of Kaunas 'for the freedom of Lithuania' of a young student, Romas Kalanta; it was his funeral on 18 May 1972, that turned into a demonstration that literally took over the city and held it for almost two days, until the troops were sent in to disperse it. More than five hundred arrests were made. The other, in October 1977, developed from a soccer match played in Vilnius between the local team and a team from the Russian town of Smolensk. On all occasions the overriding slogans were 'Freedom for Lithuania' and 'Russians out of our country'.

In Estonia a mass protest took place on 20 April 1972, in the capital city Tallinn. It started as a result of the televised hockey world championship. When the Czech team defeated the Soviet team, hundreds of people, mainly students, burst onto the streets shouting 'we won'. Mass youth manifestations took place in Tartu (Estonia) in 1976 and in Liepaja (Latvia) in 1977 over pop music events. The most significant Estonian youth demonstrations took place in Tallinn, Tartu, and some other places in October 1980 over the issue of increased time allocation to Russian lessons in Estonian schools. Subsequently, a letter from 40 prominent Estonian intellectuals expressed their full solidarity with and support for the demonstrators, who were extremely brutally dealt with by the militia and army troops.

41.   In Lithuania, protests against violations of the religious rights of the people and of the Catholic church itself, accompanied by appropriate demands, were systematically launched from 1968 onward. They culminated in a petition signed by 17 054 Lithuanian Roman Catholics and calling for an end to violations by Soviet authorities of the right of the people to exercise their freedom of conscience, guaranteed by the Soviet constitution. The petition demanded termination of the practice of gross civil discrimination against religious believers. In December 1971 it was sent to the UN and, via its offices, to Soviet leaders in Moscow. (For the English text of this petition, see Vardys, *The Catholic Church,* pp. 144–9.) In 1972 the publication of *The Chronicle of the Lithuanian Catholic Church* had started; it reflected the course of the systematic, massive, and regular struggle of Lithuanian Catholics for their rights. In Latvia, similar mass developments took place, mainly insofar as the rights of the Baptists were concerned, but Latvian Catholics were actively involved in protest activities, too.

    In Estonia, recorded protests about the lack of free access to information and of freedom for culture-creating activity go back to 1958 and are connected with the activities of the leading Estonian dissident, Mart Niklus. In Latvia, similar acts could be traced to the early 1960s, in connection with the 1961 trial of the prominent Latvian poet, Knuts Skujenieks (later, other cultural figures were also tried). In Lithuania, such cases were recorded only in the early 1970s, as, for example, the 1972 memorandum of Jonas Jurašas, the Chief Director of the State Theatre in Kaunas, who refused to comply with the dictates of the authorities and pledged to work only in accordance with his own conscience. Similarly, the poet and architect Mindaugas Tamonis refused to inspect and restore crumbling monuments to the Red Army on nationally and religiously significant Lithuanian sites.

42.   For the full English text of this petition, see *UBA Information Service,* news release no. 330/331, 11 November 1979 (supplement). Most of the 45 signatories were arrested, tried, and received heavy penalties. There were reports that 35 000 signatures in support of this petition were gathered in Lithuania alone.

43.   For its text in Russian, see Radio Liberty, *Arkhiv samizdat,* no. 70.

44.   The Herzen Foundation in Amsterdam published it in Russian in 1970 as a separate pamphlet, '*Programma demokraticheskogo dvizheniia Sovetskogo Soyuza*'.

45.   See his letter, 'The Duty of a Communist', addressed to M. Suslov, in A. Brumberg, ed., *In Quest of Justice: Protest and Dissent in the Soviet Union Today* (London, 1970), pp. 129–32.

46.   Ibid., pp. 359–60.

47.   For details, see *Delo Kovaleva,* a documentary report published as a separate pamphlet in New York in 1976 by 'Khronika-Press'.

48.   For the records of his interrogation by the KGB, see *Index on Censorship,* no. 3 (Autumn 1975): 56–61; more details on his case are available in *Delo Tverdokhlebova,* a documentary report published as a separate pamphlet in New York in 1976 by 'Khronika-Press'.

49.   For a more detailed review of the links between Lithuanian and Russian dissenters, see Vardys, *The Catholic Church,* pp. 151–5. The various ties

between Estonian and Russian dissenters are explored and perceptively assessed by Sergey Soldatov, himself an Estonian and a Russian dissident at one and the same time. See his 'Estonskii uzel' [Estonian Knot], *Kontinent,* no. 32 (1982): 223–38.

50. No. 15, 1975; quoted from *Lietuvos Katalikų Bažnyčios Kronika* [The Chronicle of the Lithuanian Catholic Church], vol. 2 (Chicago, 1975), p. 357.

51. This idea I expressed in a number of previous writings. See, for example, A. Shtromas, 'Prospects for Restoring the Baltic States' Independence: A View on the Prerequisites and Possibilities of Their Realization', in *Journal of Baltic Studies,* 17, no. 3 (Fall 1986).

Part II
From National Reawakening to Statehood

5 The Resurgence of Nationalism
Graham Smith

During the late 1980s the Baltic republics underwent a nationalist reawakening which transformed the whole character of social, political and economic life in the region. Although triggered off by the election in March 1985 of a reform-minded leadership in Moscow, what was to prove central in structuring the nature of this sea change was the emergence in the region of grassroots-based social movements. Beginning as movements in support of Gorbachev's reform agenda, these self-styled 'Popular Fronts' quickly developed into nationalist movements committed to the re-establishment of independent statehood. In this chapter we examine the nature of this nationalist revival, the conditions which gave rise to the emergence of the popular fronts and the reasons why these movements were able to mobilise support for national self-determination from their respective nations so quickly and effectively.

POLITICAL STASIS AND ETHNIC TENSIONS

Most of the conditions necessary for nationalism to emerge as a political force were present in the Baltic republics before the mid-1980s. Firstly, as previous chapters have indicated, all three Baltic nations, unlike most other peoples of the Soviet Union, could draw upon a rich variety of pre-Soviet national symbols, embedded not only in century-long national cultures but also in memories of national statehood. While Moscow attempted to restructure this sense of nation-ness to fit the template of a new form of communal identity compatible with maintaining Soviet rule, the role played by such pre-Soviet national symbols during the late 1980s national reawakening would firmly suggest that a collective imagination of wishing to reconnect with a pre-Soviet past had not simply passed into history. For many imbued with a sense of being Estonian, Latvian or Lithuanian, such symbols continued to strike some form of emotional chord, albeit with different meanings for sub-groups depending on their situational contexts. Secondly, as highly urbanised and educated societies, all three republics possessed a flourishing native cultural intelligentsia – writers, poets, teachers, journalists – linked to a tradition of intellectual dissent which in one way or another was bound up with concerns about the social reproduction

121

of their national languages and cultures and with the erosion of national freedoms under Soviet rule. It was this stratum which was to emerge as the social entrepreneurs of the nationalist resurgence and as the leaders of their nationalist movements. Finally, by the mid 1980s a multiplicity of grievances had already been amassed against Moscow, ranging from concerns about cultural survival to centralised control over local political affairs. By complementing ethnic and territorial interests and divisions, such grievances imparted a distinctive emotional edge, easily translatable into national grievances, with the potential to be effectively utilised as ammunition to forward the cause of national self-determination.

Yet throughout the two decades preceding the late 1980s nationalism had shown little sign of threatening Soviet rule in the region. There were a number of reasons why this had not occurred. Crucial was the role played by a coercive central state apparatus in ruthlessly suppressing any attempt to propagate nationalism in the region or to allow the republics the necessary political scope to pursue any meaningful autonomist claims. Consequently, nationalism was largely confined to the margins of dissident politics where it was relatively easily contained by a state willing and able when necessary to use coercion. There were however other reasons why Baltic nationalism remained on the fringes of political life. Underlying this was the centre's preference for preserving the status quo over engaging in social and economic reform and of the way in which such a regime of political stasis incorporated and attempted to manipulate those sub-groups within the Baltic population with the greatest potential to undermine rule from Moscow. Reflecting this conservatism characteristic of Brezhnev's rule was the detectable emergence of a set of centrally managed practices which contained some of the hallmarks of corporatist politics.[1] As Bunce has argued, the Brezhnevite state represented 'a corporate vision of a consensual society, in which conflict could be managed by deals struck between the state and functionally based interests'.[2] In order to secure the conditions necessary for this corporatist vision of a consensual society, in which emphasis was placed on national cohesion, steady economic growth and social stability, the Brezhnevite state in effect entered into a tacit contract with the Baltic political leadership. In return for maintaining social stability and implementing central policies within their regions, the Baltic political leadership were granted a number of concessions. This most certainly included relative stability in office for political élites, a degree of personal autonomy over their territorial fiefdoms and fulfilment of the republics' plans reflecting the centre's concern with securing steady rather than overly demanding rates of overall economic growth. In short, Brezhnevism favoured the political leadership in the republics, rewarded their conservatism and aided in the stability of the local political machines that they headed.

Moscow had little to fear from such political incumbents, who displayed none of the autonomist tendencies which had periodically surfaced during the late 1950s. In Estonia and Latvia those political leaders who had taken advantage of Khrushchev's policy of decentring limited economic powers to the regions, to forward national over state-wide interests, had been replaced by the early 1960s by more Russified Estonians and Latvians. These incumbents were disproportionately drawn from either native Russians or Balts who had lived outside their republics for a considerable proportion of their lives. In Lithuania, First Party Secretary, Antanas Sniečkus, who throughout the 1950s and 1960s had practised a more subtle form of promoting republic self-interest in preventing the runaway industrialisation which had precipitated Russian immigration in Estonia and Latvia, was replaced, following his death in 1974, by a mediocre and intensely loyal Moscow apparatchik, Petras Griskevicius. Yet throughout the 1970s and early 1980s, this intensely loyal leadership was allowed a flexibility in pursuing republic interests, but only in so far as such lobbying did not undermine the Brezhnevite compromise. The behaviour they displayed within the arena of fiscal matters was therefore not simply of obedient lieutenants carrying out Moscow's policies but rather of leaders who recognised that their positions of power were also bound up with securing as large a share of budgetary allocations for their republic as possible.[3] In short, Moscow's greater trust in this political stratum made the upper echelons of both party and state life in the Baltic less uncertain and more comfortable. In return these ruling élites could be relied upon to ensure ethno-regional stability. This was evident during the early 1980s when echoes of unrest following the rise of Solidarity in neighbouring Poland were quickly and forcibly dealt with by the local leadership, especially in Catholic Lithuania.[4]

Throughout the Brezhnev years, the centre, as part of a policy of greater trust in native cadres, also permitted a degree of indigenisation of personnel within the local party-state apparatus. Although the indigenous nationalities continued to be grossly under-represented within Party life more generally,[5] a large proportion of the state apparatus was in the hands of indigenous personnel, with natives generally well represented in relation to their overall numbers. By the late 1980s, Estonians held 82.2 per cent of administrative-managerial posts (comprising 61.5 per cent of the overall population), Latvians 63.1 per cent (52 per cent of the population) and Lithuanians 91.5 per cent (79.6 per cent of the population).[6] Such trends in effect reflected the urbanised and increasingly highly educated character of all three eponymous societies and must also have gone some way to satisfying native career prospects. Yet such trends sat uneasily with their overall disproportionate under-representation within their respective Communist Parties.

Corporatist features of centre–union republic politics were however not just confined to the arena of formal centre–union republic politics. A number of centrally declared social commitments within the general material and cultural spheres of social life also existed which, no doubt, the regime saw as vital to maintaining regime legitimacy and which must have had some bearing on stabilising the region. Thus full employment continued to be created for the eponymous nationalities within their own republics even where an over-abundance and over-concentration of particular skills existed. This was particularly notable within the arena of the cultural professions where, despite on-going urbanisation and the expansion of higher education, natives with specialist skills were, at a considerable economic cost to the regime, guaranteed continued employment within their own republics. Similarly, regime stability was purposely linked to a steady improvement in living standards. By the mid 1970s all three Baltic nations were better off than at any time during Soviet rule.[7] And finally, the Brezhnev regime adopted a more cautious and pragmatic nationalities-policy compared to its predecessor. The centre's commitment to the long-term goal of erasing nationality differences (*sliyanie*) was dropped from major policy speeches. While continuing to single out the importance of the regime's commitment to furthering the 'coming together' (*sblizhenie*) of nations, Brezhnev went to some lengths to emphasise that such a process was an objective one, and that the Party was against forcing such integration.[8] This tacit acceptance of a multicultural dimension to Soviet society was also reflected in the decision to maintain the nationality-based federal structure despite calls leading up to the redrafting of the 1977 federal constitution for its abolition. As Brezhnev noted, 'We should be taking a dangerous course if we were artificially to accelerate this objective process of rapprochement between nations'.[9] For the Baltic Republics this was important, because union republic status went hand in hand with facilitating the preservation of a whole array of native institutional supports, most important of which were those connected with the preservation of the eponymous languages. As Table 5.1 shows, these increasingly urbanised peoples did not forego their native languages or cultures for Russian although knowledge of Russian as a second language was a precondition for most specialist employment. Consequently, as Zaslavsky suggests, 'the potentially explosive ethnic situation, when educated members of ethnic minorities find their social mobility blocked by the majority group, was by and large avoided'.[10]

Table 5.1 Linguistic affiliations of the eponymous nationalities, 1959–89

	Percentage claiming the eponymous language as their native language				Percentage point change 1959–89	Percentage claiming knowledge of Russian as a second language[a]			Percentage point change 1970–89
	1959	*1970*	*1979*	*1989*		*1970*	*1979*	*1989*	
Estonia	99.3	99.24	98.99	98.61	−0.69	27.55	23.06	33.57	6.02
Latvia	98.4	98.09	97.80	97.37	−1.03	45.35	58.30	65.72	20.37
Lithuania	99.2	99.51	99.69	99.59	0.39	34.83	52.19	37.36	2.53

[a]The 1959 census did not include a question on knowledge of Russian as a second language.

Sources: *Itogi vsesoyuznoy perepisi naseleniya SSSR 1970 goda*, Gosudarstvennyy Komitet SSSR po Statistike, Moscow, 1974; *Itogi vsesoyuznoy perepisi naseleniya SSSR 1979 goda*, Gosudarstvennyy Komitet SSSR po Statistike, Moscow, 1989; *Itogi vsesoyuznoy perepisi naseleniya SSSR 1989 goda*, Gosudarstvennyy Komitet SSSR po Statistike, Moscow, 1990.

Yet corporatist politics masked a multiplicity of underlying tensions which, due to regime stasis, were becoming increasingly difficult to manage.[11] Firstly, the Baltic republics were managed by a centralised production system which stifled local professional initiative and which seemed oblivious to the far-reaching negative economic and environmental consequences of its decisions within the localities. Moscow's policy of building up heavy industry in the republics, especially in Estonia and Latvia, despite the fact that the region was devoid of a raw material base was one such source of long-standing concern. Another was the harmful ecological consequences generated by those Moscow-based ministries in charge of heavy industry.

Secondly, concern also focused on a migration policy which increasingly brought Russians and other outsiders into competition with the titular nationalities for urban jobs, based on Moscow's lack of understanding of local labour markets and insensitivity towards the increasing inability of the local authorities to provide adequate urban services and housing. Particularly affected by immigration were Latvia and Estonia, where in some years throughout the period net migration, especially of Russians, accounted for a larger share of population growth than the republics' already low levels of natural population increase. Concerned about the self-preservation of their national cultures, Latvians had seen their share of their republic's population falling from 77 per cent in 1939 to 52 per cent by 1989, while in Estonia in the same period the Estonian share of their republic's population had been reduced from 90 per cent to 61 per cent (Figure 4). In contrast, the Russian presence had increased from about one-tenth in both pre-war republics to one-third in Latvia and by a quarter in Estonia. By comparison, Lithuania, being less developed and with a substantial rural population surplus was not subject to the same scale of uncontrolled Russian immigration. Consequently Lithuania remained a more ethnically homogeneous republic, with four-fifths drawn from the eponymous nationality, a proportion unchanged from the interwar years.

Thirdly, from the late 1970s Moscow began reinstituting policies aimed at greater cultural standardisation These included the central authorities insisting upon greater fluency in the Russian language for local professional employment and expanding opportunities for the teaching of Russian in republic kindergartens, schools and universities. For the first time during Soviet rule Russian was being taught in the first grade of native language schools. Such policies did much to heighten concerns over the likely future role of the local languages and cultures as reflected in growing dissident activities during the early 1980s connected with issues of linguistic Russification. And finally, by the late 1970s, in the absence of centrally-initiated

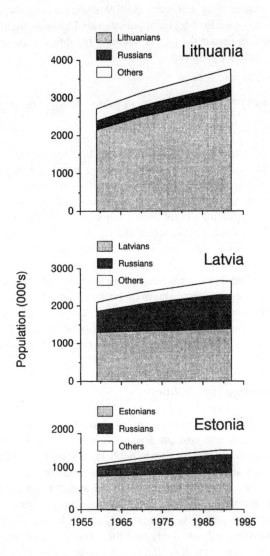

Figure 4   Ethnodemographic trends in the Baltic Republics, 1959–92

economic reform, what gains there had been in living standards during the Brezhnev years were eroding. For many Balts this was particularly galling, given that a centrally-managed regional policy geared towards fiscal redistribution continued to favour the poorer southern republics at the expense of the more economically prosperous.[12]

THE NATIONALIST MOVEMENTS: FROM PERESTROIKA TO SECESSION

It was however only as a result of the actions of a reform-minded leadership in Moscow that nationalism was able to emerge as an organised, mass-based political force capable of challenging Soviet rule. Activated primarily by the need to redress the ailing performance of the Soviet economy, Gorbachev's unfolding 'revolution from above' developed into a programme of wholesale economic, social and political restructuring which inadvertently triggered off a resurgence of nationalism throughout the borderland republics. Although at the forefront of this 'revolution from below', the Baltic Republics were not immediately secessionist in their aims. Rather we can identify three stages in the development of nationalist politics: a period of national reawakening (1986–8) followed by the emergence of nationalist movements in the form of the popular fronts (1988–90), and finally, formal republic institutional support for territorial secession (1990–1).

National Reawakening: Issue Politics

From 1986 until 1988 we can identify a period of national reawakening. As a result of the advent of glasnost (or openness), for the first time during Soviet rule the Baltic peoples were able to publicly rediscover their history, to bring openly into sharp relief the long-held national beliefs and prejudices rooted in the collective imagination, and to re-examine through debate and discussion the reality of past and current ethnic inequalities. At this stage, the national, territorially-organised, media began to play an important role, providing a distinctively republic-based focus on issues and events which did much to crystallise discussion within 'a national context' and to raise the consciousness of peoples around national-republic concerns. It was also a period marked by public shows of defiance linked to so called 'calendar demonstrations', notably the anniversaries of the Molotov–Ribbentrop Pact, commemorations of previous Independence Days, and the mass deportations of their peoples by the Stalinist regime.

At this particular stage, oppositional politics was usually of the single-issue type, in which organised opposition was mobilised against particular developmental projects which carried, in particular, environmental ramifications. This included opposition to the proposed expansion of the Ignalina nuclear power station in Lithuania, plans to construct a hydroelectric power station on Latvia's Daugava river, proposals to develop a phosphate plant in northern Estonia, and plans to construct a subway in Riga. Even where oppositional politics seized upon other issues, such as those linked to human rights or religious freedoms, their reference points were national in content. However, despite their national frame of reference, overall the politics and political actions in which civil society engaged were issue-specific with only limited inter-group co-ordination and organisational capability. This in effect was a product of a society experimenting with the politics of the possible in which particular issues, actions and agendas were judged as less likely to result in retribution by either Moscow or the local party-state machine.

This, in part, explains the high profile of ecological concerns. Although following the Chernobyl disaster of April 1986 there was a genuine concern about environmental questions, such concerns were given a higher profile precisely because they could be presented solely as issues of rational economic efficiency and technical planning rather than as direct assaults on regime legitimacy. Yet environmental issues were to play an important part in eventually bringing down conservative-minded local political leaders in both Estonia and in Lithuania, and in providing an organisational basis, oppositional know-how and political leadership for promoting the cause of national self-determination. And in all three republics, but especially in Latvia and Estonia, environmental organisations played an important part in the setting up of what became their respective nationalist organisations, the popular fronts. As Dainis Ivans, President of the Latvian Popular Front put it, 'In Latvia, everything began with the movement to save the environment. The Club (for the Defence of the Environment) was founded. Individual fighters arose, prophets. The great awakening had begun'.[13]

The Popular Fronts and National Self-Determination

The second phase (1988–90) marked a period of political take-off linked to the eventual establishment of grassroots-based social movements espousing the goals of greater economic, political and cultural autonomy. Crucial to understanding why such movements were permitted to develop first in the Baltic Republics lies in Moscow's perceived receptivity of the region to the nature of the reform programme. Certainly the enterprise culture was no stranger to the Balts. Both private enterprise and the co-operative idea had formed an integral part of their national economies during the interwar years. Under successive post-Stalin regimes, the Baltic republics had proved to be receptive laboratories for market-oriented experimentation. The idea of opening up Soviet trade through joint ventures with foreign companies was also attractive to a region with a long history of western trade and which could foresee the material benefits likely to accrue from such a reorientation. Moreover unlike Russia and many other Soviet republics, there already existed a pre-Soviet civic culture of democracy, embedded in the years of independent statehood, and one judged as likely to be more conducive than most other republics to facilitating political participation and pluralism. Gorbachev's five-day 'meet the people' visit to Estonia and Latvia in February 1987, which included visits to factories and farms where co-operatives, private enterprises and new and more effective work practices were already in place, must have underlined for the General Secretary the potential receptiveness of the region to perestroika.[14] Yet in all three republics, the conservative-minded political leadership were reluctant to engage in change.

It was the Baltic intelligentsia – Gorbachev's natural constituency of support in the region but also the traditional bearers of Baltic nationalism – which seized upon the opportunities opened up by glasnost to revitalise the agenda for reform in the republics. In April 1988 at a Plenum of the Estonian Creative Societies, which brought together members from the creative intelligentsia, support for speeding up the process of perestroika was declared. In Latvia, at the Plenum of the Writers Union on 1–2 June 1988, the local party and government also came in for particular criticism over their slow handling of perestroika.[15] The following day, Lithuanian intellectuals also met to discuss common grievances and a course of political action. Thus in all three republics, these forums provided the launching pads for the establishment of mass-based movements. Estonia led the way with the establishment of its popular front in April 1988, with Latvia and Lithuania following with the establishment of parallel organisations in May and October of that year. Thus in all three republics popular fronts were born as movements in support of perestroika whose goals were to ensure the effective implementation of Moscow's programme for restructuring. Forming the centre-piece of their aims was to achieve sovereignty in all areas of republic life within the context of the Soviet federation.

Moscow opted to accommodate such developments, no doubt viewing the popular fronts as loyal grass-roots based facilitators of local structural change. The visit of Gorbachev's emissary, Politburo member Alexandr

Yakovlev, to the Baltic republics in August 1988 provided an opportunity for Gorbachev to be briefed on developments and for both the fledgling popular fronts and the republic leaderships to get a response from Moscow of the permitted parameters of manoeuvrability. In a candid speech to representatives of Latvia's intelligentsia, Yakovlev did however warn of confrontationalism of the intelligentsia and mass media against the local party apparatus, and against proposals to redefine the notion of republican citizenship based on 'selectiveness, exclusion or isolationism'.[16] Although emphasising unity and patience, in paraphrasing Lenin, he seemed to leave the Baltic republics in little doubt of what a reconstituted relationship between them and Moscow could mean in the foreseeable future: 'a state in the form of a union must have a common defence and foreign policy. All the rest ... ought to be the prerogative of the republics'.[17]

The popular fronts that emerged were umbrella organisations whose membership frontiers were defined by their nationality/republic with each movement subsuming most of the issue-oriented interest groups which had dominated earlier oppositional politics. At the founding congresses of all three movements in October 1988, a variety of diverse organisations were represented, including environmental movements, heritage societies, religious organisations, those active in human rights, groups committed to re-establishing political independence, and members of the Communist Party. That between a fifth and one-third of their respective Congress delegates were drawn from the Communist Party must have offered some reassurance for Moscow that the activities of the popular fronts would reflect the nature and scope of Gorbachev's reforms. However the overwhelming majority of the fronts' members were from the eponymous nationalities. This was particularly marked in the case of Lithuania's Popular Front (more popularly known as *Sajudis* meaning 'movement'), where at its Founding Congress, 96 per cent of its delegates were Lithuanian.[18] Within only a few months of their establishment, all three organisations could legitimately claim to be truly mass-based movements.[19]

The establishment of popular fronts occurred more or less simultaneously with the removal in the three republics of conservative first party secretaries although it was only in Estonia and Lithuania that the two events were directly linked. Consequently, with the appointment of reform-minded leaders in the Autumn of 1988 – Vaino Valjas in Estonia, Jan Vagris, followed soon after by Anatolii Gorbunovs, in Latvia, and Algirdas Brazauskas in Lithuania – the republics were able to move towards greater co-operation with the popular fronts, albeit not unmarked by occasional confrontation. By late 1988, the authorities in all three republics were implementing measures linked to calls to relocate their eponymous peoples at the centre stage

of local political, cultural and economic life. In the early months much of
the legislation passed was bound up with important symbolic victories:
making the indigenous languages state languages of the republics, reintro-
ducing their own national flags and national anthems, and formalising the
concept of republic-based citizenship.

It became quickly apparent, however, that for the popular fronts in particular, especially those organisations and individuals within their ranks
who advocated a more radical stance on national self-determination, that
what was at stake was not simply the democratisation and economic
restructuring of their republics, but the possibility, for the first time in half a
century, of 'home rule'. No doubt during these early months the more moderate stance taken by the popular fronts on national sovereignty was in part
conditioned by tactical limitations. Certainly there is evidence to suggest
that from the outset of their organisations' formation, many of their leaders
had clearly set their sights on achieving nothing short of independent statehood.[20] By August 1989, no doubt spurred on by the success of the revolutions in Eastern Europe, all three popular fronts had acquired sufficient
confidence to call publicly for independent statehood. That the popular
fronts so quickly became separatist in their aims and in the process were
able to convince their peoples so easily of the rightness of their cause were
in one way or another linked both to the way in which powerful national
symbols were drawn upon and equated with a pre-Soviet past and of the
material benefits which such sovereignty might again provide. In particular, the myth of incorporation, the economic viability of republic statehood
and the question of cultural self-preservation, all became invaluable nationalist resources, providing bases upon which nationalist leaders could
capture the sovereign imaginations of their peoples.

The most powerful of these nationalist resources centred on the myth of
voluntary incorporation into the Soviet federation. From the late 1980s,
this myth received its first public airing, with reform-minded historicist
educators emerging to play a key role.[21] In all three republics, for the first
time during Soviet rule, Baltic historians began to challenge publicly the
twin myths of Soviet official historiography, that Stalin's motives for signing the Non-Aggression Pact with Hitler in 1939 were purely intended to
secure peace, and that the peoples of the Baltic States welcomed incorporation into the Soviet Union as an alternative to the continuation of authoritarian rule in their own respective republics. At the founding congresses of
all three popular fronts, demands were voiced for endorsing the illegality of
forced incorporation and thus the call for the reinstatement of independent
statehood. In August 1989, in an unprecedented show of solidarity between
the peoples of the Baltic States, the popular fronts organised up to two mil-

lion people to form a human chain stretching from Estonia to Lithuania to show their condemnation of the Molotov–Ribbentrop Pact. In a joint communiqué issued by the popular fronts, the Pact was described as 'criminal' and 'unlawful'.[22] Such a powerful weapon for mobilising support behind independent statehood also provided a major boost in late 1989 when the Supreme Soviets of all the Republics officially declared incorporation illegal. By December of that year the Congress of Peoples Deputies had declared the secret protocols as 'legally untenable and invalid from the moment they were signed'.[23] Thus for the separatist cause there was a sense that history was again on their side. Moreover, unlike the other Soviet republics the cause of national self-determination could be couched in a language of a people seeking to regain the independence which had illegally eluded them. Theirs was 'a lawful struggle' against 'occupation' by 'a foreign power'. In short, the nationalist cause could appeal to rectificatory justice further legitimised by an international community, including the United States, who had never officially acknowledged their *de jure* incorporation into the Soviet Union.[24] Once Moscow had acknowledged this fact, emphasis shifted from the struggle for autonomy within the Soviet federation to demands for the restoration of independent statehood.

The second nationalist resource focused on the viability of economic self-determination and the benefits which might accrue to their republics and peoples with independent statehood. Although Gorbachev had inadvertently begun the process by calling for greater economic autonomy for the republics as a way of improving the Soviet Union's sluggish economic performance, reform-minded Baltic economists quickly seized the initiative, formulating a far more coherent and radical economic model for autonomy than that proposed by Moscow. It included proposals to decentre fiscal and other economic activities to the republics, single out market principles as the basis of economic reform and devolve ownership of natural resources to the republics. By the summer of 1989, the supreme soviets of all three republics had adopted laws concerning economic autonomy. In referring to these laws, the Chairman of the Council of Ministers of the Estonian Republic, Indrek Toome, seemed in no doubt that they provided 'the green light for the development of economic independence'.[25] The notion of economic sovereignty was exploited to the full by the nationalist leadership, linked to the notion of reconnecting with the form of economy which had existed during the inter-war years. This necessarily meant redressing what were identified as the irrational and inefficient imbalances induced by Moscow-based rule, namely between market and plan, heavy and light manufacturing industry, and urban and rural investment. Thus in Latvia, much was made of the 'unjustified priority development of industrial production over agricultural production' during Soviet rule and of the need to reorganise the countryside along more individual and co-operative lines, emphasising the importance of again recreating a country of small farmers.[26] Emphasis was put on the Baltic republics' rejoining a trading regime of European partners, resembling Finland or Denmark more than the traditional Soviet model. While it was recognised that economic sovereignty did not mean deprioritising the Soviet market, the potential for new trading arrangements was highlighted with active steps taken to revitalise Western contacts. In September 1989, in yet another exercise in regional solidarity, the popular fronts met in Panevežys, where they called for closer economic integration between their republics in order to secure greater economic prosperity for all.

The optimism that such visions of potential economic wellbeing generated contrasted sharply with the increasing inability of Moscow's reform programme either to produce economic change or to redress falling living standards. An economically faltering core, unable to provide the resources or leadership necessary to guarantee living standards, must have acted as an important catalyst in swaying particularly those who did not identify with the core national cultures to the perception that materially they were likely to be more secure in an independent and more westward-oriented and reform-minded Baltic state than as part of a Soviet Union which looked increasingly incapable of affecting economic change. Yet Gorbachev's emphasis on the non-economic viability of geopolitical divorce, particularly the issue of Baltic dependency on Russian energy and raw material supplies, must have made many Balts cautious about leaving the Soviet federation. However, the attempt by Moscow to claim the moral high ground in arguing that post-war economic rehabilitation of the republics had been assisted by the entire Soviet federation probably did more to fuel than dampen the nationalist resolve.[27]

The third but most problematic nationalist resource centred on the issue of cultural self-preservation. It was based on the simple notion that the most effective way of protecting and regenerating the eponymous national cultures was through establishing a protective ring-wall in the form of their own polities. In one way or another, be it in relation to centralised control, industrial development, environmental degradation, language or immigration, the nationalist movements were united in linking the self-preservation of the eponymous national cultures and ways of life with greater control over their own political, economic and cultural affairs. Thus at its Founding Congress, the Estonian Popular Front called for 'the defence of national identification and a halt to the process of assimilation'.[28] Yet within these movements existed a politics of nationalism reflecting two identifiable modes of national consciousness.

The most demagogic and powerful was a form of *ethnic* nationalism which appealed to a more primordialist sense of nation-ness. Grounded in abstract notions of 'the people' and in 'blood notions' of genealogical descent, it reflected a desire to obtain, as nearly as possible, a coterminous nation-state. The need to introduce such measures as restricting citizenship to the eponymous culture were called for, as were policies to 'suppress the migration that threatens to make Estonians a minority in their own lands'.[29] For some delegates, the language was uncompromising: Russians were referred to as 'the civil garrison' of 'the occupying power', 'as colonists' and as 'rootless migrants'. One resolution passed by the Latvian Popular Front described the republic's Russians as 'a huge mass of badly qualified and uncultured people' who threatened to swamp the ancestral territory of the Latvian peoples.[30] A handful of delegates even went so far as to advocate the repatriation of Russian communities.[31]

This conception of nation-ness contrasted with a *civic* nationalism. In keeping with a tradition of pluralist citizenship and tolerance towards ethnic difference as found in the Baltic States during the 1920s, emphasis was placed on the importance of individual as much as national rights. It was an inclusionary conception of community, designed to mobilise all those who lived and worked within the territories of the republics, to identify with and feel that they had a stake in national self-determination. It was reflected in efforts by moderates within the popular fronts to de-emphasise national exclusivism which included establishing pluralistically-structured cultural associations within their movements, with the explicit aim of broadening membership to include ethnic minorities. Yet despite efforts to project the idea of moving towards a multi-ethnic polity, the Russian communities, particularly in Latvia and Estonia, remained decidedly uneasy about supporting a nationalist cause whose rhetoric and legislative actions reflected concern about their presence in an alien homeland.

The ascendancy of ethnic nationalism however had a further reactive effect among minorities within all three republics, formalised in late 1988 with the establishment of Russian dominated counter-movements. At the Founding Congress of the Estonian counter-movement, *Interdvizhenie*, held in March 1989, delegates complained about the 'Estonianisation of Soviet Estonia' and in particular of language and citizenship laws which threatened their social marginalisation. Similar fears of 'nativisation' were voiced by counter-movements in Latvia (*Interfront*) and in Lithuania (*Yedinstvo*) where the republics' large Polish majority were also active. Unlike the popular fronts however, support for the counter-movements was more limited, both to particular places (especially strong in the large industrial cities and in north-east Estonia where Russians comprised over four-fifths of the population) and to particular social strata (blue-collar workers, army officers, economic managers, party apparatchiks). For the Balts these characteristically conservative pro-federal movements symbolised at best an attempt to halt the transition towards greater national self-determination and at worst a return to Brezhnev-style rule. Yet there is evidence to suggest that such limited support as existed among the Russian communities for the counter-movements was giving way to support for independent statehood. This sea-change was evident in all three republics including the region's largest Russian community, in Latvia. By 1990, nearly two-fifths of Russian speakers in the republic were supporting independent statehood, a proportion even higher among younger Russians.[32] This trend towards supporting statehood was also later confirmed in the March 1991 Latvian referendum.[33] Although the one-third of Russians who declared their support for independent statehood was markedly lower than the overall 73.7 per cent of the population who voted 'yes', it was nonetheless significant insuring majorities for independent statehood even in those cities, like Riga and Daugavpils, where Russians predominated (Figure 5). Despite the envisaged prospects of becoming 'second class citizens' in a Latvian-dominated polity, it is probable that for many Russians life in a Western-style economy was judged as more favourable than remaining part of a Soviet Union unable to guarantee basic housing, employment and essential services.

Declarations of Independent Statehood

The third and final phase in the development of the secessionist movements was characterised by the popular fronts gaining control of the republic supreme soviets and of the peripheralisation of the Communist Parties as instruments of central control. In this final stage, which led to formal declarations by the supreme soviets of independent statehood, Lithuania led the way and on 11 March 1990 proclaimed the restoration of the sovereign powers of the Lithuanian state. The supreme soviets of Estonia and Latvia followed on 30 March and 4 May respectively although only going so far as to declare their intention to re-establish independent states.

There were two major preconditions to the Baltic States reaching this historic stage. The first were the 1989 and 1990 elections to the supreme soviets, the first democratic elections to be held since the inter-war years. In all three republics, popular front backed candidates won majorities in their respective legislatures with support for *Sajudis* being particularly striking, winning 100 of the 136 seats in the March 1990 election.[34] The second major development was the Baltic Communist Parties' split with

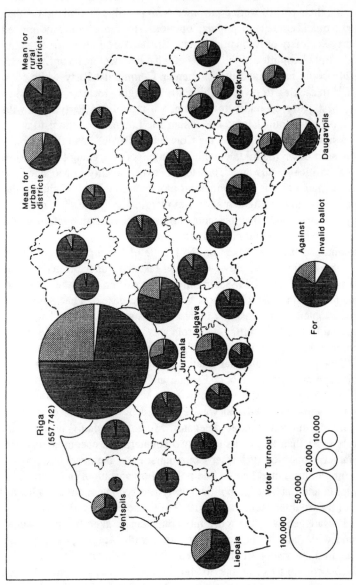

Figure 5 Latvia's referendum, 1991

Moscow. Throughout 1989, all three parties had seen many of their members go over to the popular fronts. Local Party leaders therefore acknowledged that their parties were confronted with possible annihilation if they could not quickly adapt to popular opinion. The more radically-minded First Party Secretary of Lithuania, Agidas Brazauskas, drew to the attention of the Central Committee of the CPSU of what that decline meant. In 1989, only 824 people had joined the Lithuanian Communist Party while 6500 had left.[35] In seeking to revitalise his Party's flagging fortunes, Brazauskas was the first party secretary to announce a republican Party split with Moscow. A few months later, the Estonian and Latvian Communist Parties followed suit. As a consequence, the Communist Parties in all three republics were split down the middle, with only a minority arguing for retention of the geopolitical status quo. Thus torn between loyalty to Moscow and support for national self-determination, most communists had chosen the latter course. With the fragmentation and marginalisation of the Communist Party, it was unlikely that the centre's influence over Baltic affairs could have been regained without military intervention.

Lithuania had therefore taken on the mantle of leading the secessionist cause in the Baltic States. However it had taken it rather belatedly from Estonia which from April 1988 certainly, if not earlier, had taken the lead but, no doubt fearing that it had more to lose in the case of a backlash from Moscow, adopted an increasingly more cautious stance.[36] What had however secured Lithuania's cutting-edge role was its less complex ethnopolitical demography. Unlike its Baltic neighbours, Lithuania did not have to deal with the precarious national balance of ethnic politics. This contrasted with the supreme soviets of both Estonia and Latvia, where the struggle between those who defended the status quo and the proponents of change was more evenly balanced and was reinforced by the presence of more conservatively minded Russian delegates. Moreover *Sajudis'* power base was far broader than that of its other two counterparts, encompassing not only a larger proportion of former Communist Party members but also an ethnic community united behind one political organisation. In contrast, in both Estonia and Latvia ethnopolitical unity had become more complex as a result of the establishment in early 1989 of the so called 'congress movements'. Dissatisfied with the more moderate stance taken by the popular fronts and with their willingness to negotiate with Moscow, these movements secured mass support among their ethnic constituents for resurrecting 'citizen committees' similar to the 'committees of correspondence' which prepared the way for the American Revolution of the 1770s. In calling up the legitimacy of the pre-war republics as the basis for the next step towards independent statehood, they argued that only those citizens and their descendants of the pre-1940 republics should have the right to declare their nation's future. In both Estonia and Latvia, they succeeded in registering most of their respective eponymous ethnic groups. So although the 'congress movements' did much to radicalise nationalist politics in Estonia and Latvia, they nonetheless exposed a tension within the secessionist cause between radicals and moderates. In Lithuania, by contrast, *Sajudis* was able to move quickly towards endorsing the secessionist cause, taking with it both moderates and radicals.

MOSCOW'S RESPONSE

The Baltic republics represented a paradox for Moscow throughout this transitional period. On the one hand, of all the Soviet republics it was Estonia, Latvia and Lithuania that were envisaged as likely to be most receptive to perestroika. Indeed Gorbachev gave his blessing to the setting up of grassroots-based movements in the region precisely because the Baltic was considered as the most likely flagship which the other republics would follow. Consequently, for the first time in half a century Baltic civil society was invited to participate in an experiment in socio-economic and political reform. On the other hand it quickly became apparent to Moscow that the Baltic peoples wanted to go much further down the path to national self-determination than the centre's reformers had envisaged or were prepared to allow. So underpinning this paradox was Moscow's miscalculation both of the scale of national feeling in the least Sovietised of the republics and the effectiveness of a programme of reform that assumed that embarking upon economic and social restructuring would somehow automatically resolve the question of Baltic national self-determination.

From the outset, the Gorbachev administration provided little indication that nationalism was likely to prove problematic in the Baltic republics or elsewhere in the Soviet Union. At the 27th Party Congress in 1986, in his first major pronouncement on the nationalities question, Gorbachev showed little sign of departing from the Brezhnevite line. Much continued to be made of a united Soviet people (*Sovetskii narod*), 'cemented by the same economic interests, ideology and political goals'[37] although he did acknowledge that such achievements 'must not create the impression that there are no problems in the national processes. Contradictions are inherent in any kind of development, and are unavoidable in this sphere as well'.[38] So while accepting that there did exist a problematic side to the nationalities question as manifested in occasional 'national isolationism, localism and parasitism',[39] such behaviour did not warrant sufficient concern to be incorporated into the reform programme. Indeed it was not until early 1988, following some twelve months of ethnic demonstrations in the Baltic Republics and of riots in Transcaucasia and Kazakhstan that Gorbachev was prepared to acknowledge that there was a nationalities problem. But even at this stage he seemed reluctant to tackle the question head on. This was also reflected in the belated setting up of a Special Party Platform to look into the nationalities question. Although its formation was announced in early 1988 it was not until the summer of 1989 that the Platform eventually met and only then to go so far as to recommend 'a revitalised socialist federation' which by that time fell far short of the more radical expectations of the Baltic Republics. And even as late as January 1990, in a visit to Vilnius designed to convince Lithuanians of the problems of moving further down the path toward secession, Gorbachev managed to add more fuel to the nationalist fire by declaring that 'the national question is not the most important issue in human affairs'.[40]

In the absence of a nationalities policy towards the Baltic States, Moscow in effect practised the politics of muddling through, in which it simply reacted to events as they unfolded in the region. As Tarasevich, Chairman of the Commission on National Policy and Inter-Ethnic Relations of the USSR Supreme Soviet was to note in December 1990, throughout Moscow 'was overcautious ... it did not seize the initiative that was coming from the republics'.[41] Thus due to its inability to accommodate questions of national self-determination raised in the Baltic, Moscow rapidly lost control of events. The first clear sign of this came in Gorbachev's mishandling of the so-called Estonian constitutional crisis of November 1988 following proposals to revise constitutional relations between the centre and union republics but which excluded the right of the republics to secede from the Union.[42] The Estonian Supreme Soviet was quick to respond by adopting a declaration of sovereignty by which Estonian laws were to be given precedence over All-Union legislation. Estonia could in effect veto Soviet laws that violated the rights of its republic. Although Moscow reacted by declaring the Estonian declaration to be invalid, in effect it backed down. In seizing the initiative, Estonia had won an important victory over Moscow.

While initially Moscow seemed prepared to practise limited appeasement, from the autumn of 1989 it began to take a tougher and less flexible position. In response to what was interpreted in Moscow as intransigent 'nationalist hysteria' in the Baltic Republics, concern was voiced by conservatives and reformers alike that the region was sliding towards political anarchy. On 26 August 1989, following 'the human chain' demonstration of Baltic solidarity, the CPSU Central Committee warned of the disastrous consequences of going down the road of independence: 'The fate of the

Baltic peoples is in serious danger', it noted. 'People should know into what abyss they are being pushed by nationalist leaders. The consequences could be disastrous for these people if the nationalists manage to achieve their goals. The very viability of the Baltic nations could be called into question'.[43] It was, however, following Lithuania's declaration of independent statehood that the Gorbachev regime's commitment to keeping the Baltic republics as part of the Soviet federation at any cost became most apparent. Gorbachev refused to negotiate with the Lithuanian authorities until the latter undertook to suspend its independence declaration. Although no doubt military intervention was considered by Moscow against the recalcitrant republic, instead Gorbachev opted for the imposition of economic sanctions. Faced with enormous economic difficulties, including the cutting-off of its energy supplies, Lithuania had little option but to agree to a moratorium on its independence declaration in return for Moscow lifting the blockade. It was, however, to be the centre's first and last victory. Although Moscow had attempted to regain the initiative, it no longer possessed either a loyal local party machinery to rescue a power base in the region or the inclination to bridge the gap between the political demands of the Balts and its own intransigent position on secessionism. In a last-ditch attempt to appease the secessionists, the USSR Supreme Soviet had adopted a law on secession in April 1990. Given however that for secession to occur support from two-thirds of its permanent residents was necessary, as well as a five-year waiting period, this was generally interpreted in the Baltic States as a strategy designed to prevent secession.[44] Paradoxically, however, just as it had been events at the centre which had set in train the national reawakening, so it was the failed August 1991 coup in Moscow that finally brought to an end 50 years of Soviet rule in the Baltic republics.

ACKNOWLEDGEMENTS

The author wishes to thank both the Institute of Peace Studies, Washington DC and the Leverhulme Trust for their financial support.

NOTES

1. G. Smith, 'The State, Nationalism and the Nationalities Question in the Soviet Republics', in C. Merridale and C. Ward (eds) *Perestroika. The Historical Perspective* (London, 1991), pp. 202–16.

2. V. Bunce, 'The Political Economy of the Brezhnev era', *British Journal of Political Science*, 1983, p. 134.
3. D. Bahry, *Outside Moscow, Power, Politics and Budgetary Policy in the Soviet Republics* (New York, 1987).
4. V.S. Vardys, 'Polish echoes in the Baltic', *Problems of Communism*, vol. 32 (4), 1983, pp. 21–34.
5. By the mid 1980s the eponymous nationalities were still under-represented in their respective communist parties. In Latvia, Latvians constituted 52 per cent of the population but only 39.7 per cent of party members (*Padomju Latvijas Kommunists*, no. 6, June 1989, p. 29), in Estonia, Estonians made up 64.7 per cent of the population but only 50.8 per cent of Party members and in Lithuania, Lithuanians comprised 80.0 per cent of the population and 70 per cent of Party members (R. Misiunas, 'The Baltic Republics: Stagnation and Sovereignty', in L. Hajda and M. Beissinger (eds), *The Nationalities Factor in Soviet Politics and Society* (Boulder, Colo., 1990), pp. 204–27.
6. L. Rybakovskii and N. Tarasava, 'Migratsionnyi potessy v SSSR: Novye yavleniya', *Sotsiologicheskie issledovaniya*, no. 7, 1990, p. 40.
7. G. Schroeder, 'Nationalities and the Soviet Economy', in L. Hajda and M. Beissinger (eds), *op. cit.*, pp. 43–71.
8. *Pravda*, 22 December 1972.
9. *Pravda*, 5 October 1977.
10. V. Zaslavsky, 'Success and Collapse. Traditional Soviet Nationality Policy, in I. Bremmer and R. Taras (eds) *Nations and Politics in the Soviet Successor States* (Cambridge, 1991), p. 37.
11. For a fuller discussion of ethnic tensions in the Baltic region, see G. Smith (ed.) *The Nationalities Question in the Soviet Union*, London, 1990, pp. 39–91.
12. D. Bahry, op. cit.
13. J. Dreifelds, 'Latvian National Rebirth', *Problems of Communism*, vol. 38, no. 4, 1989, p. 81.
14. *Tass*, 25 February 1987.
15. *Lietartura Maksla*, 10 June 1988.
16. *Sovetskaya Latviya*, 12 August 1988.
17. Ibid.
18. V.S. Vardys, 'Lithuanian National Politics', *Problems of Communism*, vol. 39, 1990, p. 57.
19. For summaries of the programmes of the respective popular fronts see the following: *Narodnyi Kongress: Sbornik materialov kongressa Narodnogo Fronta Estonii*, (Tallinn, 1988); *Narodnyi Front Latvii, Programma* (Riga, 1988); *Osnovnye dokumenty vtorogo s"ezda saidisa* (Vilnius, 1990).
20. Personal interview with Romualdas Razukas, Chairman of the Popular Front of Latvia, Riga, 15 September 1992.
21. See, for example, A.E Senn, *Lithuania Awakening* (Berkeley, 1990).
22. *Homeland*, 23 August 1989.
23. Vestnik Ministerstva inostrannykh del SSSR, no. 2(60), 31 January 1990, pp. 7–16.
24. A. Buchanan, *Secession. The Morality of Political Divorce from Port Sumter to Lithuania and Quebec* (Boulder, Colo., 1991).

25. Reuters Dispatch, 27 July 1989. See Radio Liberty, *Report on the USSR*, vol. 1, no. 40, 6 October 1989, p. 14.
26. *Sovetskaya Molodezh*, 7 September 1988.
27. Gorbachev's speech to the CPSU Central Committee on 19 September 1989. *Pravda*, 21 September 1989.
28. Narodnyi Kongress, *op. cit.*, pp. 171–97.
29. Ibid.
30. Resolution no. 8 as cited in E. Rundenschiold, 'Ethnic Dimension in Contemporary Latvian Politics: Focusing Forces For Change', *Soviet Studies*, vol. 44, no. 4, 1992, p. 613.
31. Ibid.
32. Rudenschiold, op. cit.
33. *Diena*, 5 March 1991.
34. *Lieutuvos Aidas*, 10 March 1990.
35. *Lieutuvos Aides*, 28 December 1989.
36. R. Taagepera, 'Estonia's Road to Independence', *Problems of Communism*, November/December, vol. 38, 1989, pp. 11–26.
37. M. Gorbachev, *Politicheskii doklad tsentral'nogo komitera KPSS XXVII Sezdu Kommunisticheskoi Partii Sovetskogo Soyuza* (Moscow, 1986), p. 101.
38. Ibid, p. 101.
39. Ibid.
40. *Pravda*, 16 January 1990.
41. *Pravda*, 10 December 1990.
42. *Rahva Haal*, 25–26 October 1988.
43. *Pravda*, 27 August 1989.
44. *Pravda*, 28 April 1990.

6 The Political Leadership
Andrus Park

Central to comprehending the nature and form that the transition to independent statehood took in the period leading up to and since the establishment of Baltic independence is the role played by the region's political leaders. There are clearly a whole variety of questions which need to be asked with regard to this political leadership. This would certainly involve considering whether it would have been possible for Baltic communist leaders to continue ruling after 1985 without paying attention to the pressures for reform; the extent to which the Baltic leadership were really connected with the Communist Party; how far the Popular Front leaders in 1988–9 wanted to reform the communist system or destroy it; whether the Baltic leadership in 1985–91 had a coherent political strategy or were mainly reacting to the opportunities of the moment; and whether or not they acted rationally, assuming that political independence is a necessary condition for successful economic reform. In this chapter, however, an examination of the political leadership in the Baltic republics between 1985 and 1991 focuses on the following three propositions: firstly, that the concept of political leadership itself becomes increasingly ambiguous during revolutionary transitions because a number of competing power centres and leaders emerge who all claim to be more legitimate than others; secondly, revolutionary transitions are usually connected with changes of leadership. In the case of the Baltic republics a number of transitions took place during this six-year period, all of which were marked by a radicalisation of the revolutionary process and in which parallels as well as differences did exist between the leadership in each republic; and finally, the Baltic experience is not unusual in post-communist transitions in that it is the intelligentsia who form a substantial part of the new political leaderships.

LEADERS AND THE PLURALISM OF POWER

In focusing on the Estonian political leadership during this transitional period we cannot readily assume who its leaders were. After all, periods of revolutionary change are usually marked by more than one power centre, by more than one group of legitimate or quasi-legitimate political leaders. Several possible approaches lend themselves to such identification.

144

Firstly, few would disagree with the claim that the real top political leadership of Estonia until at least the summer of 1988 was not in Tallinn, but in the Kremlin, and more specifically in the CPSU Politburo. According to this viewpoint, any serious study of the Estonian leadership of that period should first of all focus on Moscow. Yet, secondly, it could be legitimately argued that since most local power in 1985–91 in Estonia was concentrated in the hands of the Soviet power structures or their immediate successor institutions, the leading officials in these institutions can be identified as the top political leadership. For example, until the summer of 1988 the most powerful political position in Estonia was undoubtedly that of the First Secretary of the Estonian Communist Party (a division of the CPSU). Since 1988 the power of the Communist Party secretaries began to erode with increasing speed. After the March 1990 parliamentary elections the leaders of the different factions of the disintegrating Communist Party maintained some of their power mainly because they were members of the newly elected parliament or because of their ties with the Soviet Army or other USSR institutions. So the First Secretary of the Estonian Communist Party can be counted as a member of the top political leadership perhaps until 1988. With the decline of the Communist Party, the whole traditional communist power system (comprising the Central Committee and its *Buro*, similar committees at lower levels, etc.) also collapsed. The post of the Chairman of the Presidium of the Supreme Soviet was quite powerless at the beginning of perestroika, but became increasingly important after 1988. Following the March 1990 elections, the Chairman of the Supreme Council clearly emerged as the highest and most important state official of the republic. Of course, it is possible to debate endlessly in what sense and how much the Chairman of the Supreme Council and the Prime Minister had at different stages after March 1990 'real power'.

Thirdly, some political leaders can be identified also on the basis of the Congress of Estonia given that between 1990 and 1991 it functioned as an alternative parliament. Its members were elected in February–March 1990 by the people who were either citizens of the pre-war republic of Estonia, their descendants, or who applied for citizenship through the citizens' committees. On 11–12 March 1990 the Congress of Estonia had its first session and elected a 78-member strong Estonian Committee.[1] Although throughout the period 1990–1 the Congress of Estonia did not possess much real power, it first functioned as an important forum for the right-wing opposition to the Popular Front controlled government. Later its role was much strengthened when in August–September 1991 the Supreme Council and the Congress of Estonia formed together a 60-member Assembly to draft a new Constitution for the Republic of Estonia, to which each delegated 30 representatives.[2]

Fourthly, a number of local representative councils and government organs in the Russian-populated areas of Estonia at least until August 1991 attempted to oppose the government in Tallinn and co-ordinate their actions with the USSR authorities in Moscow. This political élite from the Russian-speaking communities can also be considered when defining the political leadership in Estonia in 1985–91. Similarly we may consider the role of various local functionaries, representing directly the powers in Moscow: officers of the Soviet armed forces, KGB officials, officials of the Soviet military-industrial complex in Estonia, and so on.

Fifthly, there was a real mushrooming of political movements and parties in Estonia in the period 1987–91 and the leaders of these organisations unquestionably represented part of the political leadership in Estonia. The number of political parties and movements as well as their alliances and ideological orientations were and are constantly changing. Before August 1991, we can divide all these parties and movements into four broad categories: right wing radical national organisations that dominated the leadership of the Congress of Estonia (The Estonian National Independence Party, Estonian Conservative People's Party, Estonian Christian Democratic Party, etc.); The popular front-related centrist organisations (Popular Front of Estonia, Estonian Social Democratic Party, Estonian Rural Centre Party, etc.); the Estonian reform-communist and quasi-communist organisations (Estonian Communist Party, Free Estonia Group); and finally, the 'Russian organisations' which until August 1991 mostly supported the communist ideology and the preservation of the USSR and most of which were banned or suspended after the coup in August 1991 (the pro-Moscow wing of the Estonian Communist Party, the Inter-Movement, the United Council of Work Collectives, etc).[3]

After Estonia gained independence in the autumn of 1991, the party-political structure changed even further. On 30 August 1991 a non-communist Russian Democratic Movement was established in Tallinn which signalled a political sea change among the Russian community; on 5 September 1991 Prime Minister Edgar Savisaar created his own Centre People's Party; on 27 September some right-wing parties (the Conservative People's Party, the Christian-Democratic Party, the Christian-Democratic Movement, the Republican Coalition Party) established an electoral bloc, 'Fatherland', which signalled a trend towards the consolidation of right-wing forces; and on 8 December 1991 a group of ministers and ex-ministers of Savisaar's government founded a new centre-right Coalition Party under the leadership of Jaak Tamm, reflecting a growing opposition to Savisaar's government among the economic establishment.[4]

Sixthly and finally, the broader notion of the composition of leadership can be identified also on the basis of public opinion polls. It has been a tradition in Estonia since 1988 to compile lists of the most popular politicians by various public opinion research organisations. Although these lists do not reflect the composition of any formal governmental or state body, they are often the best source in identifying the most powerful top political leaders.

The moral here seems to be that *the concept of political leadership itself becomes increasingly ambiguous during revolutionary transitions because a number of competing power centres and leaders emerge who all claim to be more legitimate than others*. Space precludes an analysis of all these power structures and their leadership patterns. Instead, consideration can be given to leadership changes, in which it is important to take into account Soviet structures, their successor institutions and public opinion polls.

TRANSITIONS AND LEADERSHIP CHANGES

It is a truism that revolutionary transitions are usually connected with changes in leadership. The French and Russian revolutions or Germany between 1918 and 1933 are clear evidence of this. The revolutionary transitions to independence in the Baltic States in 1917–20 and 1985–91 were also connected with changes in leadership. But both transitions to independence also indicate that often there is also some element of continuity in revolutionary transitions.

During the 1917–20 transition to independence, some of the Estonian political leadership were also part of the pre-1917 political establishment. The trademark of this continuity was represented by a number of politicians. This would include Jaan Poska (1866–1920), who was mayor of Tallinn from 1913 to 1917, then the Commissar of the Russian Provisional Government for Estonia in 1917, and subsequently Minister of Justice, Acting Prime Minister and Foreign Minister in independent Estonia.[5] In contrast, Jaan Tõnisson (born 1868) represented a career pattern not so strongly connected with the Russian pre-1917 establishment. From 1896 he was a newspaper editor in Estonia, twelve years later a member of the Russian state Duma, by 1917 member of the Estonian Provincial Assembly, and of the Estonian Constituent Assembly, Prime Minister in 1919–20, and the Estonian State Elder (i.e. the head of government) in 1927–8 and in 1933.[6] Konstantin Päts (1874–1956) symbolises even more discontinuity with the pre-1917 establishment. At the beginning of the century he was active as a lawyer and political activist in Tallinn, also editing a newspaper.

In 1905 he was an aide to the mayor of Tallinn, in 1905–11 in exile and then in prison because of his revolutionary activities. Since 1917 Päts was again active in politics as Prime Minister of the First Provisional Government (1918–19), then the State Elder for short periods in 1923–4, 1931–2, 1932–3, 1933–4. In March 1934 Päts carried out a coup, suppressing the fascist movement but ruling at the head of an authoritarian until 1940.[7] Johan Laidoner (1884–1953) is another figure worthy of mention and who exemplifies an element of continuity between the middle-level officer corps of the Russian army and the top leadership of the Estonian forces. As a colonel in the Imperial Russian Army he participated in the First World War, then served as a commander of the 1st Estonian national division (1917–18), than as Commander-in-Chief of the Estonian forces. He also organised the suppressed coup against the communists in 1924. Ten years later he helped Päts secure power, after which he acted as the highest military official in Estonia until he was arrested in 1940 and deported to Russia.[8]

In the post-1985 transitional period at least *three main changes of leadership in Estonia* between 1985 and 1991 can be detected in which elements of both discontinuity and continuity in leadership are identifiable: hardline communist leadership phase (March 1985 to June 1988); reform communist leadership (June 1988 to March 1990); and from March 1990 a period of post-communist leadership. We can consider each phase in turn.

1985–90: Two Transitions

The locus of power at the dawn of perestroika in Estonia was clearly the Communist Party. Johannes Käbin had presided as Communist Party First Secretary for 28 years (1950–1978), from the period of the Stalinist mass repressions to the era of Brezhnevist stagnation.[9] In 1978 Käbin was replaced by Karl Vaino who remained First Secretary until 1988. Vaino was born in Siberia in 1923, moved to Estonia in 1947 and became a Central Committee Secretary in 1960.[10] The post of head of the government (Chairman of the Council of Ministers) was in January 1984 – on the eve of perestroika – awarded to Bruno Saul, a native Estonian and engineer, who remained at this post until 1988. The third leading figure in 1985 in Estonia was Arnold Rüütel. He was nominated Chairman of the Presidium of the Supreme Soviet in the Estonian SSR in 1983. Born in 1928, Arnold Rüütel worked for a number of years as Rector of the Estonian Agricultural Academy (1969–77), then as one of the Secretaries of the Central Committee of the Estonian Communist Party (1977–79) and as First Deputy Chairman of the Council of Ministers (1979–83).

The hardline communist leadership of Karl Vaino lacked support from Gorbachev and was unable to adjust to the democratic opposition movement which was gradually growing in strength from early 1987. Although towards the end of his rule Vaino attempted to prolong his power by sacrificing subordinates (for example in January 1988 the unpopular Secretary for Ideology, Rein Ristlaan, was replaced by a liberal, Indrek Toome), his rule finally came to the end in June 1988.

By June 1988 however, we can identify the beginning of a second phase, that of the *reform-communist* leadership.[11] It started when the Brezhnevite First Secretary of the Estonian Communist Party, Karl Vaino, was replaced by Vaino Väljas.[12] Born in 1931, Väljas had worked since 1961 as the First Secretary of the Communist Party organisation in Tallinn and from 1971 until 1980 as one of the Secretaries of the Central Committee of the Estonian Communist Party.[13] In 1978 Väljas was one of the main contenders for the post of the First Secretary of the ECP, but the Politburo in Moscow preferred a Siberian-born Karl Väino.[14] Two years later Väljas was transferred to the post of Soviet Ambassador, first in Venezuela (1980–6), and later in Nicaragua (1986–8).

The new First Secretary co-opted a number of relatively liberally-minded scholars and cultural figures into the Communist Party leadership. Mikk Titma (born 1939), a professor of sociology at the Estonian Academy of Sciences was made a Central Committee Secretary in charge of ideology (he occupied that post until the virtual collapse of the Communist Party in the winter of 1990). A painter and a Popular Front activist, Enn Põldroos, (born 1933) and an eminent computer scientist, Boris Tamm (born 1930), were included in the Buro of the Party's Central Committee. In November 1988 Indrek Toome replaced Bruno Saul as Chairman of the Council of Ministers and remained in that office until the March 1990 elections. A wide range of changes among lower-level personalities also took place in the Communist Party Central Committee, and in both central and local government.

Vaino Väljas and his colleagues neither resisted the pressure by the Popular Front and other opposition movements toward greater republican autonomy nor later Estonia's political secession from the USSR. This reform-communist phase was marked by such moves as the Estonian declaration of sovereignty, campaigns for economic self-management, and official reassessment of the 1940 occupation of Estonia by the Stalinist regime. By the spring of 1990 the authority of the Estonian Communist party had been eroded, and it quickly disappeared from the centre stage of Estonian political life.

March 1990: The Third Transition

The final phase, that of the post-communist leadership, began following the
March 1990 Supreme Council elections in which one of the most prominent leaders of the Popular Front, Edgar Savisaar, was nominated as Prime
Minister. Savisaar was born in 1950, obtained a Candidate of Sciences
degree in Philosophy[15] and taught philosophy on a part-time basis in the
Estonian Academy of Sciences while working as a middle level official in
the Soviet Estonian state apparatus. He was undoubtedly part of the
reformist wing of the Soviet Estonian establishment. Savisaar's government was to include technocrats and specialists like the Minister of Finance
Rein Miller, academics such as the Minister of Economics, Jaak Leiman
and the Minister of Labour, Arvo Kuddo, as well as a writer (Lennart
Meri), a physicist (Endel Lippmaa), and a musician (Lepo Sumera).
Savisaar's government was to remain in power until January 1992 when it
resigned amid economic crisis and political struggles between factions of
the Supreme Council. Lippmaa and some other prominent ministers had
earlier resigned from the government.[16]

Savisaar's government was accused by right-wing critics of being socialist or semi-socialist and too accommodative towards both Russia and Estonia's Russian-speaking minorities. His personal style of leadership was
also considered by his opponents to be too authoritarian.[17] Although introducing some reforms, the Savisaar administration was unable to solve a
number of central political and economic questions such as the citizenship
issue (see Chapter 8), the fuel crisis connected with the decline of supplies
with Russia, inflation, the food crisis, and privatisation.[18]

During its tenure, the Savisaar government moved clearly to the left,
relying more on the Russian faction in parliament. To understand the
pattern of political forces in the Estonian parliament it is instructive to look
at some crucial cases of voting. The 105-strong parliament voted on March
1990 declaring the transition period to independence; 73 deputies voted
for, three abstained and 29 (mainly Russian deputies, who were against
Estonian independence) did not register to participate in the voting, so
showing their opposition to the decision.[19] With some fluctuations, similar
patterns were displayed throughout 1990–1 when independence-related
decisons were taken in the Estonian parliament. On 20 August 1991 the
Estonian Supreme Council declared the end of the transition period and the
restoration of Estonia as an independent state. There were 104 members of
the parliament at that time, and 69 of them voted for, nobody voted against
or abstained, one was present but did not vote, and 34 deputies did not
attend the session.[20] It is probable that at least nine deputies among the 34

not attending would have voted for independence, the others being deputies who would probably have opposed Estonian independence. It should be taken into account that on 20 August 1991 the coup in Moscow was still in progress and many deputies were not able to attend the session of the parliament for good reasons.

Against this background it is also important to take into account the nature of support for Savisaar's government. Ninety-one deputies participated in the vote when Savisaar was nominated Prime Minister in 1990 (54 voted for, 32 against and five abstained).[21] The opposition to Savisaar came mainly from the Russian deputies and from the pro-communist groups. On 16 January 1992 the Estonian Supreme Soviet voted to introduce a government-proposed state of economic emergency in Estonia. Prime Minister Savisaar defined the nature of the state of economic emergency as the government's right 'to run the economy with its own decrees, and even to make decisions that contradict [Estonian] laws'.[22] Given the fact that Savisaar threatened to resign unless his government got the emergency powers he wanted, the voting pattern on 16 January is illustrative of the divisions in the Estonian parliament at the beginning of 1992. The total number of deputies of the Supreme Council in January 1992 was 103 (two deputies from the original number of 105 had earlier quit their posts). There were 96 deputies attending the session; seven were absent. Fifty-three deputies had supported the resolution concerning the state of economic emergency, 37 were against, four abstained and two did not participate in the vote.[23]

The support for Savisaar's government came this time mainly from two principal sources: the Popular Front-related centrist deputies and the non-Estonian deputies. On the other hand there were also at least two distinct groups among the opponents of Savisaar's government: deputies representing an anti-communist national-radical trend and former top communist officials and their allies. So between March 1990 and January 1992 Savisaar lost the confidence of most ethnic Estonians in parliament but gained the support of the country's Russian-speaking minority.

Perhaps this change in support was decisive for Savisaar's decision to resign in January 1992 in spite of the fact that he won the confidence vote in parliament on 16 January 1992 and that his formal support since 1990 had fallen by one vote.

One of the remarkable features of Estonian politics in 1985–91 was the continuing and growing importance of Chairman Arnold Rüütel, who was (re-)elected as Chairman of the Supreme Council in March 1990.[24] Although former communist officials in many other post-Soviet states (like Russia's Boris Yeltsin, Ukraine's Leonid Kravchuk or Latvia's Anatolijs

Gorbunovs) played an important role throughout this transition phase, Arnold Rüütel was notably unique in having occupied the position of Chairman since the time of Yurii Andropov. The explanation of Rüütel's ability to transform itself from the 'third man' in Soviet Estonia's ruling *nomenklatura* into the 'first man' in independent Estonia's post-communist hierarchy needs perhaps a separate study. But it is possible to list at least some factors that may have contributed to this. This would include Rüütel's ability to display public support for greater autonomy of Estonia in 1987–8 when other members of the pre-1985 leadership (e.g. Karl Vaino, Bruno Saul) tried to resist the changes; his ability to distance himself from current economic problems; and the fact that opposition movements were unable to produce leaders who were such impressive media performers. Since Estonia is a small country, its potential pool of leaders is naturally limited and there is a considerable degree of public personal knowledge about politicians. The personal charm of Rüütel undoubtedly played an important role in his continuing popularity from 1983 to 1991.

The 1985–91 events in Estonia – the transition from hardline communist to post-communist leadership – seems to support the thesis that *power passes in post-communist transitions into the hands of more and more radical and anti-communist leaders.* Though it is impossible to predict the exact nature of the future balance of political power, at least one trend seems to be most likely: if democracy survives, then within the coming years a number of weak and short-lived centre, centre-right or centre-left governments will emerge in Estonia.

CONTINUITY AND THE BACKGROUND OF LEADERS

It would seem that Estonian developments in 1985–91 lend claim to the proposition that intellectuals form a substantial part of the new political leadership in the post-communist transitions. An opinion poll concerning the popularity of politicans was carried out in September 1991 in which 650 people were questioned and in which later the names of the 30 most popular politicians were published (Table 6.1). This list can be used to analyse the socio-political background of élite recruitment in post-Soviet Estonia. Although there are clearly limitations in the accuracy and utility of such polls, the list serves at least as some orientational basis for analysing the background of the political leaders. It also enables us to construct a four-fold typology of the political leadership on the basis of their main publicly described activities in the period before 1985.[25]

Table 6.1 The popularity of Estonia's politicians

	Politician	Past/Background	Percentage of respondents supporting each politician
1	Arnold Rüütel	Chairman of the Supreme Soviet	86
2	Edgar Savisaar	Prime Minister	73
3	Ülo Nugis	Speaker of the Supreme Council	70
4	Marju Lauristin	Deputy Speaker of the Supreme Council	68
5	Lennart Meri	Foreign Minister	67
6	Endel Lippmaa	Minister without portfolio	63
7	Indrek Toome	Member of the Supreme Council	57
7	Rein Otsason	President of the Bank of Estonia	57
9	Enn Põldroos	Member of the Supreme Council	56
10	Rein Taagepera	Professor of the University of California	55
11	Siim Kallas	Trade Union leader	52
11	Heinz Valk	Member of the Supreme Council	52
11	Tiit Made	Member of the Supreme Council	52
14	Vaino Väljas	Member of the Supreme Council	51
14	Olev Laanjärv	Minister of the Interior	51
16	Andrus Öövel	Chief of the Border Defence	49
17	Siiri Oviir	Minister for Social Security	46
17	Tiit Käbin	Member of the Supreme Council	46
19	Enn Leisson	Member of the Supreme Council	44
20	Lepo Sumera	Minister of Culture	43
21	Andres Tarand	Member of the Supreme Council	42
21	Rein Veidemann	Member of the Supreme Council	42
23	Mart Laar	Member of the Supreme Council	40
23	Jaak Leimann	Minister of Economics	40
25	Paul-Erik Rummo	Consultant to the Government	38
26	Ingar Fjuk	Member of the Supreme Council	37
26	Tiit Vahi	Minister of Transport and Communications	37
26	Mikk Titma	Member of the Supreme Council	37
26	Lagle Parek	Chairman of the Estonian National Independence Party	37
30	Hardo Aasmäe	Mayor of Tallinn	35

Source: EMOR Poll, September 1991.

The first group includes persons who in 1980–85 had top positions in the Soviet Estonian state or Communist Party structures. It includes Arnold

Rüütel, and Indrek Toome. With some simplification we can perhaps include also Vaino Väljas into that group, although in 1980 he left his Communist Party secretaryship for the post of Soviet Ambassador in Venezuela.

Secondly, there is a group of politicians who held only middle-level or low-level administrative positions in the Soviet Estonian state and economy. Edgar Savisaar can be included in this group, although, as we have already noted, he did work part-time in the Academy of Sciences and was very closely connected with the intelligentsia. Other persons who can be included in this group are Siiri Oviir (worked in the High Court), Olev Laanjarv (worked in the Ministry of the Interior), Siim Kallas (worked as a head of the Central Office of the Savings Bank), Tiit Vähi (worked as a manager of a transport enterprise) and Ülo Nugis (worked as the director of a factory). The third group comprises personalities who in the interval 1980–85 earned their living mainly as writers, composers, architects and other creative artists (Lennart Meri,[26] Enn Põldroos, Heinz Valk, Lepo Sumera, Paul-Erik Rummo,[27] Ingar Fjuk) or scholars in various fields, ranging from molecular biology to applied economic research (Marju Lauristin,[28] Endel Lippmaa, Rein Otsason, Rein Taagepera, Tiit Made, Tiit Käbin, Andres Tarand, Jaak Leimann, Mikk Titma,[29] Hardo Aasmäe). And finally there is a fourth group (active dissidents and human rights campaigners) which really only includes Lagle Parek, a political prisoner from 1983 to 1987.[30]

As in the other two Baltic states as well as in many of the other former socialist countries (eg. the Czech Republic, Hungary, Russia), one of the most obvious features of Estonian politics has been the transition of intellectuals to power. In authoritarian states intellectuals have to function in a civil society in which there is little social space for political activity. During democratic transitions, however, the role of intellectuals changes dramatically: some become politicians, other sections of the intelligentisia become engaged in areas like the free press, popular mass culture, and business. A minority will continue as producers of high culture which although no longer censored by the state is by and large marginal to a market society for economic reasons.

As already indicated, the role of the former top and middle-level communist officials in the Estonian political leadership at the end of 1991 was quite high. Yet the role of figures with a dissident background was more moderate. In this period Estonia certainly did not have its Vaclav Havel or Lech Walesa. The leadership background pattern in Estonia in 1985–91 was more akin to that of most other post-Soviet republics and less similar to that of the Czech Republic or Poland.

THE BALTIC STATES IN COMPARATIVE PERSPECTIVE

The Estonian case is in many respects is similar to that of Latvia and Lithuania, particularly with regard to the radicalisation of the leadership and the role of intellectuals. There are however some differences in the nature of their leadership transitions. The transition from communist to non-communist leadership in 1985–91 was more profound in Lithuania than in Estonia or Latvia. For example Vytautas Landsbergis, the highest state official in Lithuania until the March 1993 elections, came into politics from his university position as an anti-Communist *Sajudis* leader. This contrasts with the top leaders of Estonia and Latvia who were both former top-ranking communist officials. Latvia followed Estonia in creating a congress of Estonia-type alternative parliament, but no such structure emerged in Lithuania. The Lithuanian popular front *Sajudis* established itself as a right-wing nationalist political force, whereas in Estonia the Popular Front occupied a more centrist position, leaving the 'political space' in the right for groups like Fatherland or the Estonian National Independence Party. The left wing of Lithuanian politics was also different from that of Estonia. Following its split with Moscow in December 1989,[31] the Lithuanian Communist Party gained some legitimacy and was able to transform itself in 1990–91 into the main leftist party in Lithuania, whereas the Communist Party of Estonia played only a marginal role in that year. One commentator rightly observed in 1992 that in Lithuania 'the only two parties with grassroots support are the former communists (now renamed the Democratic Labour Party) headed by their popular leader Algirdas Brazauskas, and Sajudis, once a broad-based pro-independence movement, but now a distinctly right-of-centre political party, closely tied to Mr. Landsbergis'.[32] The Latvian case seems to be a mixture of both Estonian and Lithuanian situations although more similar to Estonia than to Lithuania.

NOTES

1. *Revue Baltique*, vol. 2, February 1991, p. 133.
2. On the Constituent Assembly see: 'Põhiseadus tulekul' (The Constitution is Coming), *Eesti Jurist*, 1991, no. 5, pp. 315–16.
3. The voting pattern of the non-Estonian population in Estonia during the 1990 Supreme Council elections is interesting. The 'Russian democrats' (i.e. Russian candidates who were supported by the mainstream Estonian political organisations) secured (according to some estimates) only 3.8 per cent of the non-Estonian votes, whereas up to 50 per cent of non-Estonians may have

voted for ethnic Estonian candidates. It seems that most 'pro-Estonian' Russians voted for Estonian candidates and therefore conservative and pro-USSR candidates were naturally victorious among the Russian candidates. See also: Oleg Samorodni, 'Stanovleniye mnogopartiinosti v Estonii v 1988–1990 gody', *Proceedings of the Estonian Academy of Sciences, Social Sciences*, 1991, no. 3, p. 224.

4. *Poliitika*, 1991, no. 11, pp. 2–3.
5. Cf. Richard Kleis, ed., *Väike entsüklopeedia* (*Small Encyclopedia*), Tartu, 1937, p. 1183.
6. Richard Kleis, ed., *Eesti entsüklopeedia*, vol. VIII, Tartu, 1937, pp. 440–3. Jaan Tonisson was arrested in 1940 by the Soviets and his date of death is not known. Some materials, reflecting his interrogation by the Soviet security organs, were recently published: *Eesti Jurist*, 1991, no. 4, pp. 270–80 and 1991, no. 5, pp. 342–53.
7. Cf. Richard Kleis, *Eesti entsüklopeedia*, vol. VI, Tartu: Loodus, 1936, pp. 1251–4.
8. Cf. Richard Kleis, *Eesti entsüklopeedia*, vol. V, Tartu: Loodus, 1935, pp. 137–9.
9. See Lembit Valt, ed., *Soviet Estonia*, Tallinn: Valgus, 1980, pp. 125–8.
10. See for example: Toivo U. Raun, *Estonia and the Estonians*, 2nd edition, Stanford, Calif.: Hoover Institution Press, 1991, p. 192.
11. Toivo Raun has rightly observed that 'the year 1988 began the transition from a one-party system to pluralism in Estonian politics' (Toivo Raun, 'The re-establishment of Estonian Independence', *Journal of Baltic Studies*, vol. 22, Fall 1991, p. 252).
12. See *Revue Baltique*, vol. 2, no. 1, February 1991, p. 132.
13. See Gustav Naan, ed., *Eesti Nõukogude Entsüklopeedia*, vol. VIII, Tallinn: Valgus, 1976, p. 509.
14. Toivo Raun, *Estonia and the Estonians*, op. cit., p. 192.
15. See his book, L. Valt and E. Savisaar, *Globaalprobleemid ja Tulevikust-senaariumid*, Tallin: Eesti Raamat, 1983, 160 pp.
16. *Riiga Teataja*, no. 43, 20 December 1991, p. 1012; *Riiga Teataja*, no. 45, 30 December 1991, p. 1054.
17. G. Sootla, 'Balti kriss, *Poliitika*, no. 5, 1991, pp. 5–6.
18. Some of the causes of the crisis of Savisaar's government are listed in *The Baltic Independent*, January 24–30, 1992, p. 1. A review of the main economic problems of Estonia is presented in Teet Rajasalu, *Estonian Economy at the Dawn of Independence*, Tallinn: Academy of Sciences, 1992, 52pp.
19. *Rahva Hääl*, 31 March 1990, p. 1.
20. *Rahva Hääl*, 22 August 1991, p. 1.
21. *Ibid.*, 4 April 1990, p. 1.
22. *Äripäev*, January 15, 1992, p. 1.
23. *Rahva Hääl*, 17 January 1992, p. 1.
24. *ENSV Valitsuse ja Ülemnõukogu Teataja, no. 12, 16 April 1990, p. 268.*
25. Biographical data is mainly taken from: Marje Jõeste and others, eds, *The Baltic States. A Reference Book*, Tallinn: Estonian Encyclopedia Publishers, 1991, pp. 66–85.

26. See also: Endel Nirk and others, eds, *Eesti Kirjanduse Biograafiline Leksikon* (*The Biographical Handbook of Estonian Literature*), Tallinn: Eesti Raamat, 1975, pp. 228–9.

27. Endel Nirk et al., eds, *Eesti Kirjanduse Biograafiline Leksikon*, Tallinn: Eesti Raamat, 1975, pp. 325–6.

28. Cf. for example: Karl Siilivask, ed., *Taartu Ülikooli Ajalugu (History of Tartu University)*, vol. III, Tallinn: Eesti Raamat, 1982, p. 284.

29. Karl Siilivask, ed., *Tartu Ülikooli Ajalugu*, vol. III, p. 242.

30. Cf. also: Mare Kukk, 'Poliitiline opositsioon Eestis Nõukogude Perioodil' ('Political Opposition in Estonia in the Soviet Period'), *Proceedings of the Estonian Academy of Sciences. Social Sciences*, no. 3, 1991, p. 238.

31. *Revue Baltique*, vol. 2, no. 1, February 1991, p. 137.

32. *The Baltic Independent*, 17–23 July 1992, p. 3. In the March 1993 General Election, Landsbergis' *Sajudis* government was defeated and replaced by the Democratic Labour Party under Brazauskas.

7 Economic Restructuring
Michael Bradshaw, Philip Hanson and Denis Shaw

This chapter examines the relative significance of Western and Eastern influences upon the evolving structure of the Baltic economies and what those influences might mean for the future. While incorporation into the Soviet state led to an industrialisation of the Baltic economies to suit the needs of planners and politicians in Moscow, the historic importance of Western contacts and the memory of independence mean that the Baltic states are better placed than most other parts of the former Soviet empire to respond to the demands of economic transition.

The future 'economic viability' of the newly independent Baltic states will depend upon their ability to shape a role for themselves within the international division of labour. In the short term the collapse of inter-republican relations and continuing dependence upon Russian energy resources will exacerbate the economic problems posed by the transition to the market. In the long term the Baltic states will have to exploit their location as an entrepôt between West/Central Europe and Scandinavia and Russia and the other successor states. As much as the Baltic states might like to turn their backs on Russia and join the New Europe, they will have to accept that their future economic prosperity will depend, in large part, upon maintaining good relations with Russia. If the Baltic states are to pursue an outwardly-oriented development strategy, then Russia, not Europe, is likely in the long run to be their most important market, provided the Russian economy is restructured and begins to grow.

SOVIET INDUSTRIAL POLICY AND THE BALTIC ECONOMIES

Soviet annexation of the three Baltic republics in 1940 set the stage for the second major reorientation of their economies in just over twenty years. Whereas the republics had previously been turning their faces westwards and away from the enormous territories lying to their east, they were now to undergo an abrupt about-turn. Soviet policy was very much influenced by the determination to integrate the Baltic states both economically and politically into Moscow's sphere. Strategically and politically this was deemed essential if the USSR was to retain its hold on this militarily vital region. Ideologically, too, it would not have been possible to permit these states to continue along a capitalist development path. The Baltic republics were seen to possess important characteristics which would aid in the development of the USSR as a whole. These included an established infrastructure and a skilled population. Their continued development, along lines set by Moscow, was thus regarded as very much in the Soviet interest.

The fact that the Baltic states were now to be developed in the interests of the USSR did not mean that Moscow was to pursue a carefully considered and integrated regional development policy in the area. Being integrated into the Soviet centrally planned economy meant being integrated into an economy administered by economic sectors mainly from Moscow. Not only did the Baltic republics lose the chance to influence their own economic development in any meaningful way, but there was also little attempt to co-ordinate that development at the local level. Only between 1957 and 1965, essentially during the Khrushchev period, was any real attempt at co-ordination made. As Chapter 5 noted, due to an upsurge of nationalism in Latvia and Estonia, in the Baltic republics this reform was curtailed even earlier. This was the period when the central industrial ministries were abolished and a regional economic council (*sovnarkhoz*) was set up in each of the Baltic states to manage most industry locally. From 1957 about 80 per cent of Estonia's industrial production and about 83 per cent of Lithuania's industry was managed in this way.[1] This produced particular advantages in the case of Lithuania, whose industrialisation was still under way at that stage and which was therefore in a position to pursue some far-sighted development and locational policies.[2] Even so, many important decisions continued to be made in Moscow. By 1965, with the final abolition of the *sovnarkhozy* it once more became clear that the development of the republics was to be very much determined by industrial branch ministries based in Moscow.

Soviet attempts to remodel the Baltic economies began with the initial occupation in 1940. They were soon to be interrupted by the outbreak of war and the German invasion. Soviet reoccupation towards the end of the war allowed the process of Sovietisation to continue, although the enormous physical damage (Estonian industrial capacity was down to 55 per cent[3]) and population losses obviously made the task of economic development that much harder. Nationalisation of industry was completed by 1947 and restoration of war-damaged capacity forged ahead, aided by the installation of equipment from dismantled German plants. Allowing for some adjustment to the official Soviet data, calculations suggest that pre-war industrial production levels had been reached by 1949 in Estonia and Latvia and by 1952 in Lithuania.[4]

The pattern of economic development during the Soviet period was the product of the interplay between Soviet priorities on the one hand and locally available resources and opportunities on the other. At one level, opportunities were limited by the somewhat scanty natural resources of the region. Thus apart from the oil shales of northern Estonia, local energy resources are limited to peat, some hydroelectric potential and unsubstantial quantities of oil. Although forest covers between 26 per cent (in Lithuania) and 38 per cent (in Latvia) of the territory,[5] the resource is characterised by an excess of immature stands, the result of past overcutting, wartime losses, and wind-damage in coastal regions. Labour has also been in short supply, necessitating (given the output targets and the productivity levels attainable in the Soviet system) the immigration of Russian labour especially into Estonia and Latvia. Lithuania, however, was long characterised by a slower rate of industrialisation and by higher birth-rates, and was thus a labour surplus area. It was to make use of this surplus that additional industrial capacity was located in the republic from the 1960s onwards.

To offset these disadvantages, the republics possessed many positive features to encourage industrialisation. In addition to skilled labour and an established infrastructure, Moscow was quick to capitalise on the region's long-standing experience in such branches as machine-building, woodworking, chemicals, food and light industries. Fresh water, so essential to certain industries, and building materials, are in adequate supply. And the republics' coastal location proved especially significant for the development of foreign trade and fisheries, particularly after the 1960s when the USSR began to emerge from its long-enduring policy of economic autarky.

Given the priority Moscow attached to heavy industry, it was inevitable that the Baltic republics would to some extent move away from their traditional emphasis on consumer industries such as textiles, food and light industries. However, the energy deficit would have to be dealt with if heavy industrialisation was to proceed unhindered and this problem could no longer be solved in the traditional manner, by imports from abroad. An early aim was therefore to speed up the exploitation of Estonian oil shale which was now to be developed not merely to serve Estonian needs but also those of the energy-hungry Leningrad (St Petersburg) region. From 1948 gas began to be piped from the oil-shale field at Kohtla-Jarve to Leningrad, and some years later a further pipeline began to serve Tallinn. Production was rapidly expanded both through shaft mines and open-cast pits and stood at 3.5 million tons in 1950, 15.8 million in 1965 and over 31 million by 1980. There then followed a decline to just over 23 million in 1988. Much of the production is used in two large-capacity thermal power stations built in the vicinity of the shale fields between the late 1950s and the early 1970s. This permitted the export of electricity to Leningrad and also southwards to Latvia.

Other energy-related projects of the Soviet period included the building of a number of hydroelectric power stations, notably at Kaunas on the Nemunas River; at Kagmus, Stucka (the Plavinas station) and Salaspils on the outskirts of Riga, all on the Daugava River; and at Narva in Estonia. These supplemented the pre-existing peat- and coal-fired power stations. The Ignalina nuclear power station (of the same design as Chernobyl), at Snieckus in Lithuania, began commercial operation in 1983.

The most significant energy-related development, however, was the piping into the region of natural gas from other parts of the Soviet Union. The gas, which came initially from western Ukraine and later from the Moscow–Leningrad transmission system, reached Lithuania in 1961 and Latvia the following year. From 1969 the flow of gas along the Kohtla–Jarve–Leningrad pipeline was reversed and natural gas essentially solved the Baltic energy deficit, albeit at considerable cost in capital investment.

One further energy-related project of importance was the completion in 1968 of a branch of the 'Friendship' oil pipeline from Polotsk in Belorussia to the port of Ventspils in Latvia. Ventspils subsequently became the major export terminal for the Volga-Urals crude oil pipeline and a refinery was built at Mazeikiai in northern Lithuania to process the crude oil, in part for local needs.

These developments greatly increased Baltic dependence on energy imported from other parts of the Soviet Union and also had profound consequences for the region's economy.[6] Industry was now able to develop in response to Soviet priorities. One such priority from the late 1950s, for example, was the expansion of the chemical industry to supply fertilisers to the lagging agricultural sector and to provide the new materials and substances required by a modern industrial economy. Estonia and Latvia in particular had previous experience of chemical industries, but the coming of natural gas (used as a raw material as well as a fuel) and imports of other necessities such as apatite from the Kola Peninsula in north European Russia allowed for significant growth and the development of new processes. The production of fertilisers particularly flourished, including gas-based nitrogenous fertilisers (as at Jonava in Lithuania, which began production in 1964) and phosphate fertilisers (as at Maardu in Estonia, based partly on local phosphorite deposits and also on Kola apatite). Other chemical industries which developed or expanded from the 1960s include artificial fibres (for example at Kaunas in Lithuania and Daugavpils in

Latvia), plastics (as at Olaine in Latvia and Kohtla-Jarve in Estonia), pharmaceuticals, paint and varnish.

Given the Baltic states' long tradition in the machine building and engineering industries (particularly in Latvia and Estonia), and the centrality of these branches to the Soviet economy, it was unavoidable that they would have an important role to play in the Soviet era. Given the absence of a significant steel industry (there is only one steel plant, at Liepaja in Latvia, dating from 1882 and based largely on scrap), plans from the 1970s began to emphasise the development of non-metal-intensive branches, although the expansion of heavy engineering was by no means entirely prevented. Important branches included such traditional ones for the region as the manufacture of railway rolling-stock and locomotives, buses and excavators (the first three having a long tradition in Riga), shipbuilding and repair. Branches of the industry also appeared in Lithuania as part of the attempt to industrialise that republic (for example, machine tools and electrical equipment in Vilnius and Kaunas). And traditions of skilled engineering and the presence of an educated workforce and of high quality scientific personnel ensured that the Baltic republics would have an important role to play in the policy of modernising the Soviet economy by moving towards the latest production methods and high technologies. Hence the Baltic states began to play an important role in the production of a wide range of electrical equipment and appliances, in instrument-making and electronics.

Other Baltic industries are traditional to the region. Although many of them, being consumer-oriented, suffered from low priority during the Soviet period, they still played an important role in the local economy. This was partly the result of the deliberate Soviet policy, which became apparent in the 1960s, of placing greater emphasis on the consumer sector in order to improve incentives for the population. Unfortunately, this policy change was insufficient to challenge the vested interests behind the producer goods industries and the Baltic consumer continued to suffer in consequence. The continued importance of these industries probably exacerbated local labour shortages since many are labour intensive. The industries concerned include textiles and other light industries, food processing, woodworking (including pulp and paper production and furniture making), fishing and fish processing.

Table 7.1 indicates industrial employment structure for the three Baltic republics and the USSR for 1985. This shows that Baltic employment easily exceeded the USSR average in food and light industries and to a lesser extent in wood and paper, but fell well below it in iron and steel, non-ferrous metallurgy and military industry. Estonia exceeded the USSR average for employment in fuel industries, but the other republics fell well below

Table 7.1 The Baltic States and the USSR: Employment by sector, 1985

Sector	USSR	Estonia	Latvia	Lithuania
			(Percentages)	
Energy	2.14	3.6	1.8	2.4
Fuel	4.8	8.8	0.8	1.0
Iron and steel	4.1	–	1.0	0.4
Non-ferrous	1.2	–	–	–
Chemical	3.2	3.5	5.4	2.4
Machine-building	25.7	20.4	23.1	26.4
Wood and paper	6.8	11.8	8.1	7.2
Stone and clay	4.9	5.2	4.0	6.7
Glass	0.8	2.9	0.5	0.4
Light industry	14.4	21.8	21.2	21.3
Food	7.6	14.0	12.0	12.9
Grain and agro-chemical	0.6	0.5	0.6	1.0
Medical	0.5	0.1	0.7	0.4
Printing	0.6	1.1	1.1	0.9
Miscellaneous	1.4	2.6	2.4	3.9
Residual (defence)	21.2	5.0	15.2	12.5

Source: Goskomstat (unpublished) .

Table 7.2 Structure of gross industrial output, 1988 (percentage of total in 1982 prices)

	USSR	Estonia	Latvia
Fuel energy	10.9	8.4	1.7
Engineering & metallurgy	28.4	14.9	29.4
Chemicals & timber	11.2	8.9	13.3
Building materials	3.8	3.7	3.3
Light industry	13.8	26.6	19.3
Food industry	15.4	23.8	25.3
Other	16.4	13.7	7.7

Sources: P. Hanson, *The Baltic States: The Economic and Political Implications of the Secession of Estonia, Latvia and Lithuania from the USSR.* (London: Economic Intelligence Unit, Special Report no. 2033 March 1990, p. 14); *Latvijas PSR Tautas Saimnieciba*, Statistikas Gadagrámata, (Riga, 1989), p. 175.

Table 7.3 The Baltic states and the USSR: industrial production, 1940–88

	1960	1970	1980	1988
		(1940 = 1)		
USSR	5.2	12	21	28
Estonia	11	28	48	60
Latvia	11	27	45	59
Lithuania	10	31	58	84

Sources: Narodnoe khozyaistvo SSSR za 70 let (Moscow, *Finansy i statistika*, 1987), p. 132; *Narodnoe khozyaistvo SSSR v 1988 g.* (Moscow, *Finansy i statistika*, 1989), p. 339.

Table 7.4 The Baltic states and the USSR: industrial production, 1980–88

	1980	1988
	(1980 = 100)	
USSR	100	134
Estonia	100	145
Latvia	100	132
Lithuania	100	126

Source: Narodnoe khozyaistvo SSSR v 1988 g. (Moscow, *Finansy i statistika*, 1989), p. 339.

average in this category. Employment in chemicals and machinery was about average, but these are of course very broad categories. Table 7.2, which depicts the structure of industrial output for Estonia and Latvia in 1987, again indicates the importance of food and light industries. Tables 7.3 and 7.4 show industrial growth trends in the Baltic states and the USSR in the post-war period. Even allowing for the dubious growth statistics for the Baltic states between 1940 and 1960, their overall performance has been very respectable relative to the USSR as a whole. Lithuania's rapid growth reflects its lower starting point and the availability of surplus labour in the early period.

THE RURAL ECONOMY

Before the Second World War agriculture played a dominant role in the economies of all three Baltic republics. Since then its relative significance has diminished, though it is still important, accounting with forestry for over 12 per cent of employment in Estonia, 15 per cent in Latvia and 18 per cent in Lithuania (1988 figures; USSR average 19 per cent). Agriculture's contribution to the value of social production in 1988 was about 18 per cent in the case of Estonia and over 20 per cent in that of Latvia (USSR average 17 per cent).

As we saw in Chapter 2, land reform had been one of the first items on the agenda of the independent Baltic governments after 1918. The result was to enhance the importance of the small-scale peasant farm. Under Soviet rule, the splitting up of land-holdings was initially to be taken even further, but only as a prelude to ultimate collectivisation. Thus the land reforms and redistributions which began in 1940 were mainly directed against the larger holdings, those in excess of 30 hectares. This process continued after the war, accompanied by a creeping collectivisation which reached a frenetic pace by 1949. Farmers were forced into collective farms by various land distribution measures, punitive levels of taxation, compulsory delivery quotas levied upon private farms, and 'dekulakisation'. Thousands of individuals and families fled the countryside for the cities while others were deported against their will to remote regions of the USSR. By the end of 1949, about 93 per cent of Latvia's farms and 80 per cent of those in Estonia had been collectivised.[7] In Lithuania the process was somewhat more protracted. The human and economic costs of collectivisation were considerable. Not only had the countryside been denuded of some of its most productive labour, but the new farms were afflicted by continual interference by state officials, poor management by the newly empowered farm authorities, lack of needed raw materials and equipment, lack of livestock, confiscatory delivery quotas and other problems. Continual reorganisation of farms further exacerbated the low morale of the workforce. The net effect was to set back production by about a decade (Table 7.5).

Despite the problems of the early Soviet period Baltic agriculture began to improve slowly from the 1950s. It has been suggested that a continuing peasant mentality among the farmers, some of whom still lived on individual farmsteads in spite of regulations to the contrary, and the protection given by local Baltic officials from some of the worst excesses of interference by Moscow, helped this recovery.[8] Eventually, agriculture benefited from additional allocations of capital and resources and gradually rising rural living standards, the latter particularly apparent by the mid-1960s. Also important was the greater encouragement now given to private plots. Private plots played a larger role here than in most other areas of the USSR and added significantly to the income of state and collective farmers. Farm

Table 7.5   Agricultural production in the Baltic States, 1950–88

	Estonia	Latvia	Lithuania
		(1940 = 100)	
1950	0.88	0.77	0.85
1960	1.20	1.06	1.30
1970	1.49	1.35	1.89
1978	1.69	1.38	2.21
	Value of production (average per year at 1983 prices)		
	(millions of rubles)		
1966–70	–	2104	3407.5
1971–75	1480.4	2293	3848.6
1976–80	1670.9	2442	4022.7
1981–85	1736.6	2738	4289.1
1988	1778.6	2940	4774.7[a]

[a]1987

Sources: R.J. Misiunas and R. Taagepera, *The Baltic States: Years of Dependence, 1940–1980* (London 1983), p. 287; *Eesti NSV Rahuamajandus 1988. Aarstal* (Tallinn, 1989), p. 116; *Latvijas PSR tautas saimnieciba: statistikas gadagramata '88* (Riga, 1989), p. 207; *Narodnoe khozyaistvo Litovskoi SSR v 1987 g.* (Vilnius, 1988), p. 47.

income was also enhanced by the common occurrence of subsidiary economic activities such as food processing and the manufacture of consumer goods and services. Considerable state investment went into land improvement, especially drainage schemes, the three Baltic states having by far the highest percentages of drained land in the USSR. In consequence of such improvements, agriculture became relatively intensive by Soviet standards and both productivity and quality were good. The Baltic states became reasonably efficient producers of animal products and of many vegetables, although the costs of producing grain were high. Food production, however, was hampered by the lack of a well-developed food processing industry.

By international standards, however, Baltic agriculture has been far from efficient or productive and it continues to suffer from numerous, characteristically Soviet problems such as labour deficits (given the systemic constraints on labour productivity) and an ageing workforce. Much of this can be explained by the typical deficiencies of Soviet-type agriculture. Interest in the possibility of improving this situation through various kinds of reform continued to grow as the 1980s advanced.

URBANISATION AND LIVING STANDARDS

With 72 per cent, 71 per cent and 68 per cent respectively of their populations living in urban places in 1990, Estonia, Latvia and Lithuania were among the most urbanised republics in the USSR, (in part reflecting their relatively industrialised character. Compared to other parts of the Soviet Union, all three also enjoyed higher living standards, particularly their capital cities (Tables 7.6 and 7.7). Yet for the Balts, primarily for historical and cultural reasons, their comparative reference point was the Western capitalist countries, especially the Scandinavian states. Once integrated into the USSR, Baltic economic development patterns inevitably paralleled those of the Soviet Union as a whole. The resulting bias towards heavy industry and relative neglect of consumer services exposed the Baltic peoples to many of the disadvantages – housing shortages, poor quality consumer goods, unreliable domestic services – which were suffered by Soviet citizens elsewhere. The fact that Baltic living standards are somewhat higher than the Soviet norm no doubt reflected the Baltic republics' long industrial histories, Europeanised cultures, and perhaps Moscow's desire to counteract secessionist sympathies. But in the minds of many Baltic citizens this scarcely compensated for the privations of Soviet-type development. In any case, the relatively attractive mode of life in the Baltic republics acted as a stimulant to the immigration of non-Baltic peoples, especially Russians.

Table 7.6 Selected quality of life indicators in the USSR and the Baltic republics, 1988 and 1989

Indicator	USSR	Estonia	Latvia	Lithuania
National income used per capita	100	109.8	119.0	117.2
Retail trade turnover per capita[a]	1282	1609	1831	1965
Life expectancy	69.5	71.8	70.4	70.6
Infant mortality	22.7	10.7	11.1	14.7
No. of doctors per 1000 residents	116.9	126.7	126.5	115.7
Living space per resident[a]	15.1	18.7	19.2	21.1
Av. salary for workers and employees	235.8	242.7	260.9	300.9
Rural telephones per 1000 persons[a]	32	78	119	97

[a]1988

Source: J. Tedstrom, *USSR–Baltic Independence: The Economic Dimensions* (Munich, 25 January 1991), p. 4.

Table 7.7   Selected quality of life indicators for the Baltic capitals and USSR, 1988

Indicator	USSR	Tallinn	Riga	Vilnius
Living space per capita	14.7[a]	18.4	17.3	15.4
Retail trade turnover per capita (rubles)	1586[a]	2380	2233	2252
Doctors per 10 000 population	43.8[a]	78.1	86.2	61.5
Hospital beds per 10 000 population	131.3[a]	179.2	159.7	130.7

[a]Calculated for the urban population only.
Source: Vestnik statiskiki, 1989, no. 11, pp. 69–80.

PERESTROIKA: ECONOMIC RESTRUCTURING AND ECONOMIC SELF-DETERMINATION

As integral parts of the Soviet economy, the Baltic states could not escape the consequence of the economic slowdown which became particularly apparent by the late 1970s. The much-heralded attempt to move the economy from an 'extensive' pattern of development, reliant on commensurate increases in resource inputs for each increase in output, to an 'intensive' one with much greater emphasis on productivity growth, failed to achieve the necessary results. Despite some progress in introducing new technologies and production methods, the Baltic economies continued to be dominated by resource-demanding heavy industries and the raw materials and energy required to supply these industries came increasingly from elsewhere. The high costs of transporting energy and raw materials into the region, and the local labour shortages, are but two of the consequences of 'extensive' growth.

When Mikhail Gorbachev came to power in 1985, the underlying economic malaise which afflicted the entire country began to be tackled in a far more serious way than hitherto. However, his economic and political reforms eventually fomented the instability which was so much feared by Communist hard-liners. Gorbachev no doubt hoped that the Baltic states, with their long industrial traditions, skilled labour forces and higher than average productivity, would play a key role in his policies of economic transformation. In the wake of a growing national self-confidence, the Balts turned out to be highly receptive to restructuring. Gorbachev's encouragement of the notion of regional self-management found particular support. A group of Estonian intellectuals were the first to elaborate an economic autonomy programme, in the form of the original IME proposals of 1987. IME stands for Ise-Majandav Eesti, a self-managing Estonia. This was a well-chosen acronym. 'Ime' is Estonian for 'miracle'. For some time afterwards, IME was the name given to the package of economic reform measures being introduced in Estonia.[9] The main changes sought in the early programmes were the transfer of many enterprises from all-Union (Moscow branch ministry) control to Estonian administration; an increase in Estonian budgetary autonomy by simplifying budget transfers between Estonia and Moscow into a single channel through which a fixed percentage of tax revenue would be handed over; and scope to proceed with substantial institutional reforms on Estonian initiative.[10]

At this stage, Estonia was in the lead so far as Baltic proposals for economic autonomy are concerned. There was nonetheless pressure on Moscow from Latvia and Lithuania as well. In March 1989 the USSR Council of Ministers produced a draft programme on republic economy autonomy, with a title of Brezhnevian ponderousness: 'General Principles of Restructuring of the Management of the Economy and of the Social Sphere in Union Republics on the Basis of a Widening of their Sovereign Rights, of Self-Management, of Self-Finance'.[11] The Moscow draft envisaged an increase in the share of industry that would be administered within the republics. In the case of the Baltic states, the change proposed was quite substantial: from republic administration of between 7 and 9 per cent of gross industrial output to a range of 57–72 per cent. Correspondingly, taxes on the enterprises thus transferred would have shifted from the Union to the republic budgets. The republics would also get a share of the taxes on Union-subordinate enterprises as well, and, on the spending side, more discretion over welfare expenditure. Despite these concessions, the Moscow draft still contained provision for substantial powers of control from the Union level. These included, for example, continued output-targeting in Moscow of the total net output of all branches in the republic.

The Baltic leaders (at this stage still the Party leaders, but increasingly responsive to local demands) wanted more. Eventually, a USSR Law on the Economic Autonomy of the Lithuanian, Latvian and Estonian Soviet Socialist Republics was passed. It was a messy compromise, relying on formulae such as 'will be arranged by agreement between the republics and the centre'. Crucial issues such as the treatment of property rights in land and natural resources and in the 'all-Union' systems on republic territory (military bases, gas pipelines, etc.) were fudged. The all-important supply system and price control remained in Moscow's hands. The arrangement was workable only in the political sense that it left both sides able for the time being to claim that they had got what they wanted.

In the medium term, the late-1989 deal was not a stable one. Moscow had conceded enough to whet Baltic appetites, in both the economic and political spheres. Ad hoc negotiations continued. Estonia got – or rather, its leaders thought they had got – a simplified, transparent, single-channel fiscal transfer arrangement with Moscow. Local reforms moved ahead, with Estonia, in particular, legislating in 1990 for the transformation of state enterprises into joint stock companies on 1988 Hungarian lines.[12] In 1990, when Sajudis had come to power in Lithuania and was adopting a strong secessionist stance, the Soviet leadership attempted an economic blockade of the upstart republic. The Lithuanian economy suffered, and *Sajudis* made some modest concessions, but the results of the blockade, and its abandonment after three months, testified to Moscow's own weakness as well. Many Russian enterprises did business with Lithuania despite Moscow's best endeavours. Mutual dependence was widely believed to have been demonstrated, *inter alia*, by perceptible worsening of food supplies to Moscow from Lithuania.[13]

In the face of a weakening centre, and with their own elected leaderships, all three Baltic republics embarked in 1990–1 on economic policies and reforms of their own. Their room for manoeuvre was of course limited. But the fact that Estonia, for example, had largely decontrolled prices during 1991, before the Yeltsin-Gaidar team had done so in Russia, is one striking example of the powerful Baltic will to pursue independent economic policies.

The drift towards independence of the various Soviet republics in the late 1980s focused attention on the extent to which they were economically interdependent. In consequence, a considerable amount of data was published for the first time, indicating the nature of the Baltic republics' interrelationship with the USSR and the rest of the world.[14] Because the republics are small, imports and exports have played a bigger role in their production patterns than has been the case for larger Soviet republics. Thus in 1988 exports accounted for between 24 and 25 per cent of production in the Baltic states, compared with only 11 per cent for the RSFSR. The comparable figures for imports were 27–29 per cent and 14 per cent respectively.[15] The Baltic states have been particularly dependent on the rest of the USSR for the import of energy and raw materials. Thus in 1985, Latvia imported about 91 per cent of its total fuel and energy requirements, and Lithuania 88 per cent.[16] Only Estonia, with its oil shales, imported less. Similarly, with 2.8 per cent of the Soviet population in 1989, Baltic steel production was only 0.4 per cent of the Soviet total, necessitating considerable imports. In addition to energy and ferrous metals, all three republics import considerable quantities of machine tools, and Estonia and Lithuania large amounts of chemicals. On the other side of the coin, all three republics export many products of the light and food industries to the post-Soviet republics. Because of the characteristic Soviet tendency towards monopoly production (not always apparent from branch-aggregate statistics), the Baltic states may have been of overriding significance to the Soviet economy for the production of some specialist items. From the bald statistics for 1989 it is apparent that the republics, with 2.8 per cent of the Soviet population, produced well above their share of the following items: ac electric motors, metal-cutting machine tools, livestock and feed products, woollen and linen fabric, stockings and stocks, knitting products, radio receiving systems, televisions, washing machines, furniture, meat, fish and fish products, butter and conserves (over 6 per cent of total Soviet production in each case).[17]

THE BALTIC ECONOMIES IN TRANSITION TO CAPITALISM

As we have noted, incorporation into the Soviet Union resulted in the further industrialisation of the Baltic economies to suit the needs of the Soviet system. The economic development strategy orchestrated from Moscow not only promoted industrial expansion, it also tied the Baltic republics into the complex system of inter-enterprise trade that resulted from the dominance of the all-union industrial ministries over republican authorities. As a direct consequence of the nature of the Soviet central planning system, despite their newly-won political independence and the decision not to enter into an economic treaty with the other republics of the former Soviet Union, the Baltic states still find their economic fate closely entwined with that of the other newly-independent states of the former Soviet Union, most particularly Russia.[18]

As they seek to transform their economic systems, the post-independent Baltic states face two key challenges. The first is linked to the development of foreign trade; the second to the reorientation of their domestic economies to meet the needs of the domestic market and to establish their place in the new Europe. Clearly these two challenges are inseparable. The small domestic market of all three states means that their future economic prosperity is dependent on the pursuit of outwardly-oriented development strategies. Therefore, the successful restructuring of the Baltic economies is dependent, in large part, upon attracting foreign investment and securing access to export markets. Many of the problems currently facing the Baltic states are due to the collapse of the centralised Soviet trading system. Therefore, the starting point in this analysis of the prospects for economic transition is an assessment of the economic legacies of the Soviet system, in particular the structure of foreign trade relations.

Prior to the collapse of the Soviet Union inter-republican trade was managed by the central planning system, with the key actors being the all-union industrial ministries. At the same time, foreign economic activity was the sole responsibility of the Ministry of Foreign Trade in Moscow. As a result, upon independence the governments of the Baltic states inherited trade relations which were not of their making; more than that, the distortions of the Soviet pricing system and the inadequacies of statistical services meant that there was no clear picture of the true nature of trade relations between the newly-independent Baltic states and the rest of the former Soviet Union. The data that have been released are subject to price distortions and under-reporting, but they do provide a general indication of the domestic (inter-republican) and foreign economic relations of the Baltic states. The data in Table 7.8 provide details on trade relations with the rest of the former Soviet Union. Two aspects are noteworthy: firstly, for all the Baltic states the Russian Federation is the most important trading partner; secondly, there is a modest level of trade between the Baltic states. This is because they have similar economic structures and been developed to serve the Soviet market, rather than the development of a relatively self-sufficient Baltic economic region. Because of the pricing system and the methodologies employed to calculate the value of trade, it is very difficult to make precise statements about the balance of trade between the individual Baltic states and the rest of the former Soviet Union. Data on inter-republican trade made available by Goskomstat SSSR on merchandise trade only show that in 1988 the Baltic republics ran a deficit with the rest of the Union in the region of 2.9 billion rubles.[19] Those same data, recalculated by Goskomstat on the basis of so-called 'world prices' produced a much increased deficit of 6.3 billion rubles. This is largely due to the underpricing of Russia's energy exports and suggests that at world prices, assuming the structure of trade remained the same, the Baltic states would have substantial difficulties financing their trade with the Russian Federation. The recent Swedish government study of the Baltic states has reworked these trade data to include turnover tax, subsidies and cross-border traveller's purchases, when expressed in world market prices and converted into US dollars at the average 1988 official rate, the balance of trade is as follows (US $ billion): Lithuania 4.7, Latvia 1.2, and Estonia 1.6 (Baltic total 7.5).[20] By including fees from transit services, estimated to be worth $1.3 billion, and tourist revenue and income from workers abroad, the deficit is reduced to $5.7 billion. This represents a substantial burden on the finances of the Baltic states. Since 1988, the collapse of inter-republican trade and the potential for cost savings due to the removal of Soviet troops may have reduced the size of the deficit to $3.0 to $4.5 billion a year, but, at the

Table 7.8   The distribution of inter-republican trade, 1987 (percent of trade)

	Estonia		Latvia		Lithuania	
Republic	*Exports*	*Imports*	*Exports*	*Imports*	*Exports*	*Imports*
Slavic	*78.4*	*79.7*	*73.7*	*74.4*	*75.3*	*86.1*
Russia	60.5	58.5	50.0	53.5	53.6	64.9
Ukraine	13.0	14.4	16.0	11.6	13.1	11.5
Belarus	4.9	6.8	7.7	9.3	8.6	9.7
Baltic	9.7	9.7	9.8	14.8	11.0	5.4
Estonia	na	na	4.1	4.2	2.0	1.2
Latvia	7.2	6.0	na	na	9.0	4.2
Lithuania	2.5	3.7	5.7	10.6	na	na
Uzbekistan	1.7	1.7	3.0	0.7	3.3	0.8
Kazakhstan	3.7	1.9	4.7	1.8	3.2	1.1
Georgia	1.2	1.0	2.3	2.1	1.4	1.7
Azerbaijan	1.0	0.8	1.5	0.8	1.1	0.6
Moldova	1.6	2.6	1.7	3.3	1.6	1.7
Kyrgyzstan	0.5	0.4	0.6	0.7	0.9	1.2
Tajikistan	0.5	0.8	0.8	0.2	0.6	0.5
Armenia	1.3	0.8	1.3	0.7	1.1	0.7
Turkmenia	0.3	0.7	0.7	0.5	0.8	0.2

Sources: IMF, *Economic Review: Estonia* (Washington DC, 1992), p. 44; IMF, *Economic Review: Latvia* (Washington, DC, 1992), p. 69; IMF, *Economic Review: Lithuania* (Washington, DC, 1992), p. 71.

same time, demands on the budget have increased and tax revenues have declined. Thus, the trade relations inherited from the Soviet Union continue to drain the Baltic states of revenue needed to finance economic restructuring.

The data in Tables 7.9 and 7.10 provide information on the structure of inter-republican trade. The structure of exports (Table 7.9) reflects the all-union specialisation identified earlier in this chapter. Similarly, the structure of imports reflects the high level of dependence upon imported energy and raw materials. In sum, the legacy of incorporation into the Soviet economic system is a high degree of dependence upon the Slavic republics of the former Soviet Union, both as suppliers of energy and raw materials and as the principal markets for the products of Baltic enterprises. As the blockade of Lithuania revealed, the Baltic states are extremely vulnerable to the

Table 7.9   Commodity structure of exports for the Baltic states, 1988 (per cent of total)

Sector	Estonia Domestic	Estonia Foreign	Latvia Domestic	Latvia Foreign	Lithuania Domestic	Lithuania Foreign
Industry	98.6	99.7	93.8	91.3	97.9	99.9
Electric power	4.8	0.0	1.7	0.0	3.0	0.0
Oil and gas	0.2	0.8	0.1	0.0	5.7	33.9
Coal	0.0	0.0	0.0	0.0	0.0	0.0
Other fuels	0.5	0.2	0.0	0.2	0.0	0.2
Ferrous metals	0.2	0.3	2.3	3.2	0.6	0.5
Nonferrous metals	0.3	0.0	0.3	0.1	0.2	0.0
Chemicals & petro-chemicals	11.7	4.2	14.0	9.6	6.6	2.1
Machinery	19.7	13.5	28.1	35.8	32.5	26.9
Wood, paper & pulp	4.7	10.4	3.0	9.1	4.5	4.4
Construction materials	1.1	0.9	1.3	1.2	1.3	1.4
Light industry	29.4	22.0	17.7	3.3	25.8	3.4
Food industry	23.9	46.1	22.0	27.9	17.0	26.9
Other industry	2.0	1.3	3.4	0.3	0.9	0.3
Agriculture	1.1	0.2	2.3	2.8	2.0	0.1
Other sectors	0.3	0.1	4.0	5.9	0.1	0.0

Source: B. van Arkadie and M. Karlsson, *Economic Survey of the Baltic States* (London, 1992), pp. 173–4.

collapse of inter-republican trade. Unfortunately, while the Baltic economies remained through 1992 open to the CIS, they were still isolated from
the international economic system. On average, during the 1980s, trade
with foreign partners accounted for about 10 per cent of the trade turnover
of the Baltic economies. Of that 10 per cent, half was with members of the
now defunct CMEA, the rest was with market economies and the developing world. All such trade was managed by the foreign trade monopoly and
its system of foreign trade organisations located in Moscow. The Baltic
states, therefore, now find themselves in a doubly difficult situation, on the
one hand having to manage with the negative consequences of the collapse
of the Soviet Union, while, on the other hand, assuming responsibility for

Table 7.10 Commodity structure of imports for the Baltic states, 1988
(per cent of total)

| | Estonia | | Latvia | | Lithuania | |
Sector	Domestic	Foreign	Domestic	Foreign	Domestic	Foreign
Industry	97.7	79.5	97.3	84.6	98.7	83.8
Electic power	1.0	1.6	2.9	0.0	1.5	0.0
Oil and gas	8.6	0.0	10.6	0.0	16.8	0.1
Coal	0.1	1.1	0.1	2.5	0.3	2.9
Other fuels	0.0	0.0	0.0	0.0	0.1	0.0
Ferrous metals	4.6	2.1	8.7	1.0	5.9	1.9
Nonferrous metals	2.9	0.1	2.9	0.0	2.9	0.4
Chemicals and petro-chemicals	14.9	10.9	13.6	9.4	12.3	5.6
Machinery	32.7	22.3	33.8	11.6	34.8	29.0
Wood, paper & pulp	2.7	1.4	3.0	2.2	3.5	1.5
Construction materials	1.3	1.3	1.6	0.4	1.4	0.8
Light industry	16.6	24.8	10.9	27.1	12.6	21.3
Food industry	10.1	13.5	6.80	29.3	4.8	20.0
Other industry	2.2	0.6	2.5	1.0	1.8	0.5
Agriculture	1.9	18.9	2.5	15.2	1.3	16.2
Other sectors	0.5	1.7	0.2	0.1	0.1	0.0

Source: B. van Arkadie and M. Karlsson, *Economic Survey of the Baltic States* (London, 1992), pp. 175–6.

foreign trade relations and having to attract foreign investment and secure export markets. Obviously, the creation of joint ventures and the attraction of foreign capital are crucial components of economic transition. Unfortunately the collapse of the Soviet Union and the political and economic instability that now characterises the republics of the former Soviet Union, as well as global recession, have severely constrained investor enthusiasm.

At the end of 1991 the Baltic states were complaining that while they had met their obligations to deliver products to Russia, the Russian Federation had supplied only 40–50 per cent of the fuel it had promised.[21] During early 1992, having decided not to join the CIS, the individual Baltic states sought to renegotiate their trading agreements with the Russian Federation.

These agreements take the form of barter agreements based on the 'traditional' pattern of trade between the republics. For example, in April 1992 Latvia reached agreement with the Russian Federation on the mutual exchange of goods and raw materials based on the principle of clearing. Under this agreement Russia is to supply petrol, diesel, liquid natural gas and other energy resources worth $326.62 million (calculated in the basis of an exchange rate of 35 rubles to the US dollar). In return Latvia was to supply meat and meat products, milk and milk products and other agricultural products and some consumer goods worth $326.62 million.[22] A similar agreement was reached between Lithuania and the Russian Federation. Such state-controlled barter agreements can only serve, at best, as a temporary solution.

In practice, they have been substantially underfulfilled. The privatisation of economic activity and the marketisation of the economy will inevitably lead to the decentralisation of foreign trade activity to the enterprise level. Governments will then have to rely on a regime of taxes and tariffs to manage and influence the structure of foreign trade and manage the balance of payments. There are already indicators that the decentralisation of the Russian economy is fostering new direct trade links with the Baltic states. For example, the Estonian government signed an agreement on 10 June 1992 with the Nadymgazprom production association in West Siberia to purchase 210 million cubic metres of natural gas in which all payments were to be made in hard currency at world prices.[23] Agreements such as this raise additional problems, namely which prices to employ and whose currency to use. The Russian government has been pressured by the IMF to free energy prices. In early 1993, while introducing substantial prices increases, the Russian government had resisted liberalising domestic prices, but had promised to move to world prices over the next year or so. But it is understandable that Russia should charge world prices for oil exports to the Baltic states which are not part of the CIS and have left the ruble zone. While Latvia has exercised leverage by increasing the cost of shipping Russian oil from Ventspils, Russia is already seeking to construct its own oil export terminal southwest of St Petersburg. Already the Baltic states are suffering an energy crisis due to the physical reduction of energy supplies.Substantial price increases will only aggravate the financial crisis facing the region.

One of the reasons for the introduction of separate currencies, which in 1992 had been accomplished by Estonia and were planned for Latvia and Lithuania, is the need to isolate the Baltic economies from the inflationary pressure being experienced in the ruble zone and to gain control of the domestic money supply. At present (early 1993), the Estonian Kroon, introduced on 20 June 1992, is not directly convertible into rubles. Instead, the

Deutschmark (DM) is used as an intermediate currency. Thus, the price for a ton of oil is converted into deutschmarks at the market DM/ruble rate and then into Kroon on the basis of the DM/kroon rate. More importantly, the Kroon was pegged to the DM at 8Kr = DM1 under arrangements close to those of a currency board. (In a full version of a currency board system, the cash circulation is required by law to be 100 per cent backed by the reserve currency, so that the cash base of the monetary supply is rigidly and automatically determined by the foreign-currency reserve.) The Estonian Kroon retained its DM anchor through the summer and autumn of 1992, giving Estonia the chance of becoming an island of monetary stability within the dangerously inflationary ruble zone. The introduction of separate currencies, if successful, provides a degree of isolation, but increases the transaction costs involved and may prompt Russian enterprises and traders to demand payment in convertible currencies.

Whatever the financial arrangements, it is clear that as Russia has moved to charge world prices in convertible currencies for its energy exports this has had negative short-term impact upon the Baltic economies, further depressing production, increasing unemployment and generating further inflation. However, if they are to be internationally competitive, in the longer run the Baltic economies must face the true cost of energy imports. High energy costs will lead to greater energy conservation and the closure of the more energy- and raw material-intensive sectors of the economy. This would have a positive impact upon the environment, reducing atmospheric and water pollution. However, the unemployment generated by such restructuring would likely fall disproportionately upon the urban-based ethnic Russian workforce. To avoid economic collapse and social unrest, increasing unemployment in the manufacturing and heavy industrial sectors of the economy must be parallel by the expansion of light industrial and service sector activities. Here the actions of the individual governments and their ability to attract foreign investment are likely to be key determinants of success.

The majority of Baltic joint ventures between Soviet and Western firms, which got under way as part of Gorbachev's economic reforms and in which the Baltic states led the way, are located in Estonia. This reflects the positive attitude towards foreign investment adopted by the Estonian government, as well as their close relations with Finland. By the end of 1991 foreign investments accounted for about 3 per cent of Estonia's gross national product. This was twice the corresponding share in Latvia and 16 times that in Lithuania which had adopted a rather negative attitude to foreign investment.[24] Since then, however, foreign direct investment has risen substantially in Estonia, and to a lesser extent in Latvia, as both have reduced inflation to about two per cent a month (by mid-1993) and proceeded quite rapidly with privatisation.

On 1 May 1992 agreement was reached on the establishment of a free trade area among the Baltic states. However, because of the limited complementarity between the three economies, this is likely to have limited immediate impact. In fact, unless, as the experience of ASEAN suggests, the three states can agree on a degree of specialisation among themselves they are likely to be in competition with one another for foreign investment and foreign aid.

In the absence of sustained foreign investment, successful economic restructuring will be dependent upon the creation of new types of economy activity. Unfortunately, the collapse of inter-republican trade has reduced the economic viability of many state enterprises, substantially reducing the chances of successful privatisation. In reality, it is more contructive to support the creation of new privately-owned enterprises, rather than support bankrupt state-owned enterprises that have lost their traditional sources of supply and no longer have a secure market. The rate of creation of co-operatives provides one indicator of the potential entrepreneurial base of the three states. The number of co-operatives in the region had increased from a handful in 1987 to several thousand in each republic by 1990. As of 1 July 1991 there were 2421 co-operatives in Estonia employing 47 100 persons; 4797 cooperatives in Latvia employing 158 600 persons; and 4605 co-operatives in Lithuania employing 77 900 persons.[25]

The immediate problems facing the Baltic economies are daunting; however, it is not for the first time that the population of the region has had to readjust to face an entirely new reality. The continuing collapse of the Soviet empire contributed to the 1990–3 economic decline in the Baltic states. What however will be crucial to their future economic prosperity will be their ability to exploit their strategic position between Europe and Russia. Access to Russia's market will be crucial. According to one view popular in the Baltic states in 1991–2, their future may lie as a prime location for the production of goods for the CIS market and Central Europe. The presence of a relatively skilled workforce and developed infrastructure should provide the basis for attracting multinational enterprises to set up production facilities in the Baltic states to serve the Russian market. In a sense, this represents a qualitative consolidation of the role the Baltic region played in the all-union territorial division of labour. Such a strategy is dependent upon providing a fiscal environment that is more advantageous than actually locating within Russia and upon the Baltic states negotiating some sort of free trade agreement with Russia. It is true that the governments of the Baltic states have negotiated free trade agreements with the Scandinavian countries. In late 1993 it was possible that this could be a source of advantage in relations with the EU, if at least some of this access to Scandinavian markets could be incorporated in their

Scandinavian partners' EU accession deals. The reality remains that without access to Russia's markets the Baltic states will find it very difficult to enjoy sustained and rapid growth. Having decided not to join the CIS, in the short term the best they can hope for is bilateral agreements with the individual republics. Should the CIS lead to the creation of a durable ex-Soviet economic community, then the Baltic states will have to negotiate an agreement similar to that recently reached between EFTA and the EU. Assuming market access can be guaranteed, the individual governments must create conditions attractive to foreign investment and encourage the emergence of new forms of economic activity. In particular they must resist the temptation to support insolvent state enterprises which have no viable future. The consequences of such an economic strategy will inevitably be high unemployment and a sectoral and spatial redistribution of the workforce. The end result will be a new geography of economic activity in the Baltic region and a pattern of trade reflecting a balance between West and East, the West providing the capital and the know-how, the East access to energy and raw materials and a market for the Baltic states' products.

CONCLUSION

The world which the newly-independent Baltic states are entering in the 1990s is a very different place from that which faced them in the 1920s. In some ways, indeed, their current economic difficulties are more severe, given the enormous complexities of transition from a centrally planned economy to a market one. Equally, however, they are unlikely in the foreseeable future to face such formidable enemies as Germany and the Soviet Union proved to be in the 1930s. Given a favourable international climate, and some wisdom on the part of their governments, their problems will no doubt prove surmountable. They can take a certain amount of comfort from the fact that their difficulties are likely to prove rather less intractable than those facing many of their neighbours to the east.

REFERENCES

1. R.J. Misiunas and R. Taagepera, *The Baltic States: Years of Dependence, 1940–1980* (London, 1983), p. 179.
2. Ibid., pp. 179–80.
3. Ibid., p. 71.
4. Ibid., p. 109.

180   *Michael Bradshaw, Philip Hanson and Denis Shaw*

5. P.E. Lydolph, *Geography of the USSR* (Elkhart Lake, Wis., 1990), p. 363.
6. T. Shabad, *Basic Industrial Resources of the USSR* (New York, 1969), pp. 207–13; I.P. Shneidere, *Sotsialisticheskaya industrializatsiya v Latvii* (Riga, 1989), pp. 208ff; V. Klauson, *Gody sozidaniya* (Tallinn, 1976), pp. 37ff; *Litva v sisteme*, 1982, pp. 132ff; E. Jarvesoo, 'The Postwar Economic Transformation', in T. Parming and E. Jarvesoo (eds), *A Case Study of a Soviet Republic: The Estonian SSR* (Boulder, Colo., 1978), pp. 137–90.
7. Misiunas and Taagepera, 1983, p. 99.
8. B. van Arkadie and M. Karlssen, *Economic Survey of the Baltic States* (London, 1992).
9. The *Byulleten' IME*, published in Tallinn in Estonian, Russian and, latterly, English, gave details of economic reform proposals and legislation during 1989–91.
10. See *Byulleten' IME* I and II; M. Titma, *Estoniya: chto u nas proiskhodit?* (Tallinn, 1989).
11. *Ekonomicheskaya gazeta*, 1989, no. 12. See also J. Tedstrom. 'USSR Draft Program on Republican Economic Self-Management: An Analysis', *Report on the USSR*, vol. 1, no. 16 (21 May 1989).
12. *Byulleten' IME* II.
13. D. Reid-Thomas, *The Economic Blockade of Lithuania*, 1990, MSocSc dissertation, Centre for Russian and East European Studies, University of Birmingham, 1991.
14. A.R. Bond and M.J. Sagers, 'Adoption of Law on Economic Autonomy for the Baltic Republics and the Example of Estonia: A Comment', *Soviet Geography*, 31, 1990, pp. 1–10; M.V. Belkindas and M.J. Sagers, 'A Preliminary Analysis of Economic Relations among Union Republics', *Soviet Geography*, 31, 1990, pp. 629–56; M.J. Sagers, 'Regional Aspects of the Soviet Economy', *PlanEcon Report*, nos 1–2, 15 January 1991.
15. J. Tedstrom, *USSR–Baltic Independence: The Economic Dimensions*, Munich, 25 January 1991, p. 6.
16. J. Tedstrom, 1991, p. 6.
17. J. Tedstrom, 1991, p. 3.
18. *International Herald Tribune*, 14 October 1991.
19. *Vestnik statistiki*, 1990, no. 4, p. 49.
20. B. van Arkadie and M. Karlssen, 1992, pp. 182–3; UN Economic Commission for Europe, *Economic Bulletin for Europe* (New York, 1992, pp. 74–86; and A. McAuley, 'Economic constraints on devolution: the Lithuanian case' in A. McAuley (ed.) *Soviet Federalism Nationalism and Economic Decentralisation* (London), pp. 169–78.
21. R. Kionka, 'Baltic States Develop a New Ostpolitik' *RFE/RL Research Report*, 21, February 1992, pp. 21–5).
22. *BBC Summary of World Broadcasts, Former USSR*, 3 April 1992, p. C1/3.
23 *BBC Summary of World Broadcasts, Former USSR*, 19 April 1992, p. C1/1.
24. R. Kionka, 'Estonia: A Break with the Past', *RFE/RL Research Report*, 3 January 1992, pp. 66.
25. B. van Arkadie and M. Karlssen, 1992, p. 265.

8 Statehood, Ethnic Relations and Citizenship

Graham Smith, Aadne Aasland
and Richard Mole

The Baltic nations are hardly exceptional in national self-determination leading to the establishment of multi-ethnic polities rather than nation-states. Yet as the experiences of post-colonial states only too vividly show, where nationalists aspire to the idea of the model nation-state in which the dominant nation and national homeland are considered as one and the same, independent statehood is unlikely to become the panacea for resolving multi-ethnic tensions.[1] How the new polity defines the contours of citizenship will be especially critical to determining ethnopolitical stability. As Enloe has observed, 'During political integration national ethnic groups are likely to be looked upon as alien, having less right to the rewards of national sovereignty than indigenous groups'.[2] This is likely to be especially problematic where the nation, having fought for independent statehood, perceives an ethnic minority within the new sovereign polity as inseparable from that nationality which enjoyed a privileged role during colonial rule.

In this chapter we examine how the struggle for national self-determination and the re-establishment of state sovereignty has reconstituted ethnic relations by focusing on what has emerged as the most burning political issue, that of the citizenship question. Firstly, we consider the various debates on citizenship. This enables us to flush out the role that differing ideologies and factions have played in reconceptualising the relationship between the nation, ethnic groups and normative meanings of citizenship, and the factors which have shaped the outcome of these debates. Secondly, as independent statehood has resulted in the ethnic reconstitution of power relations, it is necessary to examine afresh ethnic relations in the new multi-ethnic polities, especially how citizenship is redefining their character. We explore the utility of various models of interethnic relations and assess their applicability to the situation in all three states. And finally, we examine the reaction of the Russian communities to their redefined positions within the new polities, particularly their reactions to citizenship legislation.

CITIZENSHIP AND NATIONAL SELF-DETERMINATION

From their very inception, the popular fronts signalled the importance of citizenship in their desire to secure greater national self-determination for their peoples. At the founding congresses of all three movements in October 1988, delegates discussed citizenship-related issues but refrained from adopting actual resolutions on citizenship itself. However, what clearly emerged from discussions at these founding congresses was the importance of redefining citizenship in order to safeguard the homeland and cultures for their indigenous peoples. At all three congresses, speakers underlined support for the indigenous language to be linked to republican citizenship. As one prominent speaker at the founding congress of the Estonian People's Front noted: 'Over many years, language and citizenship have been artificially separated from other signs of national existence: the community of territory, the community of economic and political life for all people inhabiting this territory. And now we wish to close this gap.'[3] Speakers at the initial congress of the Latvian Popular Front echoed this sentiment, calling upon the Latvian Supreme Soviet 'to pass without delay a law to the effect that the Latvian language is the foundation of the statehood of the sovereign republic and the foundation of national culture, and to acknowledge it as the state language of Latvia'.[4] At all three congresses, the question of citizenship was also linked to immigration which should, as one Estonian delegate observed, be reconstituted in order to 'help regulate migration processes'.[5]

Differing attitudes towards citizenship, however, quickly began to emerge between more multi-ethnic Estonia and Latvia on the one hand and Lithuania on the other. This was in part reflected in the Declarations of Republican Sovereignty and in the subsequent constitutional amendments in which Estonia and Latvia laid much more emphasis than did Lithuania on the need to safeguard a secure homeland for the titular nationalities. Underlying this divergence was the fact that for reasons of ethnodemographics, the popular fronts in Estonia and Latvia felt far less comfortable than their counterpart in Lithuania with the multi-ethnic nature of their societies. Throughout the Soviet period, Estonia and Latvia had been exposed to a massive influx of immigrants. This ethnodemographic metamorphosis had contributed to the Latvian share of its population declining from 75.5 per cent in 1939 to 51.8 per cent by 1989. In Estonia it was even more marked, with the pre-war proportion of its titular population falling from 90 per cent to 64.7 per cent by 1989. In contrast, the Lithuanian proportion of its republic remained relatively unchanged at around 80 per cent, a product of both an economy which during the Soviet period industrialised at a slower pace and which therefore did not justify a large migrant labour force, and of a relatively high rate of native population growth which contrasted with that of Estonia and Latvia where the rate of demographic reproduction remained extremely low. Indeed this fear of demographic extinction and of the need to protect the core nation from its unfavourable demographic situation became a dominant theme in the nationalist discourse of Estonia and Latvia. In contrast, it did not play a prominent part in the programme of *Sajudis*.

Lithuania: the Politics of Inclusion

Lithuania's more accommodating stance was consolidated with the adoption on 3 November 1989 of its law on citizenship. Keen to harness the support of the non-indigenous population, Lithuania's 'zero option', which based the conditions for citizenship upon territorial and not primordial factors, aimed to contribute towards and not result from the struggle for national self-determination. As outlined by Sajudis, the law set out 'to contribute to the creating of a legitimate opportunity to defend the interests of the Lithuanian SSR and to create conditions ... to restore a sovereign Lithuanian state'.[6] No reference was made to saving the nation, as the non-indigenous population did not constitute a threat to the former's continued existence. In order to appease the national radicals within the government, however, deputies did point out that the law on citizenship did not mean that pre-war Lithuanian citizenship had become invalid, thereby acknowledging the fact that the Republic of Lithuania was a restored and not a new state, despite the 'new state' model of citizenship adopted.[7]

After independence attempts were made by neo-nationalists to narrow the range of residents eligible for automatic citizenship, in part fuelled by anti-Russian feeling following Moscow's economic blockade. The then President, Vytautas Landsbergis, however, declined to hold a referendum on the legitimacy of granting citizenship to those who arrived in Lithuania during the Soviet period. For him this would not only side-track what he considered more pressing problems facing the country but would also 'aggravate the political situation in the republic, stir up ethnic animosity, lead to civil confrontation and strengthen the underground CPSU and KGB structures'.[8] Nevertheless, on 5 September 1991, the Sajudis-led Supreme Council imposed direct rule over two Polish-dominated districts and one Russian-dominated town. Although the parliament justified its action as necessary due to the local councils having supported the leaders of the August 1991 *coup d'état*, Russians and Poles in these areas accused Vilnius of using this as an excuse for persecuting national minorities because of their desire for greater autonomy.[9]

Estonia and Latvia: the Politics of Exclusion

As in Lithuania, two traditions also competed for the high ground of nationalist politics in Estonia and Latvia. On the one hand, there was the tradition of civic nationalism. This type of nationalism, embodied in the inter-war national constitutions, was based on a conception of plurality which emphasised the values of cultural coexistence and the importance of universal citizenship for all social groups and classes. On the other hand, the late-1980s national reawakenings had also given rebirth to an ethnic nationalism linked in part to ethno-national insecurity and which grew in opposition to and in conflict with the polity of which it was a part. It was a form of nationalism based on ethnic or primordial ties and which stressed the exclusivist and symbiotic relationship between the core nation, home-land and citizenship. Whereas nationalist politics in Lithuania reflected a view that it could move unhindered towards a more multi-ethnic and less exclusivist stance on who should or should not be a citizen of their recon-stituted polity, the prevailing view of nationalist politics in Estonia and Latvia was that circumstances justified a more exclusionary stance.

This tension was reflected within both the Estonian and Latvian popular fronts. On the one hand, there were those who believed the national self-determination should not be exclusivist and that all those who lived and worked within the territories of Estonia and Latvia had the right to become full and equal members of the body politic. No doubt such a belief was reinforced by a pragmatism based on an acknowledged need to secure broader ethnic support for the separatist struggle in polities whose core nations did not have the same commanding ethnodemographic base as in Lithuania. It was how-ever the formation of the Citizens' Committees in Estonia and Latvia which did much to radicalise the debate. By registering the names of all the citizens of the inter-war republics and their descendants, the citizens' committees advocated a conception of political community based firmly on descent. These radicals resented Russian immigrants enjoying equal status with the indigenous populations, and 'considered unfair the participation in the fate of the region of all the residents of the republics'.[10] Bowing to such conflicting pressures, the popular fronts opted for a more conciliatory and pragmatic strategy. This was underlined by the publication in July 1989 of 'The Latvian Popular Front's ideological platform, based on the idea of creating an inde-pendent and democratic Latvia, for the consolidation of various nationalities living in Latvia' which stressed that

> the Latvian Popular Front advocates that all residents of Latvia, regard-less of their nationality, social situation, or religious affiliation, who

have chosen freely to support the creation of an independent Latvia become citizens of Latvia. Likewise, the Latvia Popular Front advocates that the citizenship of independent Latvia be granted to all permanent residents of Latvia, who at the time of citizenship registration, have lived in Latvia at least ten years.[11]

At its third Congress, in October 1990, the Popular Front attempted to distance itself from more radical nationalist elements by emphasising the importance of avoiding the arrogance of one nation over another, as well as chauvinism, anti-Semitism and Russophobia.[12]

Following the proclamations of independence, there was a shift of focus in the citizenship debate in both republics.[13] With the transitional phase towards independence under way, discussion in Estonia and Latvia subsequently centred upon the need to determine the boundaries of the citizenry. The way forward was back to the future. By acknowledging that the Baltic states should not be considered *new* but *restored* states, the Estonian and Latvian governments argued that the same applied to the citizenship question, with citizenship being restored only to the original citizenry and their descendants of the inter-war republics. Consequently 'exclusionists' in Estonia underlined the fact that the republic was not the legal successor of the Estonian SSR and was, therefore, under no obligation to accommodate those who had settled in Estonia during the years of Soviet rule.[14] It was a viewpoint which had also been held by delegates at the Congress of Estonia who were adamant that 'only the citizens of the Estonian republic and their descendants have the right to participate in its restoration'.[15] In their opinion, all those who arrived in Estonia after 1940 were immigrants, whose naturalisation would depend upon strict language and residence requirements, calculated from the date of the republic's restoration. As one nationalist explained, the indigenous population simply wanted to feel at home again in its own republic: 'We are tired of having people come up here and tell us how to run our country and what to do with our land. ... Decisions about Estonia should be made by Estonians'.[16]

This exclusionary stance was also evident in Latvia. At the Latvian Citizens' Congress, delegates criticised the inclusive nature of the Lithuanian citizenship legislation and stressed that there should be 'an ethnically pure attitude towards citizenship, there should be no hypocrisy, there is nothing shameful in a Latvian-like Latvia'.[17] National radicals in Latvia, therefore, also insisted that the national government reinstate the pre-war law on citizenship, with all the norms for naturalisation of immigrants envisaged in it. The greater danger of 'national extinction' in Latvia, however, led to the call for even more stringent residence requirements for those seeking naturalisation. This fear also resulted in political actors in Latvia supporting the introduction of quotas, whereby a priority list would be drawn up with regard to acquisition of citizenship: ethnic Latvians without citizenship would be given priority, followed by the spouses of citizens and those who contributed actively to Latvian independence. By definition, ethnic Russians would find themselves at the bottom of such a list.

There seems little doubt that the drift of nationalist politics in Estonia and Latvia towards a more exclusionist stance understandably polarised relations with many Russians although not sufficiently to prevent sizeable numbers supporting the cause of independent statehood. Russian organisations, in particular, felt that severe inter-ethnic tensions would ensue were citizenship legislation to be given retroactive force. As the leader of one Russian political organisation in Estonia explained: 'No civil accord can be obtained by a society in which a sizeable proportion would have the status of non-citizens'.[18] In Latvia, as in Estonia, many proponents of the 'zero option' argued that the Baltic republics ceased to exist as a result of the Soviet annexation in 1940. Consequently, they felt that the new polity should have proclaimed a second Republic in August 1991; it would then follow that all those permanently resident in Estonia or Latvia on the day of the independence declaration would be entitled to citizenship, as citizens of a new state. As a result, the 'inclusionists' opposed all forms of residence and language requirements for citizenship.

The citizenship debate took on a new dimension in the summer of 1992, when the parliament of the Russian Federation declared its intention to take up the cause of ethnic Russians living in the Baltic states. With regard to Estonia, the parliament in Moscow expressed no objection to Russians taking an oath of loyalty to the Republic, but criticised the fact that citizenship was dependent upon passing an examination in the Estonian language. On 17 July 1992 the Russian Parliament passed a resolution on infringements on human rights in Estonia, instructing the government to consider 'temporary economic sanctions against the Estonian Republic in case its authorities continue discrimination against ethnic Russians'.[19]

Similarly, Moscow censured the Latvian parliament for its treatment of the republic's Russian population. Latvian politicians, however, countered the accusation, laying the blame for the fate of Latvia's Russian minority with the parliament of the Russian Federation: 'At the moment Russia is demonstrating a cynical reluctance to withdraw the troops. If Europe demands liberalism without demanding that Russia speed up the withdrawal of troops, then that could generate among the people unnecessary radicalism and lack of confidence in European structures'.[20]

The issue of republican citizenship had developed from a purely domestic political concern to a factor in geopolitical inter-state relations. By insisting that the situation in Latvia warranted 'the possible granting of interim powers to the Russian military in regulating its presence in that country', the Russian President, Boris Yeltsin, linked the withdrawal of Russian troops from the Baltic states to amendments being made to local citizenship legislation. As he later emphasised: 'Russia has no intention to sign any agreement regarding the withdrawal of Russian troops from Latvia or Estonia until these countries bring their legislation into line with international standards'.[21] This was reiterated in his Vancouver speech in April 1993: troop withdrawals would be delayed until these countries ended the persecution of minorities[22]. Although officially both the Estonian and Latvian governments refused to link troop withdrawals with citizenship matters, Russia's eventual willingness to withdraw its garrisons was successfully concluded by April 1994, primarily due to Western pressures concerning economic aid. This was despite the lack of negotiations between Russia and the Baltic States on issues related to the status of the Russian speaking communities.

More influential were western pressures, bound up with the desire of the Baltic States to reconnect up with Europe, of being able to sell themselves as democratic states 'living by modern European conditions' in order to secure the benefits of both Europe's economic market-place[23] and from membership of its geopolitical security structures. Interstate organisations such as the Conference on Security and Co-operation in Europe (CSCE) and the Council of Europe were an especially moderating influence[24]. While being seen by some Western human rights organisations such as Helsinki Watch as being too accommodative, nonetheless such international organisations did play an important role in effecting modifications to citizenship legislation, specifically with regard to amending Estonia's June 1993 Law on Aliens which would have required all non-citizens to obtain residence and work permits within two years if they wished to remain in the country[25]. Responding to criticisms of the CSCE, on 8 July 1993 the law was amended to guarantee work permits to any alien who had settled in Estonia prior to 1 July 1990 and had been registered as a permanent resident. Similarly, Western pressures also played a part in influencing Latvia's 1994 Citizenship Law which saw the abandonment of proposed citizen quotas and the residency qualification being reduced from sixteen to ten years.

THE STATE, DEMOCRACY AND CITIZENSHIP

For the Baltic states, the relationship between ethnicity, citizenship and democracy is still uncertain. As polities still in transition, their emerging political systems do not lend themselves to easy labelling or classification. Three models, however, are particularly apposite.

Firstly, there is a disparate school of thought which suggests that Estonia and Latvia display the characteristics of a system of social apartheid. This model would assume that ethnic minorities are excluded on the basis of ethnicity or race from integrating fully into the body politic. Linked to securing the hegemony of the core nation, citizenship rights (political, civil and social) are limited to individuals on the basis of ethnicity; consequently, democracy is enjoyed only by members of the core nation. While some Western observers argue that denial of political rights, notably the right to participate in and stand for national elections, points towards the possibility of Estonia and Latvia sliding towards another South Africa,[26] Baltic Russian activists suggest that this situation has already arrived.[27] It is also the official view of Russia, where its President, Boris Yeltsin, has argued that 'a form of apartheid' directed against Baltic Russians is bound up with attempts at 'ethnic cleansing' designed to secure more ethnically homogenous polities.[28] If this model has utility we would also expect its repercussions for institutionalising ethnic divisions to extend beyond political participation to producing differentiated upward mobility, a greater cultural division of labour within the work place, political favouritism, and socio-spatial segregation.

The applicability of this model is problematic. First, membership of the citizen-state is not based on ethnic or racial criteria but rather between citizens of the interwar republics and their descendants and other residents. Thus Estonia's February 1992 citizenship law requires two years of residence (plus a one-year waiting period) before a migrant qualifies while Latvia's 1994 citizenship law stipulates a 10 year residency requirement. Hence for the Russian community this in effect means that 'historic Russians' automatically qualify for full citizenship while most 'Russians migrants' do not. Thus in Latvia, about a quarter of those who have registered as citizens are non-Latvians, having qualified through being either citizens of the former Latvian state or through family ties to a former citizen.[29] According to the newspaper *Estoniya*, approximately one-sixth of Russian speakers in Estonia qualified by 1992 for citizenship.[30] Second, like Lithuania, residents in the other two Baltic states, irrespective of their ethnicity, have the potential to become citizens. It has been argued that all states have residency requirements and that compared to many liberal democracies the time frame for acquiring citizenship in Estonia is less stringent. Thus in theory, Estonia's two-plus-one residency requirement would mean that if all non-Estonians had registered by 30 March 1990 for citizenship, for non-Estonians the residency requirement would be a non-issue. In practice, however, only 30 000 did register by this date. Finally, exclusion from citizenship within the Baltic states does not automatically relegate Russians residents to the status of stateless persons. Russia's adoption of an extra-territorial definition of citizenship includes its Russian diaspora. However this policy has been used by Baltic ultranationalists as justification for both the exclusion of Russians from Baltic citizenship and as a basis for encouraging their emigration.

In some respects Lithuania comes closer to resembling a second type of model: majoritarian-type democracy. This model is usually considered as being particularly appropriate to societies which are ethnically not deeply divided.[31] Although ethnic tensions still manifest themselves, the core nation is sufficiently secure to prevail as a majority in the political, economic and social life of the polity, to let ethnic groups keep or drop their sub-cultures, or live apart or mix. Emphasis is on aspiring to a polity in which citizens are mobilised into a national political community irrespective of ethnic affiliations. Thus what is aspired to is not 'the Lithuanian nation' but 'the nation of Lithuania'. Emphasis is placed as much on rights associated with individual well being as on support for ethnic communalism. It can lead to national party formations reflecting a high degree of 'nationalisation' within society.

Elements of this model may have some applicability to Lithuania: its citizenship laws are by far the most liberal; it is a highly homogeneous society (over 80 per cent Lithuanian); ethnic and linguistic differences are politically less problematic than in Estonia and Latvia due to a higher degree of social interaction between ethnic groups; and support for political parties is less ethnically partisan, although the adoption of a complex system of proportional representation does allow ethnic minority parties, like the Polish Union, the opportunity for representation in Parliament. The election to government in February 1993 of the Democratic Labour Party (LDDP) illustrated that not only was a major political party capable of attracting support from a broad spectrum of ethnic groups but also that, compared with Estonia and Latvia, ethnic politics was no longer judged the most salient socio-economic issue. Yet in such majoritarian democracies feelings of deprivation may persist, owing to the inevitable 'tyranny of the majority' under this system.

The third model, that of ethnic democracy, might have more applicability to Estonia and Latvia. It encapsulates three central features.[32] Firstly, an ethnic democracy accords an institutional superior status to the core nation beyond its numerical proportion within the national territory. Secondly, certain civil and political rights are enjoyed universally. This can include the right of assembly and association, freedom of the press, an independent judiciary, a multi-party system, and a change of government through fair elections. And thirdly, certain collective rights are extended to ethnic minorities. In combining some elements of civil and political democracy with explicit ethnic dominance, an ethnic democracy attempts to preserve ethno-political stability based on the contradictions and tensions inherent in such a system. For many multi-ethnic polities emerging from coercive rule and where the transition to democracy is unlikely to be either automatic or easy, adopting such a model has its own inner logic. As Smooha and Hanf note, 'Since nationalism in Eastern Europe tends to be integral and exclusionary as opposed to western nationalism which tends to be open, inclusive and coterminous with citizenship, there is a strong possibility for some of the democratising states there to become ethnic democracies'.[33]

In the transition towards independent statehood, the secessionist movements were clear that in a future polity, the core nation, because of its unique symbiotic relationship to the national homeland, should occupy a privileged place. Thus as early as 1989, Latvia's declaration of sovereignty strongly emphasised that the 'territory of the Latvian Soviet Socialist Republic is the ... only place on earth where the Latvian nation can fully exercise its right to statehood and develop without hindrance the Latvian language, national culture and economy'.[34] What in particular has been crucial in safeguarding the institutional hegemony of the Estonians and Latvians has been the scope of political rights and language laws.

Whereas in Lithuania all permanent residents have the right to participate politically and to stand in national and local elections, in Estonia and Latvia this right extends only to local political representation.[35] In the 1993 national elections no ethnic Russian representatives were found in Estonia's parliament, only seven in Latvia[36] (out of a 100-strong parliament), while in Lithuania ten non-Lithuanians secured seats (out of a parliament of 141 deputies). In urban government the situation differs, as non-citizens have the right both to vote in and stand for elections. In Riga, where over half the population is non-Latvian, only 10 per cent comprise non-Latvians. In Daugavpils the situation is slightly better; non-Latvians make up 50 per cent of the local council and 87 per cent of the population. A similar situation is evident in Estonia. In Tallinn, the non-eponymous population makes up 18 per cent of the council but in Narva, where the non-Estonians constitute 96 per cent of the population, 39 of its 42 deputies are non-Estonian. In restricting the right to vote and be represented to the locality, the state provides a basis for ethnic minority representation over local affairs but one which does not threaten the core nation's political hegemony. However, such ethnic representation, especially strong in the non-eponymous enclaves of north-east Estonia and in Latgallia, provides Russians with a territorial-institutional base to mobilise local support against the centre in which issues of fiscal and other communal resources are likely to fuel ethnic tensions.

The transition towards a multi-party political system which now flourishes in all three Baltic states has not however been accompanied in Estonia and Latvia by the right of all those domiciled there to form or become members of political parties. Estonia's constitution stipulates that only citizens of Estonia have the right to become members of political parties; consequently, political party membership is highly mono-ethnic in character, ensuring the dominance of the core nations within the political life of their polities. In a handful of political parties, non-Estonians comprise between 2 and 8 per cent of members but more typically have no members at all.[37]

The elevation of the core nation language to that of the state language and of the language requirements which accompany a successful application to become a citizen also ensures the institutional dominance of the core nation. Given the extra-territorial privileges which accrued to the Russian language during Soviet rule, there was little local pressure on Russians settling in the Baltic region to learn the dominant languages of the region. According to the 1989 Soviet census, only 13 per cent of Russians in Estonia and 22 per cent in Latvia possessed a knowledge of the local languages. Thus language tests are an obligatory condition not only for most professional occupations, but also for membership of the body politic. In short, the new language policies will for most Russian-speakers act as a major barrier to enjoying basic citizens' rights and also as a brake on opportunities for membership of the professional classes. Consequently, language will function as a key resource for the strengthening and reproduction of core cultures and as an obvious social stigma.

Within the arena of other rights, notably of civil and social rights, all three Baltic states are still in the process of mapping out the social contours of membership. The May 1990 Latvian Declaration of Independence guaranteed a range of rights to all 'those nations permanently resident in Latvia' but its Supreme Council in December 1991 restricted many of these rights to citizens only, including the right to own land and other natural resources and the freedom to reside in Latvia and return there. Similar restrictions on property rights (October 1991 Land Reform Law) and on mobility exist in Estonia. Thus in both states, permanent members who are non-citizens do not have the automatic right to re-enter their country of residence: moreover the old Soviet residence permit (*propiska*), employed to restrict freedom of mobility within as well as between the former Soviet republics, is still used to regulate the movement of non-citizens. Within the arena of social rights, which were well developed during Soviet rule and available to all Soviet citizens, it is still uncertain what implications states no longer committed to guaranteeing full employment to workers or high social welfare spending will have. Yet the economic restructuring of former state-owned industries is likely to affect the Russian community in particular with no clear guidelines as to whether those who lose their jobs will be entitled to the same social security benefits as citizens. In comparison, collective rights are supported. Minorities have the right to their own languages, schools, newspapers, access to television programmes in their own language and cultural associations. Yet such collective rights do not go so far as their southern neighbour. In Lithuania a language law, for instance, stipulates that if more than a third of a locality are non-Lithuanian speakers, public institutions must also conduct their business in the language of the sizeable minority.

THE BALTIC RUSSIANS AND CITIZENSHIP

The attitudes of the Russian communities, especially in relation to the citizenship question, will be particularly crucial to determining the nature of ethno-regional stability. In a major survey of the Baltic Russians undertaken by the authors in February 1993 in four cities – Narva (Estonia), Riga and Daugavpils (Latvia), and Klaipeda (Lithuania) (Table 8.1)[38] it was found that reactions to the citizenship laws did differ between Estonia and Latvia on the one hand and Lithuania on the other. While only one-fifth of Klaipeda's respondents felt that the citizenship legislation was unfair, in the other three cities the overwhelming majority registered their disapproval (Table 8.2). Overall, however, most Russians felt that a residency requirement was an acceptable condition for citizenship (Table 8.3). Such a response is consistent with the prevailing view held among most Russian-dominated organisations and Russian activists within the popular fronts who supported the 'zero option' model, whereby the only requirement for citizenship would be permanent residency in the state at the date independent statehood was declared. There is however no evidence to suggest any relationship between length of residency among the Russians who came in during the Soviet period and support for a residency requirement even though respondents who had lived in their respective state for over 10 years (in the case of

Table 8.1 Nationality composition of the cities in the 1993 survey

	Total population ('000s)	Eponymous nationality (per cent)	Russians (per cent)
Riga	910.5	36.5	47.3
Daugavpils (Latgallia)	124.9	13.0	58.3
Narva (north-east Estonia)	77.5	4.0	85.9
Klaipeda	202.9	63.0	28.2

Source: The 1989 Soviet census.

Table 8.2 Russian responses to citizenship laws*

	Riga	Daugavpils	Klaipeda	Narva
		(per cent)		
Fair	0	10	41	8
Unfair	98	79	20	82
Don't know/No answer	2	11	39	10

*As the survey predated the 1994 Citizenship Law in Latvia, Russians in that republic were asked their views on proposed citizenship laws.

Latvia) would not be affected by a strict residency requirement. However Russians born in the republic, irrespective of their age, were marginally more supportive of residency requirements than were Russian immigrants.

What however is clear is that in all four cities Russians are generally against additional conditions for acquiring citizenship. Only one in ten respondents in the cities of Latvia and Estonia thought it should be necessary to renounce citizenship of other states, while few respondents agreed that citizenship should be restricted to citizens and their descendants of the interwar republics (Table 8.3). Only a fifth of respondents felt that applicants for citizenship should be required to give an oath of loyalty to the state. This issue has been particularly controversial among Daugavpils' large and long-established community of Old Believers whose church representatives oppose an oath of loyalty to any secular institutions.

Opposition, however, is particularly evident against knowledge of the local language as an entitlement to citizenship. This was particularly clear in the cities of Latvia and Estonia, where less than 5 per cent supported this view and where knowledge of the eponymous language is lower than in Klaipeda. Clearly most Russians fear that language legislation in particular

Table 8.3 Citizenship requirements*

	Total	Riga	Daugavpils (per cent)	Klaipeda	Narva
Residency requirements					
Yes	58	58	60	48	64
No	25	26	27	26	20
Don't know/No answer	18	16	13	26	16
Oath of loyalty to the state					
Yes	20	12	13	32	22
No	50	60	63	35	41
Don't know/No answer	31	29	24	33	37
Citizenship from the previous (interwar) state					
Yes	11	5	15	5	18
No	43	37	53	41	41
Don't know/No answer	46	58	32	54	41
Renunciation of citizenship of other states					
Yes	16	9	13	30	11
No	58	71	59	41	63
Don't know/No answer	26	20	28	29	27

*Respondents were asked whether they thought the requirements listed should be necessary in order to obtain citizenship in the state in which they reside.

makes their position especially tenuous. This is notably so in Estonia and Latvia whose language laws are tougher and where complaints about the level of linguistic requirements are greater. Yet at the same time, most Russians acknowledged that a knowledge of the eponymous language should be a precondition to working in state institutions and in the service sector (Table 8.4). In more multi-ethnic Riga, however, Russians were least keen, no doubt reflecting their greater vulnerability to losing their jobs to native speakers than in the other cities sampled, caused by insufficient knowledge of the eponymous language. As might be expected, however, Russians who were fluent or who displayed a good command of the local languages were more likely to support the principle of language requirements in particular workplaces. Not surprisingly, a clear majority in

Table 8.4   Statehood and the language issue. Respondents were asked to what extent they agreed with all or any of the following statements.

(a)   Russian should have the status of an official language in Latvia (Lithuania, Estonia)

	Riga	Daugavpils	Klaipeda	Narva
		(per cent)		
Fully agree	77	48	21	53
Tend to agree	10	27	26	22
Don't know/No answer	2	7	15	8
Tend to disagree	9	15	19	12
Completely disagree	2	3	18	5

(b)   Only people who have a knowledge of the Latvian (Lithuanian, Estonian) language should be entitled to Latvian (Lithuanian, Estonian) citizenship

	Riga	Daugavpils	Klaipeda	Narva
		(per cent)		
Fully agree	4	0	17	2
Tend to agree	0	1	14	3
Don't know/No answer	1	6	10	5
Tend to disagree	12	21	23	20
Completely disagree	83	73	37	70

(c)   People working in the service industries and in state institutions should be required to speak Latvian (Lithuanian, Estonian)

	Riga	Daugavpils	Klaipeda	Narva
		(per cent)		
Fully agree	18	32	48	28
Tend to agree	27	31	22	28
Don't know/No answer	13	10	12	12
Tend to disagree	19	19	12	20
Completely disagree	24	8	6	12

continued

Table 8.4   continued

(d) Russians who do not speak Latvian (Lithuanian, Estonian) have only themselves to blame

	Riga	Daugavpils	Klaipeda	Narva
		(per cent)		
Fully agree	3	11	47	6
Tend to agree	13	17	17	5
Don't know/No answer	1	8	13	5
Tend to disagree	20	32	12	20
Completely disagree	63	32	12	63

(e) Russian should be a/the language of inter-ethnic contact in Latvia (Lithuania, Estonia)

	Riga	Daugavpils	Klaipeda	Narva
		(per cent)		
Fully agree	75	57	35	54
Tend to agree	16	25	32	20
Don't know/No answer	5	7	20	16
Tend to disagree	2	9	9	6
Completely disagree	2	2	5	4

all four cities supported the idea that Russian should be adopted as an official language of the polity in which they reside.

Russians in Estonia and Latvia have the self-image that their exclusion from such a community of eponymous speakers is not of their making but is rather a product of circumstances beyond their control. In Klaipeda, however, where a far higher level of fluency in the eponymous language is detectable, nearly two-thirds of Russians supported the view that only Russians had themselves to blame for not knowing the local language. This would therefore seem to reinforce the more general proposition that Russians in Lithuania have become more linguistically integrated precisely because of ethnodemographics and the greater everyday pressures to communicate in the local language than in Estonian and Latvian society, where larger Russian communities – such as in north-east Estonia – were able to function with more limited social contact with eponymous speakers.

Despite concern about the citizenship and language laws, the majority of Russians in all four cities had either applied or intended to apply for citizen-

Table 8.5 Intended citizenship applicants among the Russian communities

	Riga	Daugavpils	Klaipeda	Narva
		(per cent)		
Republic citizenship				
Intend to apply	71	81	99	40
Will not apply	18	10	0	28
Don't know	9	9	1	31
No answer	2	0	1	1
Russian citizenship				
Intend to apply	27	5	8	19
Will not apply	52	73	75	48
Don't know	20	19	13	28
No answer	2	3	4	5

ship from their polity of residence (Table 8.5). In Narva, however, only 40 per cent of Russians reported that they would apply for Estonian citizenship, with almost one-third undecided. The number of Russians who intended applying for citizenship of the Russian Federation was however generally low, although in Riga it was just over one in four and in Narva just under a fifth. Although Lithuanian citizenship legislation does not allow for dual citizenship, 8 per cent of the respondents in Klaipeda had either applied or intended to apply for both Russian and Lithuanian citizenship. This can be explained by the fact that, in the two-year period during which permanent residents were required to declare their citizenship, no corresponding Russian law on citizenship existed. Not convinced of the longevity of their Soviet citizenship, and afraid of losing their right to their apartment, many Russians applied for Lithuanian citizenship. Later, when a Russian law on citizenship had been drawn up and when Russians were assured by the Lithuanian state that permanent residence was enough to secure housing ownership rights, some Russians in the republic began transferring from Lithuanian to Russian citizenship. This process has been slow, in part due to the relatively high cost of the procedure, and also to the fact that all application forms for transferral of citizenship have to be written in Lithuanian. Similarly, in Latvia, despite the unlikelihood of the state endorsing dual citizenship, 17 per cent of the respondents in Riga did intend applying for dual citizenship, whereas in Daugavpils this was an option not considered by any of the sample. Also 7 per cent of Riga's respondents and 10 per cent in Narva did not intend to apply for citizenship either in the state in which they live or in the Russian Federation.

Russians born in the Baltic republics were naturally more likely to apply for citizenship of the state in which they lived than were Russians born elsewhere. Similarly, only 2 per cent of the respondents who reported that they were born in the Baltic states had considered obtaining Russian citizenship. As could also be expected, there was a strong correlation between level of knowledge of the language of the titular nationality in the state and intentions of applying for citizenship of that state. Moreover, none of the Russians born in mixed marriages where one of the parents was of the indigenous nationality intended to apply for Russian citizenship.

Virtually all Russians living in Klaipeda were, or intended to become, Lithuanian citizens, in part a product of Lithuania's liberal citizenship legislation which also excludes a language requirement for citizenship. A higher level of integration of Russians in Lithuania than in the two other states is also a contributory factor. This contrasts with Estonia and Latvia where the citizenship issue is more controversial but where important differences between the two are detectable. First, the number of people who were citizens or descendants of citizens from the interwar republic was significantly higher in the Latvian cities than in Estonia. During registration of the population, preliminary results indicated that there were more Russians who automatically qualified for citizenship in the Latvian cities than in Narva. Second, the level of language-knowledge was significantly higher in the Latvian cities than in Narva, and many Russians in Narva probably knew that they would not pass the language examination, or found the prospects of taking such an examination humiliating. This probably made them less enthusiastic about applying for citizenship. However, four in five of the respondents in Narva who reported fluency or a good command of the Estonian language had also applied or intended to apply for Estonian citizenship. Third, the existence of a law on citizenship could be another explanatory factor for differences between Narva and the Latvian cities. Whereas Russians in Estonia were familiar with the terms for obtaining citizenship at the time when the survey was carried out, this was not yet the case in Latvia. Russians in the Latvian cities could therefore still hope that a liberal law on citizenship would be adopted, which may have influenced the way in which they expressed their preferences. Russians in Narva were also familiar with the restrictions applying to non-citizens, while in Latvia, where the likely boundaries on the rights of non-citizens were unclear, many Russians felt that the spheres in which the rights of citizens and non-citizens would differ could be broadened in the future. They were therefore likely to be more worried about the risk of ending up without citizenship and thereby losing not only political rights, but also the right to own property or freedom of movement. The higher organisational level of

Russians in Narva, combined with their ability to influence local politics without becoming citizens, may be another explanation why Russians in Narva were less interested than Latvia's Russians in obtaining citizenship of their polity of residency.

The differences between Riga and Daugavpils with regard to interest in applying for Russian citizenship would suggest that Russians in Riga were generally less well integrated into Latvian society than their counterparts in Daugavpils, who tended to have a stronger sense of local historical identity linked also to traditions as an ethnic minority in the interwar Latvian state. In contrast Riga was the major destination for Russians during the Soviet period. By the 1970s, Russians constituted the largest ethnic group in the city, a situation of particular concern to those involved in Latvia's struggle for national self-determination. Riga's Russians were therefore conscious of what they perceived as their unwanted presence: their interest in Russian citizenship might be seen as a protection against Latvian nationalism. In Daugavpils, on the other hand, where Russians and other Slavs dominate numerically, Latvian nationalism was not seen as a major threat, which might well be one reason why the city's Russians did not feel the same need to secure protection through Russian citizenship.

It would however seem that Russians have sufficient associational ties to the Baltic states to be content to remain there. Indeed our survey revealed that two out of three Russians intended to remain with only about one-fifth stating a preference for living in Russia. Thus for most Russian migrants re-emigration has limited appeal, with most Russians as settled now in the Baltic states as they were in early 1991.[39] For many, no doubt, the benefits of living in Estonia and Latvia, despite the possibility of becoming an ethnic underclass, outweigh the costs of uprooting and returning to an even less certain economic future in Russia. This is also borne out by the negligible number of Baltic Russian settlers, compared to most other post-Soviet states, who have so far returned to Russia.[40]

Nor is political secession an option favoured by those Russians in the territorially compact communities contiguous to Russia. Less than 10 per cent of Russians in Narva, Daugavpils and Klaipeda supported the secession of their local regions (Figure 6). Ethno-regional autonomy, however, is seen as a more attractive proposition, although the type of autonomy favoured and support for it does differ between the localities. Among those Russians in Riga who had made up their minds on the issues of economic and cultural autonomy, more were in favour than against. In Klaipeda the opposite was the case. The majority of Russians living there seem to feel that their cultural rights are sufficiently protected to make it of less concern than elsewhere. A large number of the city's inhabitants did however favour

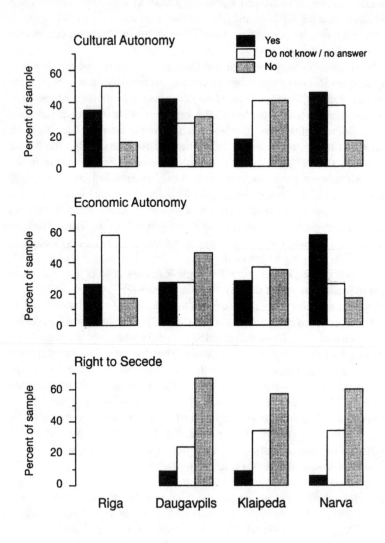

Figure 6   Regional autonomy in the Baltic States

economic autonomy, no doubt reflecting the possible benefits which could accrue to this seaboard locality from a more locally-flexible response to their advantaged location on the Baltic Sea. This contrasted with Daugavpils; located as it is in less-developed Latgallia, its local politicians fear that left to its own economic devices, and with less financial support from Riga, the region could become even more of an economic backwater. A much larger proportion of the respondents in Daugavpils were however in favour of cultural autonomy, no doubt also reflecting as much a sense of Latgallian identity as Russian identity. It is in Narva, however, that both cultural and economic autonomy enjoy most support, with about half the population in favour of both cultural and economic autonomy. This is also borne out by the position adopted by Narva's overwhelmingly Russian-dominated town council and the notably strained relations that exist between the Tallinn government and a local community whose demands for autonomy have been more clearly articulated than in any other locality in the Baltic States.

CONCLUSIONS

Labelling polities in transition is an especially precarious exercise. It would however seem that, with reservations, Lithuania displays more of the characteristics of a majoritarian-type democracy, whereas Estonia and Latvia contain many of the features of an ethnic democracy. Yet despite concern among the Russian communities in Estonia and Latvia about their polities moving towards more exclusionary-based political systems, neither republic has witnessed the scale of ethnic tension found in many other post-Soviet states. Nor is such tension translated into a high degree of organised political opposition.

The large number of social organisations with a predominantly Russian or Slavic membership gives a misleading impression of the activity level of the Russian population in the region. There is a broad range of organisations, varying from religious organisations, cultural associations and more politically orientated parties and movements. Most of these organisations have a very small membership, and the number of people taking an active part in them is even smaller. Many of the existing organisations either do not co-operate with one another or they work against each other, even though the main aims of the organisations are often similar. In the four cities surveyed there was little indication of political activity among the Russian population, with only a negligible one per cent of respondents indicating affiliations with any of the existing Russian-dominated organisations in their city or polity. Besides the obvious state-imposed limits that exist in Estonia and Latvia concerning non-citizen political activity, there are other reasons for the low level of political mobilisation and the lack of unity among Russian-dominated organisations.

Firstly, Russians in the Baltic states are far from being a homogeneous group of people, and their historical origin and attitudes to their future in the Baltic States differ widely. Those belonging to various sub-groups of the Russian population have different interests and few reasons to unite. To a migrant worker the main concern may be how to avoid unemployment and manage to feed the family; a peasant Old Believer might see the revival of his confession and his culture as the main concern; while a retired officer may be occupied with who will pay him a pension and how to keep his previously rent-free accommodation.[41] The few issues uniting them are the Russian language, their self-identification as Russians (although 'Russian' may have a variety of meanings), and the fact that they live in a post-Soviet state outside Russia. It is however doubtful whether this is enough to instil a communal sense of purpose. Indeed, many Russians argue against the formation of political organisations along ethnic lines, fearing that such organisations will increase the significance of ethnic differences and stand in the way of political integration.[42]

Secondly, in all three states Russians lack intellectual élites willing and able to champion issues of social justice. Such an élite did however exist in the independent states between the world wars and played a prominent and integrative role during that period. Their subsequent reduction during the Stalin years has had serious implications for the continuity of Russian culture in the region. Russians who came into the Baltic states during the Soviet period tended to be a technical élite, employed in economic management, administration and science. Moreover, the so-called but numerically small creative élite who came to work in the Baltic universities, other educational institutions, and administration, received their education and had been indocrinated within the Soviet system. It is in short an élite unaccustomed to the traditions of civil society and unconnected to a cultural tradition of pluralist democracy.

Finally, after Russian-dominated organisations and movements such as the Intermovements and the Communist Parties discredited themselves and became illegal after the August 1991 coup, a political vacuum developed among their former supporters. Many Russians who had seen these organisations as the only defence against Baltic nationalism quickly became disillusioned with and lost faith in politics and the ability of politicians to improve their situations.

While the Baltic Russians may well constitute 'a motley, unorganised mass, which in a political sense does not represent movements and parties but a crowd',[43] nonetheless it has on occasion shown itself capable of mobilisation against the politics of exclusion. This has been somewhat uniquely evident in Narva where already existing local political institutions – notably in the form of the municipal government and local trade unions – have provided a basis for strike action, demonstrations and calls for a local referendum on north-east Estonia's future territorial status.[44] More generally, much will also depend on local responses to economic change and the extent to which the economic rights of Russian communities will be affected by polities undergoing economic restructuring. What will therefore be crucial in determining whether the Baltic states enter the twenty-first century as ethnically stable democracies will be how secure their core nations feel about the multi-ethnic societies of which they are a part, and how well Russians can adapt to membership of polities in which they no longer constitute an ethnically privileged élite.

ACKNOWLEDGEMENTS

Graham Smith would like to thank the Institute of Peace Studies, Washington DC, and the Leverhulme Trust for their financial support.

NOTES

1. R. Tarzi, 'The Nation-State, Victim Groups and Refugees', *Ethnic and Racial Studies* 14(4) 1992, pp. 441–52.
2. C. Enloe, *Ethnic Conflict and Political Development* (Lanham, Md, 1986), p. 24.
3. FBIS-SOV-88-204; 67.
4. FBIS-SOV-88-208: 63–4.
5. FBIS-SOV-88-204: 67.
6. FBIS-SOV-89-208: 67–8.
7. FBIS-SOV-89-213: 70.
8. FBIS-SOV-91-232: 59.
9. FBIS-SOV-91-178: 69.
10. *Literaturnaya gazeta*, 19 July 1989, p. 10.
11. Radio Free Europe/Radio Liberty, *Report on the USSR*, 20 October 1989, p. 21.
12. M. Kvernrod, *Citizenship and Interethnic Relations in Latvia* (Hovedfagsoppgave, Oslo, 1993), pp. 59–60.
13. On 30 March and 4 May 1990, respectively, the Estonian and Latvian Supreme Councils proclaimed that their republics had entered transition

periods 'of unspecified duration' towards independence; Lithuania's unconditional declaration of independence was made on 11 March 1990.

14. The views of the national radicals were laid down in the resolution 'On the status of a citizen of the Estonian Republic and the status of a USSR citizen in the Estonian Republic' which was published in draft form in November 1991.

15. FBIS-SOV-90-126-S: 17.

16. *Sovetskaya Rossiya*, 5 Aug. 1989, p. 4.

17. FBIS-SOV-90-085: 89.

18. FBIS-SOV-91-184: 49.

19. FBIS-SOV-92-179: 47.

20. FBIS-SOV-92-083: 72.

21. *Rossiskaya gazeta*, 18 July, 1992.

22. *Nezavizamaya gazeta*, 13 April, 1993.

23. For example, economic organisations like the European Bank for Reconstruction and Development purposely linked development aid to citizenship, a sharp reminder of the economic leverage that the West can exercise over the Baltic States.

24. Estonia's law on citizenship was sufficient not to act as an impediment to membership of the Council of Europe, along with Lithuania, in May 1993. Latvia, however, had to wait until February 1995. In order to become a member, Latvia had to revise its 1994 Citizenship Law, dropping proposals to implement a quota system whereby only a restricted number of non-citizens could become citizens in any given year.

25. A. Sheehy (1993) 'Estonia's Law on Aliens', *RFE/RL Research Report*, Vol 2 (38), pp. 7–11.

26. See, for example, T. Milljan, paper presented at the *Conference of the Association for the Advancement of Baltic Studies* (Toronto, June 1992).

27. Former Estonian Premier Edgar Savisaar, in commenting upon Estonia's Citizen Law of June 1993, in which all residents who are not citizens will have to apply for a residence permit and thus face the possibility of being deported, fears the institutionalisation of apartheid. See *the Baltic Independent*, 25 June–1 July 1993, p. 3.

28. See, for example, *Pravda*, 24 June 1993.

29. *Diena*, 1 February 1993.

30. *Estoniya*, 30 October 1992.

31. R. Lijphart, *Democracies, Patterns of Majoritarian and Consensus Government in Twenty-One Countries* (New Haven, Conn., 1984).

32. For a discussion of an ethnic democracy and its applicability to certain ethnically-divided polities, see S. Smooha, 'Minority status in an ethnic democracy: the status of the Arab minority in Israel', *Ethnic and Racial Studies*, vol 13(3), 1990, pp. 389–413.

33. S. Smooha and T. Hanf, 'The Diverse Modes of Conflict Regulation in Deeply Divided Societies', in A. Smith (ed.), *Ethnicity and Nationalism* (Leiden, 1992), p. 32.

34. Radio Free Europe/Radio Liberty, *Report on the USSR*, 15 September 1989, p. 15.

35. Whereas a 1993 law in Estonia has now finalised the right of permanent residents to participate and stand for local government elections, the Latvian

parliament has still to ratify whether or not it intends to follow a similar course.

36.   *Baltic Independent*, 25 June–1 July 1993, p. 5.
37.   P. Jarve, 'From Estonian Popular Front to Multi-Party System: Overcoming Nationalism?' *Paper presented at the Twelfth Nordic Peace Research Conference*, Tampere, Finland, 26–28 June, 1992.
38.   The choice of the four localities was based on a number of criteria: first, cities with sizeable but differing types of Russian communities, including large immigrant populations; second, cities drawn from all three polities so as to compare and contrast responses to differing state policies on citizenship; and finally, localities where territorial secession is an option (hence Daugavpils, Narva and Klaipeda). A random sample of 517 Russians were interviewed, weighted according to age and gender. For fuller details of this survey, see G. Smith, 'Nationality and Citizenship in the Baltic States', *Report to the Institute of Peace Studies*, Washington DC, March 1994.
39.   A survey, reported in *Moskovskie novosti*, no. 4, 27 January 1991, noted that towards the end of 1990, 65 per cent of Russians in Latvia and 50 per cent in Estonia had no intention of leaving for Russia.
40.   According to official statistics, the total number of Russian speakers who left Estonia and Latvia totalled no more than 35 000 in 1991.
41.   M. Mitrofanov, 'Prichiny bessiliya russkikh', *Dinaburg*, 11 August 1992, p.2.
42.   See, for example, a presentation of different views within the editorial board of the leading Russian-language newspaper in Latvia, *SM-Segodnya, Smena* 30 March 1993, p. 3. See also Z. Katz, 'Na orekhi ot Vorontsov', *Baltiiskaya Gazeta*, 13 March 1993, p. 2.
43.   A. Semyonov, 'The Russian and the "Russian speaking" Population of the National Republics', in H. Krag and N. Yukhneva (eds), *Leningrad Minority Rights Conference, Papers*. Copenhagen, 2 June 1991, p. 117.
44.   Baltic Independent, 25 June–1 July 1993, p. 1.

Index